China's Political-Military Evolution

Westview Special Studies

The concept of Westview Special Studies is a response to the continuing crisis in academic and informational publishing. Library budgets for books have been severely curtailed. Ever larger portions of general library budgets are being diverted from the purchase of books and used for data banks, computers, micromedia, and other methods of information retrieval. Interlibrary loan structures further reduce the edition sizes required to satisfy the needs of the scholarly community. Economic pressures on university presses and the few private scholarly publishing companies have greatly limited the capacity of the industry to properly serve the academic and research communities. As a result, many manuscripts dealing with important subjects, often representing the highest level of scholarship, are no longer economically viable publishing projects--or, if accepted for publication, are typically subject to lead times ranging from one to three years.

Westview Special Studies are our practical solution to the problem. As always, the selection criteria include the importance of the subject, the work's contribution to scholarship, and its insight, originality of thought, and excellence of exposition. We accept manuscripts in camera-ready form, typed, set, or word processed according to specifications laid out in our comprehensive manual, which contains straightforward instructions and sample pages. The responsibility for editing and proofreading lies with the author or sponsoring institution, but our editorial staff is always available to answer questions and provide guidance.

The result is a book printed on acid-free paper and bound in sturdy, library-quality soft covers. We manufacture these books ourselves using equipment that does not require a lengthy make-ready process and that allows us to publish first editions of 300 to 1000 copies and to reprint even smaller quantities as needed. Thus, we can produce Special Studies quickly and can keep even very specialized books in print as long as there is a demand for them.

About the Book and Author

In recent years the People's Liberation Army (PLA) has relinquished much of its political power to China's civilian leadership and has turned to the task of professionalizing the military. The transition of the PLA into a relatively apolitical force in Chinese society has occurred alongside great progress toward military modernization, with the foundation now laid for the PLA to become one of the world's most powerful military forces. Dr. Bullard traces the PLA's extremely important and almost revolutionary transition, examines the structural changes associated with it, and assesses current military policies and trends. He discusses in detail the political commissar system, the key institution for all political-military relationships in the Chinese military system.

Colonel Monte R. Bullard is U.S. Army Liaison Officer in the U.S. Consulate General in Hong Kong.

China's Political-Military Evolution
The Party and the Military in the PRC, 1960–1984

Monte R. Bullard

Westview Press / Boulder and London

Westview Special Studies on China and East Asia

The views, opinions, and/or findings of this book are those of the author and should not be construed as an official Department of the Army or U.S. Government position, policy or decision, unless so designated by other official documentation.

All rights reserved. No part of this publication may be reproduced or transmitted in any form or by any means, electronic or mechanical, including photocopy, recording, or any information storage and retrieval system, without permission in writing from the publisher.

Copyright © 1985 by Westview Press, Inc.

Published in 1985 in the United States of America by Westview Press, Inc., 5500 Central Avenue, Boulder, Colorado 80301; Frederick A. Praeger, Publisher

Library of Congress Cataloging in Publication Data
Bullard, Monte.
  China's political-military evolution.
  (Westview special studies on China and East Asia.)
  Bibliography: p.
  Includes index.
  1. China--Politics and government--1949-   .
  2. China. Chung-kuo jen min chieh fang chün--History.
  I. Title.
  DS777.75.B85 1985   322'.5'0951   85-3258
  ISBN 0-8133-7041-8

Printed and bound in the United States of America

10 9 8 7 6 5 4 3 2 1

To Shan

Contents

List of Tables xiii
List of Abbreviations xv
Preface xvii

1   INTRODUCTION 1
    Analytical Issues 1
    Overview: The Bureaucratic Environment and
        Elite Conflict 6
    Method of Analysis 14
    Notes 16

2   THE PLA IN TRANSITION 19
    Overview 19
    Modernization and Political-Military
        Relations 20
        Chinese Threat Perception 21
        Self-Reliance 22
    Personnel and Organizational Change 22
    Personnel Change: The Three Transformations . . 22
        Modernization 23
        People's War Doctrine 23
        Revolutionization 24
        Regularization 25
        Professionalization 26
        Recruitment 26
        Training/Schooling 27
        Promotion Criteria 28
        Cadre Defined 28
        Cadre Revolutionization 29
        Rejuvenation 30
        Intellectualization 31
        Cadre Professionalization 32
        Demobilization 32
    Organizational Change 34
    Summary 36
    Notes 37

3	INSTITUTIONS, ROLES, AND RELATIONSHIPS	41
	Overview	41
	Institutions	41
	Elite Roles	46
	Party	47
	Military	49
	Government	50
	Relationships	51
	Center-Region	51
	Intraregion	56
	Notes	60
4	THE POLITICAL COMMISSAR SYSTEM: EVOLUTION, STRUCTURE, AND FUNCTIONS	65
	Overview	65
	Concept Origin	65
	Political Commissar Concept Brought to Russia	67
	The Chinese Setting	68
	Sociological, Political, and Economic Factors Contributing to the Acceptance of Political Commissars in China	69
	Political Commissar Concept Brought to China	72
	PLA Political Commissar System: Organization and Functions	73
	Summary	82
	Notes	84
5	THE INTERLOCKING DIRECTORATE--NATURE AND SCOPE	89
	Part 1: Overview	89
	Part 2: Regional Representation at the Center	91
	Central Committee	91
	Hierarchy of Province Representation	92
	Hierarchy of Military Region Representation	94
	Politburo	96
	Summary	97
	Part 3: Military Region-Province Linkages	97
	Scope of Interlocking Roles--1960	98
	Scope of Interlocking Roles--1973 and 1982	98
	Command System--1973	100
	Command System--1982	101
	Political Commissar System--1973	101
	Political Commissar System--1982	103
	Summary	104
	Part 4: Province Level Party, Government, and Military District Linkages	106
	Province Level Party Linkages	106
	Scope of Interlocking Roles: 1960-1982	106
	Summary	117

Province Level Government Linkages	117
Scope of Interlocking Roles: 1960-1982	118
Summary	126
Military District Linkages	126
Scope of Interlocking Roles: 1960-1982	127
Summary	140
Part 5: Conclusions	141
Notes	146
6 CONCLUSIONS	149
Appendix A: Party Cadre Levels	157
Appendix B: Government Cadre Levels	159
Appendix C: Military Grade Levels	161
Appendix D: PRC Elites Holding Interlocking Positions (1960)	165
Appendix E: PRC Elites Holding Interlocking Positions (1973)	169
Appendix F: PRC Elites Holding Interlocking Positions (1982)	177
Bibliography	181
Index	201

Tables

3-1	Chinese Communist Party Central Committee Members	42
3-2	Chinese Communist Party Politburo Standing Committee Members	43
4-1	Evolution of the Political Commissar Concept	74
5-1	PRC Central Committee Composition	92
5-2	Weighted Hierarchy of Province Representation at the Center	93
5-3	Weighted Hierarchy of Military Region Relationship at the Center	95
5-4	Dual/Triple Positions Held by Military Region Elites - 1960	99
5-5	Dual/Triple Positions Held by Military Region Elites - 1973	100
5-6	Dual/Triple Positions Held by Military Region Elites - 1982	102
5-7	Military Region Commander and Political Commissar Involvement in the Provinces in 1973 and 1982	105
5-8	Province Level First Party Secretaries - 1960	107
5-9	Province Level First Party Secretaries - 1973	108
5-10	Province Level First Party Secretaries - 1982	109
5-11	Province Level Party Committee Members - 1960	111
5-12	Province Level Party Committee Members - 1973	112
5-13	Province Level Party Committee Members - 1982	113
5-14	Province Level Party Committee Members (Standing Committee Members and Members) - 1973	115

5-15	Province Level Party Committee Members (Standing Committee Members Only) - 1982	116
5-16	Province Level Governors/Mayors (Government) - 1960	119
5-17	Province Level Chairmen (Government) - 1973	120
5-18	Province Level Governors/Mayors (Government) - 1982	121
5-19	Province Level Government Organization - 1960	123
5-20	Province Level Government Organization - 1973	124
5-21	Province Level Government Organization - 1982	125
5-22	Military District Commanders - 1960	128
5-23	Military District Commanders - 1973	129
5-24	Military District Commanders - 1982	131
5-25	Military District Command System - 1960	132
5-26	Military District Command System - 1973	133
5-27	Military District Political Commissars - 1960	134
5-28	Military District First Political Commissars - 1973	135
5-29	Military District First Political Commissars - 1982	137
5-30	Political Commissar System - 1960	138
5-31	Political Commissar System - 1973	139
5-32	Interlocking Directorate in the People's Republic of China (1960-1982)	143

Abbreviations

A	-- Alternate member of the Politburo
Alt	-- Alternate member of the Central Committee
Bn	-- Battalion
CAC	-- Central Advisory Commission
CC	-- Central Committee
CCP	-- Chinese Communist Party
Cdr	-- Commander
CH	-- Chairman
CMC	-- Central Military Council (State)
CO	-- Commander
DEP	-- Deputy
DPC	-- Deputy Political Commissar
DS	-- Deputy Secretary
F	-- Full member of the Politburo
GC	-- Garrison Command
GOV	-- Governor
GS	-- Government system (includes vice and deputy governors, vice and deputy mayors, standing committee members and members of province government organizations)
MAY	-- Mayor

MAC	--	Military Affairs Commission (Party)
MEM	--	Member
MD	--	Military District
MR	--	Military Region
NDSTIC	--	National Defense Science, Technology and Industry Commission
NO	--	Not a member of the Central Committee
NPC	--	National People's Congress
PC	--	Political Commissar
Pltn	--	Platoon
POS	--	Position
PS	--	Party system (includes second, deputy, acting, and alternate secretaries, secretaries, standing committee members and members of province party organizations)
REG	--	Region
RP	--	Responsible person
SCM	--	Standing committee member
SEC	--	Secretary
Sec Gen	--	Secretary General
VC	--	Vice chairman
VG	--	Vice governor
1S	--	First Secretary
2S	--	Second Secretary
3S	--	Third Secretary
1VC	--	First vice chairman
( )	--	Indicates first-listed, e.g., (1st) SEC is a first-listed secretary who is considered a first secretary in the study
(1) PC	--	Probable First Political Commissar

Preface

This book was originally written as a doctoral dissertation for Professors Robert Scalapino, Chalmers Johnson and Weiming Du at the University of California, Berkeley, in 1977. The original dissertation focused exclusively on the "interlocking directorate" phenomenon associated with the politics of the People's Republic of China. It suggested a methodological approach using the study of elite roles to examine structural change. Although the interlocking directorate was reduced in scope after 1976, the phenomenon continues to have significance in a historical context.

I have taken advantage of the past six years to add to my original study. In particular, I gained unique access to Chinese elites during my assignment as US Army Attache to the People's Republic of China from July 1980 to June 1982. I am therefore able to offer additional observations about Chinese political-military relations and the general development of the People's Liberation Army. Both of these areas are related to the original topic and provide some added insights into the direction of political and military change in China. I have also added some comments about analytical methodologies based upon perceptions I developed from participation in the US Government process of reporting on Chinese political-military affairs.

Some readers may find the scholarship in this book uneven. Since I did not have access to other authors' writings on similar topics while stationed in Taipei, Hong Kong, and Beijing, I was unable to incorporate their ideas into this work. Furthermore, since part of this book is based upon research and part is based on personal observation and loosely structured interviews, the writing style and organizational format may at times seem to lack continuity. However, I feel there are sufficient sections within the book that will stand alone and contribute to the understanding of Chinese political-military relations and elite change.

Among the problems I encountered in compiling the statistical data available for the three periods under study (1960, 1973 and 1982) were inconsistencies in data and position titles, and changing frames of reference. Nonetheless, I believe the data is reliable enough to allow valid conclusions to be reached.

Another problem was the change in Chinese terminology from year to year. This was particularly true for titles. For example, the senior government official in the provinces was known as a governor in 1960 and 1982, but as a chairman in 1973. I have attempted to clarify these changes as much as possible. The problem of romanization system was vexing. For the spelling of all modern Chinese words I used the Chinese pinyin system, but where names and words were quoted from historical references the system used by the original author was used. Thus, Mao Zedong will be used interchangeably with Mao Tse-tung throughout.

A final problem was in the terms used for province-level units. For ease of reading I have elected to use the term "province" to describe all province-level units. The five autonomous regions (Guangxi, Nei Monggol Ningxia, Xinjiang, and Xizang) and three province-level municipalities (Beijing, Shanghai, and Tianjin) are referred to throughout the book as "provinces."

I owe a great debt of gratitude to many people. Professors Scalapino and Johnson guided my original work with great care. Professors Kenneth Jowitt, John Starr, Robert Price, Kenneth Waltz, Paul Seabury, and Pat Hatcher helped me to organize my thinking process. Andrew Jameson greatly assisted in the editing of the original dissertation. Col. Carl Bernard, Dr. Don Marshall, and Dr. William Whitson inspired me to enter academia.

During the final phases of the book I also received a great deal of assistance. Bob Suettinger and Harlan Jencks offered extremely valuable suggestions to insure correct facts. The Hong Kong American Consulate's Defense Liaison Office research staff and Richard Welker helped me with much of the research in the final stages. Weber Wung, of the DLO research staff, was especially helpful in the wordprocessing and computer efforts.

I owe a special vote of thanks to Karl Eikenberry and Ed O'Dowd for a very thorough job of editing. Their critical page-by-page review added much to the clarity and accuracy of the final product.

Although I received a great deal of help in the preparation of this book, I accept all responsibility for the conclusions and any errors that remain.

Finally, it would not have been possible if it were not for the active support of my wonderful wife, Sylvia Shan Chen Bullard.

Monte R. Bullard

1
Introduction

ANALYTICAL ISSUES

Political change in the People's Republic of China in recent years has defied explanation much less prediction. Scholars have applied models, projected trends, developed intuitive hypotheses and used nearly every social science methodology available to make sense of the events of the Chinese Communist movement. To say that this topic is important and has serious implications throughout the world is clearly an understatement. Whether used as a model in comparative developmental studies or as a factor in the analysis of international relations, political change in China demands attention.

One of the most illuminating approaches to the study of political change and political-military relations in China has been elite analysis. Professor Robert Scalapino points out that by definition elites are those who manipulate power and that power is the essence of the political process.1 But once elites are selected as the focus of attention there are still major methodological questions which must be answered depending in part on the purpose of the study.

Scholars who have studied political change in China have found it helpful to construct a wide variety of models to organize data about elites. Harry Harding has recently written an excellent critique of the models.2 For purposes of this study only two of the most used will be discussed: the bureaucratic model and the factional model.

A **factional model** is defined by its focus on groups of elites in conflict within a single political system. The model stresses analysis of the characteristics of group members to identify attitudes or behavior patterns which can be correlated with policy outcomes.

A **bureaucratic model**, on the other hand, focuses on institutions and formal roles within institutions to identify changing characteristics and relationships of roles which might suggest conclusions about institutional adaptability to, or stability in, a changing political environment. This model can also be used to organize data for comparison with a Weberian ideal-type bureaucracy to explain and predict bureaucratic behavior.

There are significant variations within each general model. Factional models, for example, can be divided into two categories based on the criteria for identifying a faction or group. One category includes the factions defined by the current issue orientation (for philosophies/ideologies, organizational interests, or selfish motivations) of the members. The second category includes the factions defined by common identity-forming past experiences. Some studies include combinations of both types. More complex factional models attempt to correlate the factions with issues or events to determine influence relationships. Some of the factional models have been successful at establishing a relationship between elite types and specific political outcomes, but they are still very narrow and fail to see general political change or implications. Furthermore, the relationships are always explained from hindsight and these models have not been useful in predicting outcomes.

If the analytical purpose is limited to the prediction of succession or which policy or range of policies are likely to prevail over the short run then a relatively narrow focus on **elite conflict** is useful. This approach can say little, however, about the long range maturity and stability of the political system. If the concern is more than what domestic or foreign policy is likely to result from the ability of one individual or group to prevail, then a more fundamental analysis of the political processes and the political environment must be included. This means movement from a factional politics model to some form of bureaucratic model.3

Whether one selects the factional or bureaucratic model to organize data, the subject matter must be elites and the method elite analysis. Gordon Bennett divides elite analysis into four variables the environment (to include the time dimension), the issues, the nature of the elites, and the political outcomes of elite conflict.4 A fifth variable, the decisionmaking process, should be added.

Each of these variables includes subsets of variables, and most scholars up to this point have focused on the subsets, one or more of the five variables, or on relationships among the variables. There is no agreement as to which combination produces the best insights or predictive capacities. It is clear, however, that single factor analyses or reductionist approaches have not produced valuable conclusions, although most have developed and organized essential data which contribute significantly to more

eclectic approaches.
A critical problem still to be resolved is one of level of analysis. Most approaches can be considered micro-political analysis, but some scholars have begun to move into the level of middle-range theory and macro-political analysis. The hope of someday reaching a general theory still exists, but in the meantime middle-range theory or macro-analysis based upon data from earlier micro-analyses has contributed significantly to our understanding of politics in China. This study will fall into the category of "middle-range theory and hypothesis of intermediate scope" as advocated by Scalapino.5 But before the elements of this effort can be explained a brief review of some of the analytical problems in the field and a description of the bureaucratic environment are necessary to place this approach into perspective.

Clearly some scholars work from a narrower data base than others. It is difficult, however, to categorize research efforts by the scope of the data base. It is possible to separate works by the degree of focus on particular variables, variable subsets or relationships between variables. It is also possible to break them down by complexity as measured by the number of variables or relationships considered. Finally, most works can be distinguished by whether they fit into a factional or bureaucratic model of political analysis.

At the least complex end of the factional analysis scale are works on individual elites. These studies assume, often correctly, that the individual under study exercises significant influence over politics and that an understanding of the background, behavior, and attitudes of that person will clarify the political policies over which he has influence. A major weakness of these studies is their lack of explanation for more general political change and the rapid obsolescence of the work when the individual elite member is removed from the political scene by purge, retirement or death. Some of these works do, however, include important insights based upon factional or bureaucratic analyses as well as biographic study.

At a slightly more complex level are the works that attempt to categorize groups of elites who influence policy based upon similar ambitions or attitudes (factions), similar organizational interests (interest groups) or some type of personal relationships (cliques).6 The search is for some commonality in the group's background which is likely to cause predictable political behavior or relationships. These categories also range from very simple to very complex.

The least complicated elite groups are those defined upon left or right leanings; they include the dichotomies between radicals and moderates, reds and experts, the Cultural Revolution Group (Jiang Qing faction) and Old Cadre Group (Deng Xiaoping/Zhou Enlai), or Dengists versus anti-Dengists. Another dichotomy is the classical Marxist analysis in terms of class background; bourgeois versus proletarian. Elites are also divided by their stand on current policy. There are those revisionists who take the "capitalist road" versus those who follow the correct party line.

One of the most important problems with this approach is identifying the members of a particular faction. For example, prior to 1976, Hua Guofeng had been identified as a radical and by implication should have been purged along with the Gang-of-Four. Instead he became Premier and Chairman of the Party. Nonetheless, these analyses can be useful in the larger examination of elite conflict at the national and provincial levels because they help to clarify the issues.

There are two other problems with dichotomies. First, they are always black and white by definition when the real world includes many shades of grey. This is especially true in Chinese politics where a shade of grey is perceived or interpreted as black at one time and white at another. Secondly, it is difficult to assign more than the top few leaders who make public speeches or whose background is well-known to one of the groups. For example, in the frequently discussed dichotomy, party versus army, there are real problems in identifying the members of each group. Key army elites are also party members and many party cadre have extensive military experience. Further, many military men have held concurrent positions in key party organizations as well as in the army. Neither party nor army is monolithic; seldom do all members of the "High Command" agree on any given issue, even one dealing with the role of the military.

Most elite groups have been identified by stands on policy issues, work style or personal relationships. An increasing number of analysts have attempted to identify groups based on past identity-forming experiences. The hope has been to correlate elite recruitment or mobility with environmental factors, elite conflict over issues, political styles, or policy outcomes. These approaches require the assembly of detailed biographic data which is generally available for senior elites but sparse at lower elite levels.

The assumption is that by identifying elite types which pervade, usually by sheer quantity, key policy-making or policy implementing organizations, explanations and predictions about policy can be made. These approaches go beyond background categorization and attempt to correlate the elite nature with other variables: issues, policy outcomes, historical periods, or organizational changes.

Data and conclusions based on these forms of micro-analysis add significant depth to our understanding of the Chinese political system and elite conflict within the system. They have provided a sound foundation for more complex efforts which can begin to relate more of the variables. Nearly all approaches reach conclusions which are based upon factional approaches to analysis, although some touch briefly on elements of a bureaucratic model. They attempt to explain political change **within** the political system, not **of** the political system. It will require more effort along the lines of a bureaucratic model to move in that direction.

These two models have yielded mixed results depending partially on the questions posed. The factional model has proven more useful for short range policy explanation and prediction. The bureaucratic model offers a more comprehensive explanation and more long range predictive capacity.

The bureaucratic model or some combination of bureaucratic and factional models offers more potential for prediction. It forces the analyst to use more macro-analysis, but based on micro-analysis. It is important to look at the forest **and** the trees to avoid getting lost in the trees.

This study will examine structural change in China during the period 1960 to 1984 by looking at institutional linkages in the political-military relationship. The institutional linkages which reflect structural change are called collectively the **interlocking directorate**. The interlocking directorate, for purposes of this analysis, consists of interlocking roles between five key institutions: (1) the Central Committee of the Chinese Communist Party, (2) military regions, (3) military districts, (4) province party committees, and (5) province revolutionary committees or government organizations. Other national level organizations have been omitted from the analysis because the focus is on provincial level elites and their relationship to the Center. Some important national organizations, however, will be discussed in Chapter Three.

Schisms among the key institutions listed above have been a constant concern of the Chinese leadership and a major contributor to political disunity and national instability. During the period from 1960 to 1973 there was a clear effort to increase the number of interlocking roles probably in an attempt to reduce friction between organizations. This increase probably had the unintended consequence of concentrating too much power in the interlocking positions. As a result during the last decade the concept of interlocking directorate has come under increasing scrutiny and the emphasis has been on the quality of the interlocking roles rather than on the quantity. In other words, certain interlocking roles were identified as important to assure appropriate organizational relationships;

e.g., the first secretaries of each of the province party organizations were assigned concurrent positions as first political commissars of military districts. These patterns of interlocking roles will be explained in more detail later in this book. The significance of refining the interlocking directorate phenomenon has become a key factor in change in the bureaucratic infrastructure which supports efforts toward a more rational and stable bureaucracy.

The assertion that the motivation behind the changes in the interlocking directorate is the result of efforts to reduce schisms between key organizations cannot be proved with available data. The fact that the interlocking directorate has changed in patterned ways and has become a decisive factor in Chinese politics can be proved through the elite analysis methodology of this study. The assertion that the result of these changes will lead to a more rational and stable bureaucracy will only be proven in time, but such conclusions are warranted in light of modern bureaucratic theory.[7]

OVERVIEW:
THE BUREAUCRATIC ENVIRONMENT
AND ELITE CONFLICT

A principal contention of this discussion is that recent analysis of Chinese politics has focused too much on elite conflict in terms of factional, clique or interest group analysis. This has led scholars to neglect the more difficult and perhaps more important factor of change of the political system. The factional analysis methodological approach often proves inadequate in explaining or predicting events in Chinese politics over the long run. For example, if one posits that the motivation for political change in recent years under Deng Xiaoping has been to assure that his faction, the "Dengists", get into the key positions and squeeze out all opposition, the system cannot be said to be moving toward stability because the opposition will inevitably try to figure out a way to return and gain political power. However, if one focuses on systemic changes and assumes that Deng's focus has been on the political process itself, rather than on factions, the ultimate conclusions are quite different. As will be discussed later in this book, a good case can be made that Deng is more concerned with establishing a political system which can accomodate disagreement within key decisionmaking bodies without having to resort to convulsive purges. Thus he insists on setting up an organizational system which will assure a consensus form of decisionmaking in which "shifting coalitions" are allowed and in which no individual or group loses all the time. He insists on compromise within a collective bargaining process. If he is successful in such an attempt it would be a significant move toward stability. This is quite the opposite of the conclusions reached by political analysts who insist that Deng wins by getting rid of opponents or assuring that he has more "Deng" people in key positions.

The actual dynamics of political change in China probably include a combination of Deng's effort to establish a stable political process, the maneuverings of individual elites to assure personal security, and the lobbying of groups to assure their interests are promoted. There is no doubt that during the last two decades the personal security of individuals was not assured. The strong forces that result from individual and group efforts at political manipulation are exactly what Deng's effort seems designed to control, so as to assure a stable political development.

During the last several decades ensuring survival and personal security has become a primary goal of individual Chinese elites. Survival in a political role cannot be assumed. Elites in China could not routinely disagree on issues without considering the potential consequences of quick removal from office and disgrace. In fact, no elite could assume that support for any philosophical position (e.g., radical or moderate) in a policy dispute or identification with any particular group (e.g., Lin Biao's Fourth Field Army Group) or institution (e.g., Chinese Communist Party) would guarantee protection from purge. Nor did ability assure job security since the criteria for good performance changed frequently. The experiences of quota-laden rectification campaigns and the Great Proletarian Cultural Revolution have sensitized elites to the necessity of assuring personal or group survival first, then worrying about the resolution of issues or the promotion of interests or philosophies. Such an environment of uncertainty discourages initiative and individual willingness to make decisions and accept the responsibility of or be identified with those decisions. It encourages rationalization, routinization and centralization of the bureaucracy.8 An environment of uncertainty also encourages participants in the political process to seek collegial or consensus decisionmaking.9

In the PRC the environment has been especially chaotic. In the extreme, one element of the bureaucracy, the PLA, was used to support the widespread purge of another, the party.10 One consequence of this situation has been the development of what can be described as a bureaucratic structural solution to protect individual elite members and groups, such as the party. This solution, the interlocking directorate, will be described in detail in Chapter Five.

Conflict within the elite structure coupled with an uncertain environment are clearly important variables in the Chinese institution building process. It is important that the nature of the uncertainty and the scope of the conflict be understood.

That the Chinese leadership seeks certainty in politics cannot be assumed. Chairman Mao Zedong's personal promotion of the continuous revolution has had the practical effect of creating a high degree of uncertainty, at least in the short run. In the long run however, Mao saw certainty in uncertainty or order from disorder.11 This Maoist notion of continuous revolution is one of the principal ideas over which key Chinese leaders have disagreed in recent years. Some, labeled Maoists or "whateverists", have insisted on adhering to the concept.12 Others, led principally by Deng Xiaoping, have attempted to discredit that concept and establish political stability by establishing an organizational structure and decisionmaking process which is characterized by certainty; i.e., ending the notion of a continuous revolution. There are clearly some in the leadership who agree with Deng's approach if only motivated to safeguard their personal security.

The degree to which there is a belief in the value of certainty versus uncertainty by PRC elites is still not clear, but there does seem to be a great deal of effort to build a bureaucratic structure and develop policies which will assure more certainty and stability during political evolution.

The leadership is forced to make critical decisions which influence the direction, methods and pace of social, economic and political change. In the social realm, ideal social values must be articulated and proper social relationships between citizens must be defined. Economically, the regime must outline the proper relationship between the citizen and the means of production. It must also set priorities for economic development and the distribution of goods and services. Politically, it is necessary to determine the criteria for selecting who should rule at each level in the society. The relationship of the citizen to the government and the "rules of the game" must also be determined. Political and economic relationships with the outside world must also be defined. The policymaking process which precedes these and other important decisions is not conflict free, but the scope and type of conflict allowed can be limited, and that seems to be Deng's principal objective.13

During the transformation or takeover phase of the revolution (1921-1949) the spectrum of acceptable conflict was shortened by the elimination of those who differed radically from the central leadership in their tactics or ultimate societal goals.14

The spectrum was further narrowed from 1949 to 1978 in the consolidation phase of the revolution by a number of rectification campaigns. Even though the spectrum has been narrowed considerably, there is still much room for disagreement in the policymaking process, but the exact definition of what is acceptable conflict still eludes Chinese elites and the practical search for limits results in instability within the political system.

Mao recognized as early as 1937 in his essay "On Contradiction" that there were natural tendencies and legitimate grounds for intraparty conflict.15 He recalled Hegel's formulations of a dialectical world theory: that "contradiction exists in the process of development of all things and that in the process of development of each thing a movement of opposites exists from beginning to end."16 He went on to say that "every difference in man's concepts should be regarded as reflecting objective conditions."17 He talked of "correct" and "erroneous" ideologies within the party.18 Mao's ideas on intraparty conflict were refined as guidelines for resolving contradictions within the the party by Liu Shaoqi in his 1942 <u>Liberation Daily</u> article entitled "Discussion on Struggle within the party."19 These guidelines were revived after Liu was posthumously rehabilitated and are used today as criteria in party rectification efforts.

Mao expended a great deal of effort in identifying and labeling wrong ideologies. For example, he wrote about liberalism, right and left opportunism, and bourgeois conservatism in the 1920's and 1930's. In 1942 he identified sectarianism, subjectivism, and the Party "eight-legged essay" as evil approaches to study within the party.20 Currently party leaders are seeking a middle-of-the-road approach which identifies rightist "bourgeois liberalism" and "extreme leftism" as wrong ideologies.21 These and many other "isms" are indicators of the constant concern with intraparty conflict.

While Mao was condemning "wrong views," he was also establishing a political work style which would assure that wrong views were brought out into the open for discussion, in effect, assuring continued conflict within the party. While his goal was a unified party (certainty), his method was to arrive at a unified party through conflict (uncertainty). "Struggle is the means to unity and unity is the aim of struggle. If unity is sought through struggle, it will live; if unity is sought through yielding, it will perish."22

The Great Leap Forward was a critical period in which the struggle for unity over issues strained personal relationships and brought elite conflict into sharper focus. Each individual elite member had to examine his/her own conscience to determine whether his/her behavior should be based upon personal principles (from experience, education, or common sense), loyalty to the system when his/her principles came into conflict with the system, loyalty to individuals or groups, or pure opportunism.

The choice for any elite below the Politburo level could not have been easy. Even if he/she believed in the general communist system, it was still difficult to decipher policy from the Center since during that period there were conflicting policy statements.23 Loyalty to individuals or groups was also difficult. Motivation for selecting any specific individual or group to join could have been based on past emotional ties or the belief that that individual or group could best protect or promote one's own interest; that interest being based on principles or on opportunism. The outcome of the conflict between principle and opportunism cannot be determined by any social science method and even if it were possible, the utility would still be in question since different elites probably joined the same group for entirely different motives.

The Cultural Revolution further exacerbated elite conflict. One major effect was the identification of groups or relationships which aid in personal survival. That is to say, prior to the Cultural Revolution many elites believed that solid party status provided relatively good personal security. There had been purges or rectification campaigns within the Party which forced some elites to seek other relationships (cliques or factions) to survive, but generally party membership was believed to protect the individual's status. The Cultural Revolution showed that no group affiliation rendered any elite totally safe. Party, army, government, field army, generations, long-march veterans... no one was immune from attack. This probably reduced significantly the importance of such groups in the political process.

The one institutional base which did provide more security than the others was the army, and that caused nonarmy elites to seek some type of affiliation with it.24 The role played by the army in the Cultural Revolution must have made non-PLA elites notice the strength of the PLA as an institution, and seek structural means to form an alliance with it to prevent a recurrence of the Cultural Revolution. The **interlocking directorate**, whereby leaders held concurrent positions in two or more institutions, was probably perceived by elites as the most effective means of self-protection.

The number of political elites who held dual or triple positions increased significantly through the period of the Tenth Central Committee. The practical consequences of that increase, however, created a situation in which PLA cadre meddled in nonmilitary affairs (politics and economics) and nonmilitary elites meddled in military operations. Further, the very notion of interlocking directorate implied a concentration of power, and Chinese elites had been sensitized by the Cultural Revolution about potentially disastrous conse-

quences of power concentration.
The scope of the interlocking directorate phenomenon was sufficiently wide to compound the difficulties of recovering from the Cultural Revolution. Because of the highly centralized system and the fact that elites at mid and lower levels were intimidated and reluctant to take the initiative or accept any responsibility in reform efforts, major changes at the top were required. If it were not for the fall of the Gang-of-Four and Lin Biao, and the death of Chairman Mao, it is unlikely that any progress could have been made. But these events, combined with the reemergence of Deng Xiaoping and his relatively pragmatic followers, created an environment which allowed policies and programs for political and economic progress to occur.

The dynamics of current Chinese politics include complex interactions between factions, interest groups and cliques. Factions interact with other factions who have different attitudes or opinions and they also interact with interest groups and cliques. Boundaries defining the groups are not clear and a number of individuals may cross boundaries on a given issue. As mentioned above, Deng Xiaoping's efforts seem aimed at assuring avoidance of an overconcentration of power and at the same time routinizing conflict between these groups. Current Chinese politics might better be characterized in terms of "shifting coalitions of opinion groups." Old factional labels such as "liberals," "conservatives," "Dengists," and "anti-Dengists" are often misleading. They tend to force the analysis into overly simplistic dichotomies and do not take sufficient account of the consensus-style decision-making process now prevalent in China. This analytical style (dichotomizing) can lead to serious errors when attempting to explain or predict policy change.

Individual leaders are especially difficult to label. For example, there is a bit of reformer in most of those labeled conservative and vice versa. Organizational interests may cause a factional "conservative" to be very liberal when issues about his own organization are under consideration. Finally, China is replete with opportunists who change sides based only on perceptions of self interest. In short, scholars must be extremely cautious when attaching labels to individuals or groups of PRC elites. Care must also be taken in defining the group or generalizing about the group's attitudes.

The extremely complex structure of group interaction is complicated by the consensus-style of decision-making which contributes to a blurring of group (faction, interest group or clique) boundaries. Current Chinese politics is characterized by compromise. Decisions are reached by actively and sincerely attempting to satisfy as many constituencies as possible, rather than by confrontation in which one faction or individual wins and others lose. This is not to say that manipulation of the consensus and questionable methods of persuasion do not occur because they clearly do, especially at the lower levels. It does suggest, however, that analysis which focuses on the positions of factions or individuals are likely to overlook the efforts among groups to arrive at an acceptable consensus.

The very fact that Deng Xiaoping came to power as a result of factional politics illustrates the dynamic characteristic of politics in China. Once in power Deng seems to have focused on structure and process as opposed to factional interplay in order to develop a political process which avoids fluctuations based upon personalities. He has tried to structure the political process by institutionalizing the concept of "collective leadership". Examples of his efforts include his limiting the term of the Party Chairman to three five-year terms and mounting a full-scale attack on the notion of a cult of personality. His intent seems to have been to assure policy continuity, a former deficiency which severely harmed the political process by dampening the initiative and spirit of the bureaucracy within China and creating an image of erratic and irrational behavior abroad. He clearly wants to reduce the harmful effects of power struggles and avoid the problem of a succession crisis.

While Deng sees advantages in a consensus decision-making style he also recognizes disadvantages; i.e., the difficulty in arriving at a quick decision when that is required for purposes of operational effectiveness. As a result, compromises have begun to emerge (the synthesis in Marxist dialectical reasoning). The principal compromise can be found in the "leadership responsibility system" which was first discussed in 1981 and 1982. By December 1982 the notion was formalized in the new constitution by the 5th Plenum of the Fifth National People's Congress.25 In that document article Article 86 states: "The State Council practices the system of the Premier assuming overall responsibility. The ministers assume overall responsibility for the respective ministries and commissions under their charge."

Article 90 is also pertinent: "The ministers in charge of ministries and commissions of the State Council are responsible for the work of their respective departments and convene and preside over ministerial meetings or commission meetings that discuss or decide on major issues in the work of their respective departments." This article seems to provide an out on "major issues" for the leader to seek a consensus; i.e., collective responsibility, but it could also be a recognition that leaders have a responsibility to coordinate actions among the experts to assure the decision has

been thoroughly staffed.
The efforts to develop the idea of a responsibility system is a clear indication of the PRC leadership's concern with evolving the political system so that it can be more responsive but still avoid the pitfalls of an overconcentration of power.
This research will show that Deng has been relatively successful so far in evolving the political process away from confrontational politics and toward a more sophisticated form of consensus decisionmaking. His policy actions are the result of a motivation to ensure that the best consensual decisions are made. There is an important analytical distinction between the motivation to establish a process of consensus decisionmaking and factional politics. The key is that in consensus decisionmaking everyone wins a little, while in factional politics one side clearly loses. When one faction looses consistently there is more chance of political instability as the losers feel the need to change the process or eliminate the opposition through coup or purge.
The practical effect of this evolution of political style has been to diffuse political power. It is clear that in the key institutional locus of power, the politburo, power has begun to be spread around. Further, institutional power has evolved, to a degree, into a form of checks and balances system. While the total power of the army has declined significantly from the Cultural Revolution period, so has that of the party. At the same time the state/enterprise sector has been more clearly delineated and has gained a significant voice in the decisionmaking process. Finally, there has been some movement toward decentralization of power away from the Center to the provinces or enterprises but this effort is still going through some difficult adjustments.
The evolving political style includes an increased emphasis on traditional communist mechanisms of interest articulation (lobbying by factions, interest groups and cliques): inspection teams from higher levels; circulation of draft policy papers at many levels with trial and error test implementation in selected units; and political work conferences. Political work conferences are called by a higher level and subordinate units send representatives, who report their concerns. In some cases the delegate merely submits ideas which have in fact been prepared by senior headquarters. But ideas do often come from the masses or lower level units. Through these mechanisms individuals or groups are able to make their ideas known and are able to solicit support from others. In short, great efforts are being made to restore "democratic centralism." Current politics and even the system can be criticized in this process as long as there is no direct or indirect challenge to the "Four Basic Principles": (1) the leadership of the Com-

munist Party, (2) the dictatorship of the proletariat, (3) adherence to the socialist road and (4) the central role of Marxist/Leninist-Mao thought. These mechanisms, coupled with a strongly disciplined and centralized party system are very effective at identifying problems in the society. The system is not as effective in finding solutions to those problems and implementing the solutions.

In sum, the political tasks of problem identification, aggregation and articulation are handled well by the current regime. The systemic weakness and cause for potentially disruptive political action lie in solution formulation and implementation.

METHOD OF ANALYSIS

The principal purpose of this effort is to shed light on Chinese political-military relationships. After examining the methodologies used by most scholars and government analysts I decided to avoid factional analysis, but I still wanted to examine elite data. I selected a bureaucratic approach which considers elite roles. That study resulted in Chapter Five; but that was not enough. My experience as a student at the Chinese Nationalist Political Warfare College in Taiwan in 1968 combined with my experience interviewing PLA leaders while serving as US Army Attache to China from July 1980 to June 1982 provided me with an intuitive understanding and some additional factual data which I believe must be added to the structural analysis to make it meaningful. I therefore added Chapters Two through Four in descriptive form to help clarify the more academic analysis in Chapter Five. I recognize that this study only examines one part of the political-military question in China, but I believe that part is extremely important.

The starting point in the search for answers about political change has to be man, whether acting alone or in groups. Structural and functional analysis of institutions alone cannot provide adequate explanations. When acting alone, man's behavior must be examined by biographic psycho-social analysis. While it does not explain everything, an individual's life experience, especially his occupational experience, certainly contributes to his behavioral patterns when he is in a policymaking position.26 Analysis of those experiences helps to identify factors which determine values and explain attitudes which affect behavior in policymaking.

In Chinese politics, since important decisions are often group decisions rather than individual command-type decisions, the most useful approach for understanding must be some combination of analysis of groups and of individuals who make up the groups. The approach which draws upon both types of analysis is elite studies. But elite analysis, as was seen in the review of analytical problems above, can be approached in many ways. The most fruitful approach seems to be the middle-level approach which has been used for this study. The analysis includes an examination of elite assignments within five of the key Chinese bureaucracies (the Central Committee, military region and provincial party, army and government organizations). The intent is to clarify institutional relationships and elite role patterns by focusing on one type of institutional linkage, the interlocking directorate. Once the scope and nature of the interlocking directorate are exposed, changes in it over time (1960-1982) can be examined. A determination can then be made as to whether any structural change has taken place and if so to what extent that change is likely to affect future institution-building efforts or bureaucratic stability. It is the purpose of this study to describe some aspects of the current state of political-military relations and to fill in some of the gaps in elite studies and contribute to future efforts of China specialists.

The second, third and fourth chapters of this book are devoted to placing elite relationships (with emphasis on military elites) into perspective. Chapter Two will review current PLA efforts to modernize its force, particularly in the area of cadre or elite improvement. Chapter Three provides a description of the key institutions under study, the roles within those institutions and the formal relationships between and among the institutions. Chapter Four will describe the political commissar system in detail to highlight a finding of this book that the political commissar role is critical in institutional linkages and the political-military relationship. Chapter Five will examine the formal relationships and informal linkages in more detail by focusing on specific elites in interlocking roles as well as elite career patterns. It will include data about province-level institutions and the Center. It will describe the scope of formal institutional ties by identifying specific elites who hold positions in more than one institution. It will also identify formal linkage patterns and movement of elites between institutions. Emphasis will be placed on the military element in these relationships. Finally, Chapter Six will reach conclusions about the data presented.

NOTES

1. Robert A. Scalapino, "Introduction," in Robert A. Scalapino, ed., *Elites in the People's Republic of China* (Seattle: University of Washington Press, 1972), p. vi.
2. Harry Harding, "Competing Models of the Chinese Communist Policy Process: Toward a Sorting and Evaluation," in *Issues and Studies* XX (February 1984), pp. 13-36.
3. For factional models see Gabriel A. Almond, "Interest Groups and the Political Process," in Roy C. Macridis and Bernard Brown, eds., *Comparative Politics: Notes and Readings* (Homewood, Illinois: The Dorsey Press, 1968), pp.181-197. Also see H. Gordon Skilling, "Interest Groups and Communist Politics," *World Politics* 3 (April 1966), pp. 435-451. For the bureaucratic model see Max Weber, *The Theory of Social and Economic Organization*, trans. A. Henderson and T. Parsons (London: William Hodge, 1947).
4. Gordon Bennett, "Elites and Society in China: A Summary of Research and Interpretation," in Scalapino, ed., *Elites in the People's Republic of China*, pp. 3-37.
5. Scalapino, p. v.
6. For useful definitions which distinguish factions, interest groups and cliques, see John B. Starr, "From the 10th Party Congress to the Premiership of Hua Kuo-feng -- the Significance of the Colour of the Cat," *China Quarterly* 67 (September 1976): 480-484.
7. See Max Weber, *The Theory of Social and Economic Organization*, 1947. Also see Nicole P. Mouzelis, *Organization and Bureaucracy: An Analysis of Modern Theories* (Chicago: Aldine Publishing Co., 1967), and James D. Thompson, *Organizations in Action* (New York: McGraw-Hill Book Co., 1967).
8. See Mouzelis, *Organization and Bureaucracy*, especially his discussion of Max Weber and "The Increasing Bureaucratization of Modern Society," pp. 18-21.
9. Thompson, *Organizations in Action*, pp. 34-36.
10. Juergen Domes, "Generals and Red Guards," *Asia Quarterly* (January 1971): pp. 3-32 and (February 1971) pp. 123-160.
11. See Hua Guofeng's "Speech at the Second National Conference on Learning from Dazhai in Agriculture," translated in *Peking Review* (1 January 1977), pp. 43-44.
12. The term "whateverists" comes from a joint editorial in *People's Daily*, *Red Flag* and *Liberation Army News* on 7 February 1977 which stated: "Whatever Chairman Mao decides we will resolutely safeguard and whatever Chairman Mao instructs we will unswervingly follow from beginning to end."

13. These issues generally agree with those defined by Harry Harding as four critical categories of issues "at the heart of Chinese politics for the past fifteen years" in "Leadership Succession in the People's Republic of China," Symposium Proceedings: Perspectives on National Leadership Succession (Washington D.C.: Mathematica Inc, June 1975), p. 84.

14. For definitions of revolutionary phases see Kenneth Jowitt, "An Organizational Approach to the Study of Political Culture in Marxist-Leninist Systems," American Political Science Review 68(September 1974): 1174.

15. Mao Tse-tung, "On Contradiction," Selected Works, vol. II (New York: International Publishers, 1954), pp. 13-53. Also see Mao Tse-tung, "On the Correct Handling of Contradictions Among the People," People's Daily (19 June 1957).

16. Mao Tse-tung, "On Contradiction," p. 19.

17. Ibid., p. 20.

18. Ibid., p. 51.

19. See "Lun Dangnei Douzheng," in Liu Shaoqi, Collected Works of Liu Shaoqi (Beijing: People's Press, 1981), pp. 178-217.

20. Mao Tse-tung, Selected Works, vol. IV, p. 29.

21. See Deng Xiaoping, "Firmly Adhere to the Basic Principles,"(March 30, 1971), in Deng Xiaoping, Selected Works of Deng Xiaoping (Beijing: People's Press, 1983), pp. 144-170.

22. Mao Tse-tung, Selected Works, vol. II, p. 422.

23. Parris Chang, Power and Policy in China (University Park: Penn State University Press, 1975), pp. 170-171.

24. See Chapter Five of this book which supports this contention.

25. See The Constitution of the People's Republic of China (Adopted on December 4, 1982 by the Fifth National People's Congress of the People's Republic of China), (Beijing: Foreign Languages Press, 1983).

26. Jowitt, "An Organizational Approach," pp. 1171-1191.

2
The PLA in Transition

OVERVIEW

The People's Liberation Army is currently in the midst of a major transition. For a number of historical reasons, primarily related to elite transformation, the PLA has been slow to move from a peasant army to a professional military force. The perceived successes in the Sino-Japanese War (1945), War of Liberation (1949) and the Korean War (1953) were accomplished by extremely young PLA leaders who gained such prestige that they were able to maintain key military positions well beyond what some considered their effective years.

PLA leaders who matured during the two decades after 1935 can generally be characterized as charismatic type revolutionaries. They were brave, energetic and loyal to the Communist cause. They did not, however, possess characteristics generally ascribed to "modernizers". They were not well-educated and they did not understand the complexities of the modern world. The problem of a lack of qualified leaders was exacerbated by an efficient political commissar system (described in detail in Chapter Four) which promoted values completely inimical to the modernization process; values which emerged from Mao Zedong's "people's war" philosophy. In short, the PLA is having a difficult time moving from a poorly-equipped, cellular, decentralized peasant army to a unitary, well-equipped, integrated and centralized professional military force.

This chapter will provide a description of recent Chinese policies which are likely to have a significant impact on future elite change within the military cadre system.1 I will define some of the terms frequently used by the Chinese in describing their own developmental efforts and introduce an intellectual construct of my own to help place the various elements of the PLA modernization process in perspective. More specifically I will describe several recent PLA efforts to modernize its forces by improving the quality of its personnel and organizations. I will not include a discussion of equipment modernization. This topic is well-covered elsewhere.2 This chapter will lay a foundation for the in-depth study of the structural relationship between the PLA and civilian institutions.

MODERNIZATION AND POLITICAL-MILITARY RELATIONS

Military modernization cannot occur in a vacuum. There are a number of social, political and economic forces which have an important influence on the process. Those forces which result from the contact between the professional army and the civilian sectors of society are often discussed under the rubric of political-military relations. The subject of Chinese political-military relations includes, for analytical purposes, all areas in which the army relates to the nonmilitary sectors of society: e.g. recruitment, demobilization, defense industries, militia, party-army relations, and the interlocking directorate.

The PLA attempted to modernize and professionalize its forces in the 1950's but failed in part due to inappropriate leadership as mentioned above.3 The Cultural Revolution period can be said to have even reversed the modernization process. The beginning of the recovery from this disastrous experience began with Central Directive 18 published in July 1975. But the real effort didn't begin until December 1978 when China as a whole changed direction. The Third Plenum of the 11th Central Committee was the watershed and the point at which new social, political and economic policies made possible an environment which would allow for military modernization.4 The essence of the Third Plenum was the change in the principal societal task from class struggle to national reconstruction. The PRC leadership formally announced that the energies of the people and leadership were to be redirected from social transformation to economic transformation. This resulted in the implementation of the "four modernizations" campaign; a campaign which was initially articulated in 1975 by Zhou Enlai. Zhou identified four general areas for development (1) agriculture, (2) industry (light and heavy), (3) science and technology, and (4) defense.5

While there has been much debate about the priorities of the "four modernizations", it can be said that PLA leaders believe they will benefit from progress in all four areas. In fact, they believe that it is important to channel national resources into agriculture, industry and science and technology before emphasis is placed on defense. There are two important considerations which have contributed to this thinking: (1) threat perception and (2) a strong desire to remain self-sufficient.6

Chinese Threat Perception

After the US withdrew from Vietnam the Chinese reviewed their strategic environment. They concluded that the Soviets were more dangerous than the Americans. This feeling was strengthened when the Soviets supported Vietnam in its efforts to consolidate Indochina and subsequently established bases there. It was also reinforced by the Soviet invasion of Afghanistan and the development of closer relations between India and the USSR. China began to feel surrounded.

The Chinese analysis of the threat to China, however, resulted in different conclusions from those which might develop from a Western analyst's frame of reference. The Chinese saw the most serious threat to China as more political than military. They viewed Soviet collusion with other nations around China's borders as a greater threat than a direct invasion.

At the same time they remained quite sanguine about their ability to handle the 50 or more Soviet divisions and over 100 SS-20 missiles deployed in the Soviet Far East. They sincerely believed that they could handle any Soviet cross-border invasion of China. While they felt that they would initially suffer many losses, they believed they could "lure the Soviets in deep" and then defeat them with the general strategy of a defensive "people's war under modern conditions."7 Their belief in the efficacy of people's war was reinforced significantly by the performance of the Afghan rebels who hadn't even been trained in the fine points of people's war. PLA officers often stated that if those ragged Afghan rebels could handle the mighty Soviet Red Army then the Chinese people's warriors in the PLA would be able to defeat the Russians in time.

Some Chinese military leaders openly remarked that they could handle the Soviet military threat. They calculated that the Soviets would have to mobilize another three to five million men before they could become a serious threat to China's survival. They believed such a mobilization could not go undetected and the PLA would be suitably prepared for action.

Chinese military leaders also believed they could suffer a full-scale Soviet nuclear attack and still respond with a nuclear second strike of their own; large enough to destroy some key Russian cities. They were confident that the Soviets acknowledged this Chinese capability and that it served as a deterrent.

In sum, the Chinese developed a genuine belief that they could handle any Soviet military invasion of China. This belief translated directly into a lack of a sense of urgency to modernize the PLA. They believed they had time to develop an indigenous defensive capability, one which would not have to rely on outside assistance.

Self-Reliance

The second consideration is a strong belief in self-reliance. PLA leaders abhor dependence on outside support. They have articulated a principle of self-sufficiency which has become doctrine and is accepted almost unanimously in the PLA. They remember their difficulties when the Soviets departed in the early 1960's after the Chinese had developed such a close and relatively dependent relationship. They have therefore concluded that it is better for them to develop their own capabilities.

As mentioned above, they believe that the "four modernizations" priorities are correct. If the total gross national product increases because of a comprehensive economic investment program, they will get their fair share. There are, of course, some military leaders who are impatient for more and better equipment, but generally they agree on the overall approach of building a strong industrial base and allowing defense modernization to develop as a byproduct.

PERSONNEL AND ORGANIZATIONAL CHANGE

PLA leaders were also reluctant to go outside China and purchase new equipment or weapons systems because they knew they lacked skilled manpower. They knew they were not ready to absorb modern technology and that they would need a few years to develop a pool of sufficiently educated personnel. They also went through a self-assessment which revealed many organizational problems which resulted in weak performance. Thus, PLA leaders were content to delay military equipment modernization until they had improved the quality of personnel and organizations.

Even though personnel and organizational problems were identified as early as 1975, and some sporadic corrections were made after the Third Plenum, no significant progress was made until the early 1980's. The period from early 1979 to mid-1982 represented the time during which specific problem areas and alternative solutions were developed.

PERSONNEL CHANGE: THE THREE TRANSFORMATIONS

The general approach to these problems became known as the "three transformations" for the PLA. The three transformations were: (1) modernization (xiandaihua), (2) revolutionization (geminghua) and (3) regularization (zhengguihua).8

Modernization

The term "modernization" usually refers to equipment updating and, to a degree, changes in strategy and tactics. Current Chinese thinking about modernizing the PLA is to move toward a modern military force but not necessarily in the Western sense of the word. To the PLA "modern" means less reliance on weapons and doctrine designed around the concept of guerrilla warfare, but it does not mean the abandonment of the doctrine of people's war.

People's War Doctrine

At this point it is useful to digress and distinguish between guerrilla warfare and people's war. It is common in many analyses of China to equate the two. People's war is a broader term to the Chinese.9 It is primarily defined by the involvement of the total population in the war effort. Every villager, urban dweller, factory worker, or farmer has a role to play. There are neither age limits nor geographical boundaries to the war effort. Guerrilla warfare, on the other hand, is defined by the Chinese primarily as the fighting carried on by professional soldiers who operate in decentralized, independent units using specific tactics. These soldiers, according to the Chinese, should be totally dedicated and prepared to suffer extreme hardships. They should also be well-trained in the art of guerrilla warfare. When the guerrillas begin to involve the civilian population as intelligence or logistics sources the nature of the conflict becomes a people's war. Thus, guerrilla warfare is one component of people's war. People's war also includes political and economic warfare; even cultural warfare when possible. Finally, people's war is defined by its purposeful protracted nature.

Generally people's war is limited to the territory of one's own country and when used as a doctrine by the government in power it is defensive in character. The involvement of civilians in intelligence and logistics functions usually assumes that the conflict is within the borders of the country fighting the people's war. As of this writing, China was still following a people's war strategy and close examination of the PLA logistics system will verify its defensive nature. There are no means for "pushing" supplies more than a few miles beyond China's borders without a near total reliance on the citizens of the country in which the PLA is operating.

Thus under the doctrine of people's war, China has adopted a strategy of "luring the enemy in deep." The idea is to draw the enemy forces deep into China which, because of its vast size, will cause the enemy's forces to thin out, develop long lines of communication and become excellent targets for small independent local units. Larger main force units, which would be held in reserve, would then counterattack.

The current debate over modernization of the PLA has generally been whether to improve the effectiveness of people's war or move to some type of more modern forward defense. To this point, those who advocate the former have been in the ascendency. By improving the effectiveness of people's war they mean improving weapons and fighting techniques so they will not have to lure the enemy in quite so deep, will not be required to make such significant sacrifices in men and materiel, and will be able to reduce the duration of the war. Thus, from a Chinese perspective, there is plenty of room to move away from a force made up predominantly of fragmented guerrilla bands and toward a regular professional force made up of larger units operating in combined or joint operations without abandoning the **people's war doctrine**.

In short, it is important to avoid equating the relatively narrow concept of guerrilla war with the notion of people's war. If one examines these definitions from a Chinese vantage point, it is easy to see why the PLA is not likely to totally abandon the people's war doctrine, at least not for warfare within China. This also explains, in part, why PLA leaders are so concerned with maintaining close and correct civil-military relations. Finally, an understanding of the movement away from guerrilla warfare units to large integrated main force units within the doctrine of people's war helps to explain Chinese perspectives of the modernization element of the PLA's three transformations.

Revolutionization
―――――――――――――――

The second transformation, revolutionization, is relatively easy to explain. The ultimate goal is to unify the thinking of PLA personnel toward all important issues ranging from the role of the military in civilian society to what type of strategy or force to prepare and how to allocate the budget. This effort is described by the Chinese as assuring that everyone follows the "line, principles and doctrine" of the party leadership.

Revolutionization is primarily a question of attitude; loyalty to the system and its leaders. The belief is that proper attitudes are the sine qua non for a well-disciplined responsive force. The essence of "proper" in proper attitudes is embodied in the "four basic principles" which cannot be challenged.10

PLA leaders have singled out two main categories of

bad attitudes: (1) leftism and (2) bourgeois liberalism.11 Other categories include attitudes associated with opportunists or those who are lazy, corrupt or prone to abuse their position of power. While all have been important, the latter categories of attitudes are usually subsumed under one or the other of the two main categories.

The movement to erase leftism has been particularly vigorous. There have been two principal targets of the movement. One group includes uneducated peasant soldiers who joined the PLA during the revolution and rather than grow intellectually, fell back on blind loyalty to Mao Zedong. They are known as the "two whateverists".12 Since they are not sophisticated enough to know any better they are unable to adapt to the changing role of the PLA. They are so ignorant they could only interpret guidelines laid down by Mao in the guerrilla warfare stages of the revolution, and their interpretation is extremely fundamental and simple. They cannot understand change or more complex forms of military tactics or organization.

The second group of leftists were those who benefitted from the Cultural Revolution; those who "rose like helicopters." They were mostly uneducated peasants who gained positions because of a policy which emphasized the promotion of those with a strong worker/peasant background and a philosophy which emphasized egalitarian values. This group includes a number of opportunists as well as many idealistic true believers.

Many of the military men who might be legitimately labeled as leftist were and still are found in the political commissar system. Since the task of erasing leftism in the PLA fell to the commissar system there was an obvious conflict of interest. In other words the commissar system was told to purge itself. From 1979 to 1982 little progress was made. However, in August 1982 the director of the General Political Department, Wei Guoqing, was replaced by Yu Qiuli, a former commissar whom Deng Xiaoping believed could succeed in carrying out a rectification campaign within the PLA without turning it into convulsive conflict.13 The approach to getting rid of leftists so far has generally been to focus on professional competence, age and education level rather than attempt to classify psychological attitudes or behavior patterns. Thus, for the first time a party rectification campaign has been able to emphasize relatively objective criteria to purge the party of ineffective members or members who don't subscribe to the current policies.

Regularization

The Chinese include two areas under the term regularization: (1) professionalization (zhuanyehua) and

(2) streamlining (xiuzheng). Professionalization refers to the overall effort to improve the quality of personnel at all levels. In this case the term professionalism is mine and it conflicts with the Chinese use of the term which is usually much narrower and will be discussed below. The term streamlining refers to organizational consolidation or restructuring with the improvement of organizational effectiveness as the goal. The term streamlining also includes procedural concerns such as coordination procedures or task-oriented processes (i.e., research and development processes, troop leading and staff procedures, training methods, etc.). Finally, streamlining includes efforts to standardize organizations and procedures. While there is a great deal of effort to standardize training, leadership techniques, organizational structures, and equipment it is clearly recognized that units must be different in different parts of China. They must be tailored to the geography (i.e., more mobility and tanks in relatively open areas of the Northeast and smaller units in the mountains of Xizang) and the nature of the threat (i.e., more anti-tank capability along the Soviet border). Generally, there is a strong effort to standardize where possible.

Professionalization

For the purposes of this analysis professionalization is subdivided into four categories: (1) recruitment, (2) training/schooling, (3) promotion criteria and (4) demobilization (includes all forms of release from military service; e.g., retirement, lateral transfer, release as a result of failing to rectify political attitudes). There was significant progress in professionalizing the force during the three years from 1982 through 1984 in each of these four categories.

Recruitment

Recruitment guidelines now include educational criteria. Rural youths must usually be middle school graduates and urban youths should be senior middle school graduates. One particularly lucrative source for PLA recruits has been the pool of unemployed urban youths. Many of this group are bright young people who just missed passing the college entrance exam and are not accepting employment in order to prepare for the following year's college entrance exam. In many cases they are persuaded to join the PLA. One problem which has resulted from this effort is that urban youths represent more of a discipline problem than rural youths once they are inducted into the PLA. Rural youths are

not as bright, generally, but are much more malleable.
Although the recruitment process varies considerably
between military regions, it can be concluded that there
has been a significant increase in the educational level
of youths inducted into the PLA from 1980 to 1984.

Training/Schooling

The training of PLA soldiers has also improved
over the past four years. The time spent on training
versus political education or production tasks has been
increased significantly. At the height of the Cultural
Revolution it was said that 70% of a soldier's training
was devoted to nonmilitary and 30% to purely military
activities. By 1984 the ratio in many units was exactly
reversed: 70% devoted to military training and 30% to
political indoctrination and production tasks. The
thrust of the training effort in 1981 and 1982 was to
improve coordination in combined arms exercises; a clear
indication of movement away from guerrilla warfare as
the principal mode of combat.14 Other priorities in
training programs have been on antiaircraft and anti-
tank techniques, defense against tactical nuclear
weapons and chemical weapons and the integration of the
various PLA arms.

The movement to improve the technical competence of
PLA cadre has also made progress. No longer do new
officers come directly from the ranks without going
through a basic level school. Each of the eleven military regions has a basic level officers infantry school
which trains senior middle school graduates in military
skills. The course has been three years in duration but
some academies are beginning to develop four-year curri-
cula. In addition there are approximately 30 similar
schools which produce new officers in the branches which
require special skills; i.e., air force, artillery,
engineers, etc. At present the basic level officers
course is more vocational than educational, but there
are serious discussions about expanding the academic
curriculum.

Most military schools were physically damaged and
closed during the Cultural Revolution. After extensive
repairs (frequently accomplished by the new students)
and great efforts to reconstitute the faculties, most
schools were reopened by 1983. Not only were basic
level schools (described above) restored, but most
technical or branch schools at intermediate levels began
to function. Finally, the four senior level schools
(Military Academy, Political Academy, Logistics Academy,
and the Academy of Military Sciences) developed new
programs and increased the number of students to near
maximum levels.

Promotion Criteria

It is through the development of promotion criteria that the PLA leadership has been able to make the most progress in weeding out those who are less qualified. Under the slogan of the "four cadre transformations" they have detailed guidelines which serve as criteria for promotion.15 The four cadre transformations are: (1)revolutionization, (2) rejuvenation, (3) intellectualization, and (4) professionalization.

Cadre Defined

Before the four cadre transformations are discussed it is useful to review briefly what is meant by the term "cadre" (ganbu). The Chinese define the term as leadership or administrative personnel in "organs" (jiguan) and "bodies" (tuanti).16 The term "organ" is a general term for all party, government and army organizations while the term "body" refers to public or mass organizations such as trade unions, federations of women, or peasant associations. The title "cadre" represents an official status carrying a degree of authority, responsibility and prestige.

There are a number of modifiers for the term "cadre" which classify the broad group into different levels of categories and sub-categories. One means of classification is by party membership. There are party-member cadre and nonparty-member cadre. The party-member cadre are, as suggested by the name, those members of the party who hold cadre positions. There are about 19 million in this category.17 Since there are about 39 million party members it can be seen that not all party members hold cadre positions. Party-member cadre can hold positions in the party organizations or in other organizations (organs or bodies). There are about 21 million cadre who are not party members.18 In 1982, as a result of a structural reform program, these numbers began to be reduced. The reductions have been in the number of cadre at all levels, but especially the grassroots level. In some cases the cuts have been as much as 60%.

Within these two categories there are five sub-categories: (1) party (dang), (2) state (guojia), (3) government (zhengfu), (4) military (jundui), and (5) state/collective enterprise (guoying qiye/jiti qiye).19 Nonparty-member cadre function in all roles except within the party organization. Nonparty-members are generally found only at the lower levels.

The distinction between party cadre and party-member cadre is important. Party cadre are those who hold positions in party organizations. The only party cadre who hold positions in the army or government organizations are those who hold two or three positions simultaneously.20 Most cadre positions, however, in the army or government are filled by party-member cadre. This is particularly true at the high levels and for purposes of this study those at the high levels are defined as elites.

The new party constitution (adopted in September 1982) is explicit about the role of the Communist Party and its cadre. Party and party-member cadre are responsible at all levels for decisionmaking. They assure that all nonparty organs and bodies are operating within current policy guidelines (i.e., line, principles and policy) for national development. They ensure compliance with the current interpretation of Marxist-Leninist-Maoist socialism as adapted to China's conditions.

There are numerous other subcategories of cadre in each of the five organizations defined by different criteria. For example, there are three levels (or categories) in the national hierarchy: central (zhongyang), local (difang)(provincial, municipal, prefectural, county) and grassroots (jiceng)(neighborhood committees, small enterprises, rural production brigades and PLA companies). There are also functional categories: military, political (zhenggong), administrative (xingzheng), professional (zhuanye) and technical (jishu).

Within each organ there are further sub-categories. In the PLA, for example, one way of classification is by profession and another is by branch or service.21

The three principal organs (party, army and government) each have a pay structure which differentiates levels and indirectly establishes a rank system. The party and government organs list 30 levels of cadre while the PLA lists 24. (See Annexes A, B and C for titles and levels.)

Cadre Revolutionization

The concept of revolutionization is the same as that discussed above except in this case the emphasis is on positive rather than negative criteria. Ideal attitudinal and behavioral traits are defined, and the detailed dossiers of the cadre are compared with these. The dossiers are filled with data about the individual's attitudes and behavior patterns as reported by the commissar system.22 Commissars obtain their data by direct observation, informants and many forms of testing. An example of a test is to provide the cadre with an article to read. He must then write a critique of the article and in his critique he must display proper values or attitudes in the form of "lessons learned." Another method currently being used is called "heart-to-heart talks" in which commissars elicit information on attitudes under the guise of counselling. These methods have proven to be an effective means of examining PLA cadre at all levels. Once a cadre has been determined to have the "correct political outlook" he can then be considered against the other criteria.

Rejuvenation

The rejuvenation criteria is relatively objective and clear. According to the "PLA Cadre Service Regulations" promulgated in 1978, age limits for different military levels, staff and command, have been established.23 For example no military region commanders should be over 60, no military district cadre can be over 55, corps or army commanders and staff officers must be 50 or below, division commanders cannot exceed 45, regimental cadre must be 40 or less, battalion cadre under 35, company level cadre under 30 and platoon leaders under 25.24

Generally the PLA was quite successful at retiring overaged cadre during the period from 1981 through 1984. Except for the few over-70 cadre who were kept in place for purposes of legitimacy and continuity, the cadre elected to the 12th Central Committee as full or alternate members were on the average approximately 10 years younger than cadre in the military regions and districts. The main force units probably achieved the rejuvenation goals prior to 1983.25

The rejuvenation process started out strong in 1980, slowed in 1981 and early 1982, then picked up momentum again after the 12th Party Congress in the summer of 1982. Since the Third Plenum of the 11th Central Committee in December 1978, there have been many significant personnel changes. At the Center these include: a new chief of the General Staff Department, two new ministers of defense, two new deputy chiefs of the general staff, a new director and three deputy directors of the General Political Department, a new director and and three deputy directors of the General Logistics Department and two new commanders and a political commissar of the Navy.26

There have also been major changes within the military regions. All but one commander (Li Desheng/ Shenyang) have been replaced since 1 January 1980. Thirteen deputy military region commanders have also been replaced. All but one of the military region political commissars (Lanzhou) have changed and 11 deputy political commissars have been removed. Nine of the military region leaders were elected to the 12th Central Committee's Central Advisory Commission and all nine have since relinquished their military region posts.27

By mid-1983 commanders and commissars in the military districts had begun to be replaced by younger officers as a continuation of this process. In addition as part of the streamlining effort the total number of

key cadre, deputy commanders and political commissars, has also been reduced at the military region and the military district levels. There are usually from two to four deputies now compared to as many as ten in the earlier periods.
    The status of local force, people's armed police and militia cadre is not so clear because of their degree of autonomy and the fact that military positions are often linked to factory or commune positions. For example, the personnel director of a factory is likely to be concurrently the political commissar of the factory's militia unit and serve as the director of the Organization Department of the factory's party committee. In sum, the rejuvenation effort has been quite successful in removing overaged cadre in most of the PLA, but there are probably some exceptions in local force, people's armed police and militia units.

Intellectualization

The term intellectualization is used by PLA leaders to describe the improvement of the general educational level of cadre and soldiers. As described above, there are now minimum educational requirements for different positions in the PLA. Recruits must have a middle-school (sixth-grade) education, although there are many exceptions. Platoon and company basic-level cadre (non-commissioned officer equivalent) must be at least senior middle school graduates (twelfth-grade) and all officer level cadre must now graduate from one of the military academies. There are now many college graduates who go through one year of military training and become officer level cadre. They have served in frontline units along the Vietnam border in combat situations as well as in technical positions. Youths must be between 17 and 20 and must achieve a passing score on the college entrance examination in order to qualify for the military academies or technical schools. However, the passing score for military academies and technical schools is slightly lower than most civilian colleges.
    At the higher levels the PLA has introduced a system which requires cadre to pass an examination before they are eligible for promotion. These exams test technical knowledge as well as political attitudes. New schools and separate exams have also been introduced at the intermediate level, but they still do not play a critical role in the promotion process. Another change has been the reintroduction of after-hours classes and directed self-study courses. Finally, division-level and above cadre are required to graduate from one of the four PLA senior academies (equivalent to the War College in the United States).
    According to some sources, the personnel division of the General Political Department has adopted the

method of asking very senior commanders to write an essay without the aid of a secretary; a sort of literacy test which has been quite successful at eliminating some of the older uneducated guerrilla leaders.

While exact statistics are not available, there is one report from Hunan Military District which stated that 75% of its PLA cadre had graduated from military schools and 37.5% were college graduates.28 Even if these statistics are not representative there is no doubt that the PLA has made significant strides in the past four years at introducing minimum educational standards and expanding educational facilities.

Cadre Professionalization

Professionalization, or increasing the level of technical or managerial competence, has progressed at about the same pace as general educational development. New self-study programs and technical schools have been the principal reasons for the progress, but it has also resulted from the overall streamlining effort and personnel assignment policies. In other words, organizations are trimmed of excess cadre who meddle or take up the time of the technical cadre. Cadre of all types are now able to concentrate on learning professional skills rather than being distracted by political sessions or other nonproductive activity. Finally, assignment policies have begun to rematch skills with jobs so that individuals are now more frequently placed into jobs for which they were trained.

Demobilization

The problem of demobilization has been particularly difficult for PLA leaders. In fact, it is believed that the long delay in the reintroduction of the rank system has been due primarily to the slowness in getting rid of uneducated, overaged cadre; cadre whose experience, past loyalty and prestige make it difficult to tell them they are no longer needed. Nonetheless, the PLA leadership has identified this as a major problem and has initiated a number of measures to encourage retirement of older cadre.

The intense search for ways to separate or retire excess personnel with a minimum of personal turmoil has resulted in the development of a complicated separation system which recognizes past sacrifice and establishes benefits based partially upon hardships experienced during one's career. Those who joined the Communist side before it was popular or necessary are especially well rewarded. There are at least six categories of personnel being separated from the PLA: two categories of retirement (lixiu and tuixiu), demobilization (tuiwu), lateral transfer (zhuanye), becoming an advisor, and

going on convalescent leave.
The first category of retirement (lixiu) is for very senior cadre; usually division chiefs or above in the Ministry of Defense, the three major headquarters (General Staff Department, General Political Department and General Logistics Department), or the military district or military region headquarters. Those who retire in this category are usually over 60 years of age. They must have joined the PLA before the Anti-Japanese War. Because of their extensive experience they are not forced to retire and whether they do or not depends upon their physical and mental condition. Once they decide to retire (lixiu) they receive 100% of their pay, can still wear their uniform, and continue to enjoy all the privileges of an active cadre of equal rank.
Those who retire in the second category (tuixiu) are at a slightly lower position level. They are cadre usually between the ages of 55 and 60. The retirement pay for this group is from 75 to 100% of their last active duty salary. Those who participated in the Anti-Japanese War receive 100% of their pay. Those who fought in the War of Liberation get 90%. Their level at the time of retirement also influences the amount of pay they will receive. For example those who hold positions at regimental level and above will get 100% of their pay. This group, like the first group, gets complete medical coverage, but their access to military facilities is a bit more limited. They are not allowed to continue to wear the uniform.
The demobilization category (tuiwu) is for soldiers as opposed to cadre. Usually they have been in the PLA from 3 to 5 years, although some with technical skills (e.g. a truck driver) may have served from 10 to 12 years. This group receives no privileges upon demobilization although in exceptional circumstances a soldier will receive a lump-sum payment to get started in civilian life. Local governments are responsible for finding jobs for this group and the placement policies have changed over the years. There has been an effort during the last two or three years to encourage demobilized soldiers to return to their original homes or villages. Up until 1980 this group included a high percentage of communist party members because service in the PLA helped to get them party membership. They were therefore in a position to assume cadre jobs in the civilian community upon demobilization. After 1980, however, party membership has been awarded on a more discriminative basis, and the percentage of demobilized soldiers with party membership is much lower. This has had a negative impact on recruiting for the PLA.
The lateral transfer (zhuanye) category includes cadre at all levels. A cadre from this group is transferred to a civilian position at the same salary and position level. All ties with the military are severed.

They receive no privileges and are not allowed to wear the uniform. As with demobilized soldiers, the provincial government is responsible for finding them jobs. Most of the cadre in this category are those who exceed the age requirements at different levels (e.g., 45 at regimental level), request to leave the PLA, or do not meet minimum physical standards but still have something to offer as leaders. There have been some problems with this category because there has been a shortage of jobs available outside the PLA at the appropriate rank level. There are also many who don't want to leave the PLA because of the prestige and privileges which they must surrender. Perhaps the biggest problem is that receiving organizations don't want cadre entering their system at an advanced level, particularly those who possess only military skills. Some individuals who were eligible for lateral transfer have been allowed to retire even if they joined the PLA after 1949, but their salary and privileges have been reduced considerably.

The advisor category is not considered a form of retirement by the Chinese. Cadre who become advisors are considered active duty personnel and receive pay and privileges accordingly. They are kept on to provide their experience to the PLA. Advisors are assigned to military related institutes or schools rather than the field forces. There are some located at the senior headquarters (military district and military region), but none are assigned to the regular field forces.

The final category includes those whose physical condition has deteriorated to the point that they cannot fulfill their duties. They are allowed to remain at home or are placed in one of the many PLA sanitoriums. Once placed in this category they can return to active service, but usually do not.

Most cadre who are separated from the PLA fall within the lateral transfer or recuperative leave categories. Only about 20% have been in the two retirement categories between 1978 and 1984, although that percentage should increase in 1985 and 1986.

The PLA seems to have been quite successful at separating cadre through the above-described categories although the task probably will not be completed until mid-1985. The mark of its completion may be the reintroduction of ranks since the large number of overaged and incompetent cadre has been the major obstacle to a rank system.29 With the reintroduction of ranks, the pace of PLA modernization should increase significantly.

ORGANIZATIONAL CHANGE

The High Command has also taken steps to streamline the PLA to make it more effective. Streamlining includes three sub-categories: (1) consolidation of organizations, (2) improvement of organizational processes

(i.e., coordination procedures between and within organizations), and (3) evolution of interlocking roles.
By mid-1983 a number of organizational changes had been announced and several more were rumored. The most important was at the highest level; the formation of the new state Central Military Council (described in more detail in Chapter Three). Another important consolidation, apparently intended to improve the weapons modernization process, was the combining of the National Defense Science and Technology Commission with the National Defense Industry Commission to form the new National Defense Science, Technology and Industrial Commission.30

There were also consolidations within the operational portion of the High Command: The Artillery Corps, Armored Corps, Engineer Corps, Signal Corps and Antichemical Corps became subdepartments within the General Staff Department. The PLA Railway Corps was incorporated into the Ministry of Railways on 1 January 1984. There were rumors of complete disbandment of the Capital Construction Corps. While complete disbandment is not likely, it is likely that it will be civilianized and placed under an appropriate ministry.

Outside the Center there were also important changes. A number of local force units were changed to people's armed police units and transferred to the Ministry of Public Security. This was clearly an action to free the PLA from concern over internal disturbances so they could concentrate on external threats. This was another area of functional differentiation which is likely to contribute to an increased level of professionalization and efficiency in the PLA, particularly its main force units. This change also divides the control of armed force between the PLA and the Ministry of Public Security which is consistent with the overall effort to avoid an overconcentration of power by creating checks and balances at different levels. The people's armed police is considered an element of the PLA and even though it is under the Ministry of Public Security, it will still be under the overall control of the State Central Military Council and ultimately the Party's Military Affairs Commission.

There also appear to be major organizational changes taking place in local force and militia units, but their exact nature is not clear. The garrisons of cities under provincial jurisdiction have been converted to military subdistricts. The three traditional elements of the militia (primary, secondary and backbone), have been reduced to two (primary and backbone). Members of the primary militia are now regarded as being in the reserve military service category 2 and those of the backbone militia are regarded as being in the reserved military service category 1.31 There also seems to be some efforts to create a more regularized reserve system. Many organizational changes are taking place in the PLA and they seem to be designed to differentiate functions and make all units/organizations more specialized and efficient.

There is little information available about the PLA's efforts to improve coordination procedures. Discussions of training programs and exercises often describe the need to improve the integration of combat units, but there is little reporting on the results of these efforts. We do know from contact with the PLA during US delegation visits that compartmentation and centralization are problems that have been identified and that serious efforts to overcome these difficulties are underway. Again the results are not clear. Internal coordination procedures and processes are management problems for all armies and the PLA is no exception. The fact that PLA leaders have made it a priority task indicates there will be progress in the future.

The third element of the streamlining process is the interlocking directorate phenomenon. This will be discussed in detail in Chapter Five. Suffice it to say, it is another area where an evolution of the system is taking place and it seems to be in a direction which will rationalize the system to a greater degree.

SUMMARY

In summary, the PLA has embarked on an ambitious program to improve the quality of its personnel and the effectiveness of its organizations before priorities are turned to weapons production or acquisition. To date, it appears that significant progress has been made and by mid-1985 the PLA should be prepared to change the priority effort from personnel and organizations to technological modernization.

NOTES

1. During my assignment as US Army Attache to the People's Republic of China, I was able to travel to all of China's provinces, province-level autonomous regions and municipalities. I interviewed staff officers in eight military regions and one military district. I was able to visit three divisions (two infantry and one armor), three military schools, an arsenal, and a storage depot. I visited the Military Academy in Beijing several times and lectured there once. Facts in this chapter not otherwise cited are from these interviews and visits.
2. See David L. Shambaugh, "China's Defense Industries: Indigenous and Foreign Procurement," in Paul H. B. Godwin, The Chinese Defense Establishment: Continuity and Change in the 1980's (Boulder, Colorado: Westview Press, 1983), pp. 43-89.
3. See Harlan Jencks, From Muskets to Missiles; Politics and Professionalism in the Chinese Army 1945-1981, (Boulder, Colorado: Westview Press, 1982), pp. 1-134. Also see Ellis Joffe, "The Army After Mao," International Journal 34 (Autumn 1976), pp. 568-584; and "The Chinese Army After the Cultural Revolution: The Effects of Intervention," China Quarterly 55 (July-Sept 1973), pp. 450-477; and Ellis Joffe and Gerald Segal, "The Chinese Army and Professionalism, Problems of Communism 27 (Nov-Dec 1978), pp. 1-19.
4. "Communique: Of the Third Plenary Session of the 11th Central Committee of the Communist Party of China," Beijing Review 52, (29 December 1978).
5. "Zhou Enlai's Report on the Work of the Government," 13 January 1975 at the 1st Session of the 4th National People's Congress. People's Daily, (21 January 1975), p. 1.
6. References in this chapter to what PLA leaders "believe" or "think" are generalizations developed from my understanding of PLA elite attitudes based upon numerous interviews with PLA leaders (see footnote 1 above).
7. See Su Yu, "Great Victory for Chairman Mao's Guideline on War," Peking Review 34 (19 August 1977), pp. 6-15.
8. Deng Xiaoping, "Revolutionization, Modernization, and Regularization; Build a Powerful Modern and Regular Revolutionary Army," Selected Works of Deng Xiaoping, (Beijing: People's Press, 1983), pp. 349-350.
9. Mao Tse-tung, Selected Works of Mao Tse-tung, vol. III, (Beijing: Foreign Languages Press, 1965), p. 263.
10. Deng Xiaoping, Selected Works of Deng Xiaoping, pp. 144-170.
11. "Actively Launch Criticism and Self-Criticism," Red Flag 16 (16 April 1981), pp. 2-4,22.

12. "Study Documents Well and Grasp Key Links," Joint editorial in People's Daily, Red Flag, and Liberation Army News, 7 February 1977.
13. People's Daily, 28 September 1982.
14. "Raise Our Army's Education and Training to a Higher Level," Liberation Army News, 4 December 1980, p. 1.
15. "Revolutionization, Rejuvenation, Intellectualization and Professionalization," Constitution of the Communist Party of China, adopted by the 12th Party Congress on 6 September 1982 and found in The 12th National Congress of the Communist Party of China, (Beijing: Foreign Languages Press, 1982).
16. The research for this section on cadre definition was accomplished by the US Defense Liaison Office (USDLO) Research Staff, US Consulate, Hong Kong.
17. People's Daily, 30 June 1981.
18. This estimate is made by USDLO research staff from a combination of original source materials.
19. State cadre are those who hold positions in the people's congresses at various levels.
20. See Chapter Five.
21. By profession there are: (1) commanding cadre (zhihui ganbu), (2) political cadre (zhengzhi ganbu), (3) technical cadre (jishu ganbu), (4) supply cadre (junxu ganbu), (5) medical cadre (junyi ganbu), (6) veterinary cadre (shouyi ganbu), (7) military law-enforcement cadre (junfa ganbu), (8) administrative cadre (xingzheng ganbu and (9) staff cadre (canmou ganbu). By branch of service or arm: (1) army cadre (lujun ganbu), (2) navy cadre (haijun ganbu), (3) air force cadre (kongjun ganbu) and (4) militia and people's armed force cadre (wuzhuang ganbu). -- These titles come from the 1955 PLA Officers Regulations which are possibly being revived.
22. See Chapter Four.
23. Institute for the Study of Chinese Communist Problems, 1981 Yearbook on Chinese Communism, (Taipei: 1981), pp. 72-73.
24. Ibid.
25. Until 1984, the PLA was divided into main force units, local force units and militia. The main force units are the regular army and are mobile. Local forces stay in one location even during wartime. Militia forces complement main and local force units. Article 4 of the new Military Service Law (see People's Daily, 5 June 1984) now lists three elements: the PLA, the People's Armed Police (PAP) and the militia. The PAP and the militia are considered local forces and are part of a newly developing reserve system.
26. The changes included the following: The new chief of the general staff (Yang Dezhi in February, 1980), two new ministers of defense (Geng Biao in March 1981 and Zhang Aiping in November 1982), two new deputy

chiefs of the general staff (Zhang Zhen in January 1980 and Xu Xin in December 1982), a new director (Yu Qiuli in September 1982) and three deputy directors (Gan Weihan in April 1980, Shi Jinqian in March 1980 and Hua Nan in April 1980) of the General Political Department, a new director (Hong Xuezhi in February 1980) and three deputy directors (Xu Guangyi in September 1980, Wang Zhenzhu in January 1981, Zhang Xiang in January 1983 and Bai Xiangguo in February 1983) of the General Logistics Department and two new commanders (Ye Fei in February 1980 and Liu Huaqing in October 1982) and a political commissar (Li Yaowen in January 1981) of the Navy.

27. Wu Kehua, commander (CO), Guangzhou MR; Nie Fengzhi, CO, Nanjing MR; Zhang Caiqian, CO, Wuhan MR; Wei Jie, Deputy CO, Chengdu MR; Du Yide, CO, Lanzhou MR; Li Chengfang, 1st Political Commissar (PC), Wuhan MR; Xiao Wangdong, 1st PC, Jinan MR; and Xu Liqing, 1st PC, Chengdu MR.

28. "Members of the Hunan Military District Leading Body," Radio Changsha, 1 June 1983 (FBIS HK 060404).

29. Ranks were abolished in the PLA in 1965.

30. Resolution to establish the National Defense Science, Technology and Industry Commission proposed by Premier Zhao Ziyang was adopted at the 24th Session of the Standing Committee of the 5th National People's Congress, 23 August 1982. (New China News Agency-China, Beijing, 23 August 1982).

31. See PRC Military Service Law, People's Daily, 5 June 1984.

3
Institutions, Roles, and Relationships

OVERVIEW

Political-military policymaking and policy implementation in the People's Republic of China involve many institutions. The institutions which are central to understanding the interlocking directorate are: (1) the Central Committee of the Chinese Communist Party and the Politburo and Military Affairs Commission (MAC) within the Central Committee, (2) military regions, (3) military districts, (4) provincial party committees and (5) provincial people's government organizations. The National People's Congress (NPC), State Council, Ministry of Defense, state Central Military Council (CMC), and the national-level PLA headquarters organizations (General Staff Department, General Political Department, General Logistics Department) are not examined in detail in this book since the principal focus is the provincial level interlocking directorate. Normally discussions of the Center include all these organizations, but in this study when the Center is mentioned it refers only to the Central Committee.
The focus of this study is not on institutions but on role linkages between and among the regional institutions as reflected in the interlocking directorate phenomenon. This chapter will place those linkages in perspective by describing the institutions, key elite roles and the relationships that exist between institutions.

INSTITUTIONS

At the national level the locus of power is the Central Committee of the Chinese Communist Party. The Central Committee includes top party leaders from the provinces as well as the Center. The membership changes as a result of political power plays, purges, deaths, and the emergence of new leaders. The changes are ratified by Party Congresses which are now constitutionally required to convene every five years, but which have been held irregularly since the party gained power in 1949.1

The Eighth Party Congress met in two sessions in September 1956 and May 1958.2 At the first session, 97 full and 73 alternate members of the Eighth Central Committee were elected (see Table 3-1). At the second session, an additional 25 alternate members were elected. The Ninth Party Congress met in April 1969 and elected 170 full and 109 alternate members.3 Since the Ninth Party Congress was elected during the Cultural Revolution, it must be considered an aberration and is treated as such in this analysis. The Tenth Party Congress convened in August 1973 and elected 195 full and 124 alternate members.4 At the Third Plenum of the Tenth Party Congress in July 1977, four full members were officially dropped: the Gang-of-Four. The First Plenum of the Eleventh Party Congress met in August 1977 and elected 201 full members and 132 alternate members to the Central Committee.5 At the Third Plenum in December 1978 nine new members were elected and at the Fourth Plenum in September 1979 twelve more full members were added. The Eleventh Central Committee is reviewed only briefly in this book because it is considered as mainly a transition Central Committee between the Tenth and Twelfth. The Twelfth Party Congress in September 1982 elected 210 full members and 138 alternate members to the Central Committee.6

TABLE 3-1

CHINESE COMMUNIST PARTY
CENTRAL COMMITTEE MEMBERS

Central Committee Members	Full Members	Alternate
Eighth (1956)	97	73
Ninth (1969)	170	109
Tenth (1973)	195	124
Eleventh (1977)	201	132
Twelfth (1982)	210	138

Since the Central Committee is too large to effectively conduct day to day business, a smaller group, the

Politburo, was organized within it. The Politburo is the key decisionmaking body. In 1960 (Eighth Central Committee) there were 19 full members and 6 alternate; in 1969, 21 and 4 respectively; in 1973, 22 and 4; in 1977 23 and 3, and in the Twelfth Central Committee Politburo 25 and 3.7 The Standing Committee of the Politburo which has been the ultimate center of power within the PRC has varied from five to eleven. The size of the Standing Committee and changes in its composition are reflected in Table 3-2 below.

TABLE 3-2

CHINESE COMMUNIST PARTY
POLITBURO STANDING COMMITTEE MEMBERS

Year	Changes	Total
1956		6
1958	+1	7
1966	+4	11
1969	-6	5
1973	+4	9
1975	+1 & -1	9
1977 (Jul)	+1 & -2	8
1977 (Aug)	-3	5
1978	+1	6
1980	+2 & -1	7
1982	-1	6

Subordinate to the Standing Committee of the Politburo is the Party Secretariat which exercises operational control over party organizations at lower levels.8 There is usually a representative of the PLA in the Party Secretariat.

Another key element of the Central Committee is the Military Affairs Commission (MAC) which maintained operational control over the PLA until the new State Central Military Council (CMC) was organized in 1983. The MAC has been and will continue to be the key organization for assuring party control over the PLA.9

Although the pyramidal organizational structure of the Central Committee converges on the General Secretary of the party, the policymaking process is not so simple. It is clear that the leadership is not monolithic and that opinion or interest groups operate as high as the Standing Committee of the Politburo. It is also clear that regional elites have a significant impact on the policymaking process.10 The nature of this center-region relationship will be discussed in more detail below.

The National People's Congress is charged with general oversight of the governmental process as opposed to the party system. Since the number of representatives is so great, the daily management of government is left to the State Council. The State Council, in 1983, included 34 ministries, including the Ministry of Defense, and 22 special agencies. The Ministry of Defense is responsible for management of the military budget, general planning for PLA modernization, coordination with the other ministries of the State Council, and liaison with the military representatives of foreign governments. The State Council, with the party's Military Affairs Commission, is also charged with jointly monitoring the National Defense Science Technology and Industry Commission which is responsible for equipping the military with the best weapons and equipment affordable. It is also responsible for military research and development.

The new state Central Military Council seems to have been designed as part of Deng Xiaoping's effort to separate party, state, and army in order to avoid an overconcentration of power. The CMC is the highest decisionmaking body for the purely military or operational aspects of the People's Liberation Army. It is the governmental analogue to the party's Military Affairs Commission which is the highest decisionmaking body for political aspects of PLA policy. The new state constitution describes the CMC as a subordinate organ of the National People's Congress, but since CMC members all concurrently hold MAC positions and because of the nature of the interlocking directorate (see Chapter Five), the Central Committee of the party will continue to directly influence all military decisionmaking and policymaking.11

With the creation of the CMC, professional military leaders (as contrasted with professional commissars) will be able to take key issues directly to those who make the final decisions without going through the party apparatus (MAC and its subordinate committees). This represents a major step forward in functional specialization of the PLA High Command and should contribute to the professionalization of the military.

At the regional level four institutions are included for analysis: (1) the military region headquarters, (2) the province level military district headquarters, (3) the province level party organization, and (4) province level government leadership organizations.

The military region headquarters, in the wake of the Cultural Revolution became a significant subnational institution. While its stated mission is primarily contingency planning for wartime operations, it is clear that by the time of the election of the Tenth Central Committee it had also become deeply involved in regional politics and by virtue of the interlocking directorate, had the potential to influence politics in the provinces.12 When the Eleventh Central Committee was organized that trend was arrested. Chapter Five will discuss these trends in detail.

Until the establishment of the new Central Military Council the military regions reported directly to the party's Military Affairs Commission on all military matters. In fact military region commanders were members of the MAC. While the General Staff Department, General Logistics Department and General Political Department all had the functional equivalent of "staff supervision" over the military regions, the military region commander reported directly to the MAC. The exact role of the CMC in the chain-of-command is still not clear, but it seems likely that it will play a key role and that military regions will probably work through the General Staff Department to the CMC in operational matters.

In peacetime the military region headquarters commands the main force units (the regular army corps and divisions). It provides training and logistical support as well as staff supervision over the developing reserve system and the militia through the military district. It also has some responsibilities for recruitment and demobilization and monitoring military industry. It also prepares contingency plans to form an army group headquarters to command combat forces within its region in time of war.13

The provincial level military district headquarters is organized like the military region. The primary difference in the two organizations is that military districts are concerned with reserve forces and militia. Its principal peacetime mission is determined by the province party committee. In wartime military district forces revert to the control of the military regions or whatever area military headquarters is organized.

The province party committees, headed by the first or senior secretary, are organized much like the Central Committee but on a smaller scale.14 They are subordinate to the Central Committee but have a great deal of autonomy.

The provincial people's government organization (formerly called revolutionary committees) are organized like the State Council and it ministries but likewise on a smaller scale.15 After the 1957 decentralization decisions these organizations became subordinate primarily to the province party committees, and the role of the national level ministries was reduced considerably.16 After the Third Plenum of the Eleventh Central Committee the ministries at the central level were gradually strengthened again. But in 1983 a new decentralization process began.

These six organizations have become institutionalized to varying degrees over the years. The implications of that institutionalization lie in the potential development of parochial interests which are likely to conflict, particularly in the competition for scarce resources.

ELITE ROLES

Description of political culture or bureaucratic roles can contribute to an understanding of behavioral and/or attitudinal postures of elites. This hypothesis has been advanced by Kenneth Jowitt, who defines political culture as follows:

> Political culture refers to a set of informal, adaptive postures -- behavioral and attitudinal -- that emerge in response to and interact with the set of formal definitions -- ideological, policy, and institutional -- that characterize a given level of society.17

The level of society with which this work is concerned is the elite level, and Jowitt defines this as:

> Elite political culture refers to a set of informal-adaptive (behavioral and attitudinal) postures that emerge as a response to and consequences of a given elite's identity-forming experiences.18

We can reach conclusions about the behavioral or attitudinal identity of a given member of the elite who served in a particular role over time. In other words by placing a role in the context of a task environment it is possible to identify behavioral or attitudinal patterns.

Once the decision to study elites has been made, it is necessary to determine which elites. For purposes of this book the key elites are identified by position or role within three institutions: the party, army and government.

The roles in the Politburo and Central Committee are not occupational roles susceptible to precise definition. The Politburo is the apex of power in the People's Republic of China and within it the Standing Committee wields the greatest authority. Politburo members are active participants in the decisionmaking process, while Central Committee members are participants in a consensus-seeking body whose principal activities include ratifying decisions already made by the Politburo and clarifying questions on policy so they can assure its proper implementation in the provinces. Central Committee members also serve as a sounding board and source of ideas for many of the policies in the developmental stage. There are functional departments within the Central Committee which have more influence in the latter stages of policy development, but they are beyond the scope of this study. For the purposes of this analysis, Politburo or Central Committee membership is included only to help shed light on center-regional relationships and to assist in determining the significance of province elites in the prestigious central organs.

The roles of Military Affairs Commission and Central Military Council members are still in the process of being differentiated. It is possible, however, to anticipate the nature of those roles based on an understanding of the general organizational philosophies of the MAC and the CMC. MAC members are senior PLA officers who are concerned with assuring that military activities are within the scope of party direction and that the PLA supports the maintenance of the Marxist-Leninist/Maoist form of government. They accomplish this by establishing policy to be implemented by a whole range of occupational roles within the political commissar system. CMC members, currently the same individuals wearing different hats, are only concerned with the technical-professional aspects of preparing the military to fight. In other words the CMC is concerned about combat capability and the MAC is concerned about reasons for going to war and the political consequences of war.

Unlike the Center, the occupational roles at the military region and province levels can be identified. In the province party organization the key roles include the first secretaries, second secretaries, third secretaries, secretaries, deputy secretaries, and standing committee members.19 The principal roles in the army are found at two levels: military region and military district. At both of these levels the key roles include commanders, deputy commanders, chiefs-of-staff, first political commissars, second political commissars, political commissars, deputy political commissars and directors of political departments. In the province level government organization, the key positions are the governors/mayors, vice-governors/vice-mayors, standing committee members, and members.

Party

The first or senior secretary is theoretically the most powerful individual in the province. His power derives from two sources: his role as ultimate arbiter of the consensus within the party committee which is the locus of authority in the province and his role as a key representative of the province and seeker of resources and guidance for the province at the national level.20 Five provinces listed no first secretary in 1973, but three of those listed second secretaries.21 All but one of the first or first-listed secretaries in 1973 were members or alternate members of the Central Committee, and five were members of the Politburo.22 By the time of the Twelfth Party Congress all of the provinces listed first secretaries and all of them were members of the Central Committee. None of the secretaries, however, were Politburo members.23

The second secretary is the position of a party cadre who is senior to other secretaries and the immediate subordinate of the first secretary. He serves as acting first secretary when the first secretary is absent or when a first secretary has not been appointed. In 1973, thirteen provinces had second secretaries,24 and one of those had three second secretaries.25 After the 12th Party Congress, however, it appeared as if the position of the second secretary was being phased out. Only Shanghai had one as of early 1983.

Only one province had a third secretary in 1973.26 The position here is higher than a secretary but lower than a second secretary. This position, too, appeared to have been phased out by early 1983.

The secretaries were the third level in the provincial party hierarchy in 1973. Generally they were leaders in functionally specific areas such as labor, military, youth activities, or other mass organizations. They were sometimes the first secretaries of prefecture or municipal party committees. Two provinces in 1973 had no one listed at the secretary level, perhaps because they were still rebuilding the party organizations.27 The others had as few as one and as many as eight secretaries, with most having between three and five.28

In 1983 secretary titles were still evolving. Ten provinces listed no first secretary so a "secretary" was the senior secretary in the province party committee.29 It appears as though there is an attempt to phase out the title "first secretary." In the 19 provinces where there was a first secretary and the secretaries were listed at the second level, there were from 2 to 5 secretaries listed. This represents a significant reduction or streamlining since 1973.

Deputy secretaries occupy the next level down in the party hierarchy. They are usually assistants to the secretaries in functional areas, but they could also be in charge of a functional area or hold a key leadership position in a district, county, or city party committee. They usually have less time or stature as party members than secretaries. Only nine provinces had deputy secretaries in 1973.30 In 1983 the 10 provinces which listed no first secretary and in which a secretary held the top position each had from 2 to 5 deputy secretaries (sometimes called assistant secretaries). Standing committee members are also often assistants to secretaries in functionally specific areas or heads of lower level administrative units. Most provincial level units in 1973 listed from four to fifteen standing committee members. One however, listed sixty-two.31 In 1983 the numbers of standing committee members had been reduced, ranging from 3 to 9.

Some provinces listed members, alternate members, and responsible persons at the bottom levels of the party committee hierarchy in 1972. There is no data available about such roles but it is likely that they were filled by elites from lower levels (county or commune representatives).

The general role of the party committee in each province is to adapt national party policy to local conditions. This requires the development of more specific policy guidelines and monitoring the implementation of policy within the province. Individual party committee members are involved mostly in functionally or geographically specific areas during implementation or monitoring. It is also important to note that while general managerial or leadership ability may be useful for certain party committee roles, these roles are not defined specifically enough to suggest the development of a particular ethic or workstyle. However, although consensus decisionmaking has been promoted over "commandism," there is still some room for individual leadership styles within prescribed bureaucratic behavior patterns.32 In 1984 there were more discussions of a "leadership responsibility system" which may reduce the scope of consensus decisionmaking.

Military

Four military region and military district roles are important for the purposes of this study. Commanders and deputy commanders in the command system and first political commissars and commissars in the political commissar system. Like the hierarchy of secretaries there are occasionally second, deputy and assistant political commissars. In 1973 the numbers of deputy commanders at the military region and military district levels ranged from 5 to 15. By 1983 those numbers were cut and ranged from 2 to 5. In 1973 the numbers of deputy political commissars was slightly less ranging from 1 to 6. While the evolution is not yet complete, by 1984 it appeared as though deputy commissar positions will eventually range from 2 to 4.

It is important to distinguish between the command system and the commissar system. The locus of authority in the PLA is not as clear as that of the party. There is a complex relationship between commanders and commissars. The commander is "theoretically responsible for the technical management of his unit, its professional organization, training, direction, and performance on the battlefield."33 The commissar, on the other hand, is the party representative who assures that the PLA understands and conforms to the party line and general policies. He is also concerned with the institutionalization of the unit. He is responsible for developing the esprit, morale, and loyalty of the unit through positive appeals rather than negative sanctions. The nature of the political commissar role, in contrast to the role of the party secretary, is likely to suggest specific ethics and workstyles, and provide more tangible identity-forming experiences.

Government

The organization which manages government activities at provincial unit level is the provincial/autonomous region/municipal people's government. It was called the Revolutionary Committee through the period of the Tenth Central Committee. There are five categories of elite roles within government organizations: governors/mayors (called chairmen in 1973), first vice-governors/first vice-mayors (called first vice-chairmen in 1973), vice-governors/vice-mayors (called vice-chairmen in 1973), standing committee members, and members.

The governor/mayor is theoretically responsible for coordinating and managing government activities within party policy guidelines. The vice-governors/mayors are generally heads of various government activities or heads of district, county, or city government organizations. The numbers of vice-chairmen in 1973 ranged from 7 (Nei Monggol) to 29 (Liaoning). In 1983 the numbers ranged from 3 to 7.

Standing committee members and members are usually assistants in government activities or representatives of lower level government organizations such as communes or large factories. In 1973 there were often 30 to 40 standing committee members in the provinces. As of this writing the numbers for 1983 have not be announced but it is expected that they have been significantly reduced.

The government elite roles may be contrasted with party roles by their focus on implementation of policy more than policy formulation or adaptation.34 It takes more technical and managerial skill to execute the role properly. As a result of this focus, it is likely that individual elites in these roles are strongly affected by mission or goal orientations. When they come into frequent contact with real world obstacles to mission accomplishment, there is a tendency for elites who spend most of their time in these roles to develop more pragmatic attitudes and become less and less concerned with ideological purity.

This distinction cannot be generalized at too high a level because there are elements of the government organizations which are exceptions, e.g., those elements for which there are no objective or agreed-upon criteria of mission accomplishment, such as those concerned with education, indoctrination, training, organizing activities, or police/juridical activities. It is from these elements that elites with more concern for ideological purity are likely to emerge. On the other hand, those who spend time in roles in organizations whose product is quantifiable are likely to develop more pragmatic attitudes.

The notion that when an individual elite member spends time in a particular role, that role will begin to shape attitudes or behavior patterns, is important to understanding the concept of interlocking directorate/ roles this work. The capacity to explain or predict attitudes or behavior patterns based upon identity-forming experience is complicated by elite movement between roles or by a single elite member holding more than one role at the same time. In the latter case, different and often conflicting forces come to bear upon the individual and there is no way at present to determine which of the roles is likely to have the greatest influence. It may be possible to draw conclusions based upon the amount of time spent in a particular role, but for the purposes of this analysis it is only important to note that increased participation in interlocking roles is likely to mitigate differences in attitudes or behavior patterns based upon role experience. In fact, it is possible that when an individual elite member holds two or three different positions in which different attitudes are demanded he could adapt to each role with different and conflicting attitudes. At the very least, he is likely to be faced with contradictions. This points out the importance of paying particular attention to roles as well as personalities in elite analysis.

RELATIONSHIPS

Center-Region

Regionalism has been a major concern of Chinese leaders throughout China's history. There have been many periods of disunity in which areas within China became virtually independent and sovereign kingdoms. These periods were characterized by instability and civil war. The historical solution to this problem has been reunification of the country under a strong central leadership. In the past 100 years, however, the population and the complexities of the society have increased to such an extent that even though the nation is more centralized than in the past, there is still a search for a more effective balance between center and region.

Prior to 1949 the central task of the Chinese Revolution was the unification of the nation. During the Sino-Japanese War and the Civil War, however, the nature of the task required a great deal of decentralization. Although there was a major attempt to develop standard doctrine and policies in Yanan and even train cadre to use similar approaches, there was also a necessity to allow significant autonomy of activity in local areas. In many cases the autonomy was a compromise to coopt local leaders. It was a quid pro quo: a degree of loyalty to the Communist leadership for a degree of autonomy. Another practical cause for decentralized activity was the inadequate communications system.

Since 1949 there have been a number of adjustments in an attempt to settle on the appropriate degree of centralization. At first there was a strong move toward a high degree of centralization, but by 1957 the trend was reversed. In that year a number of decisions to decentralize authority were made to stimulate initiative and creativity.35 The idea was to set general policy at the Center and specific policy in the provinces.

The decentralization decisions were more complicated than the simple centralization-decentralization dichotomy might suggest. Franz Schurmann provides a useful description of attempts to balance center-region relationships and the following few paragraphs draw heavily from that description.

The decentralization decisions were the result of a debate between groups headed by Mao Zedong and Chen Yun.36 Both groups agreed that some degree of decentralization was needed, but they did not agree on the exact level of critical decisionmaking. A balance between the Center, the province and the production unit had to be reached.

The debate was complicated by discussions of the effectiveness of two styles of command relationships: vertical or dual rule.37 Vertical rule meant party control over the ministries at the central level which in turn controlled policy formulation and implementation from the Center through provincial agencies to production units. This was extreme centralization based upon functional areas of specialization. Dual rule meant the establishment of parallel party committees at the provincial and production unit level and allowing important decisions to be made at the lower levels. This also signified that the provincial party committees would be responsible for a wider range of decisions (functionally diffuse). Dual rule had the practical effect of strengthening the role of the party. Party influence over the government at only one point, the top, was much weaker than party control over decisionmaking and policy implementation at all levels. The debate centered on whether decisionmaking powers should be delegated to the producing units (communes/enterprises)38 or to middle-level administrative units (provinces).39

The Eighth Party Congress of 1956 began the call for dual rule which "paved the way for decentralization in 1957."40 The Third Plenum of the Eighth Central Committee (20 September to 9 October 1957), which included first secretaries from the provinces, "ratified the decisions made by the Politburo in September 1957 for a far reaching decentralization of the economic system."41 The Third Plenum wanted to make the province level unit the locus of decisionmaking.42 The effort was intended to strengthen the position of province level elites. It resulted in the State Council announcing on November 18, 1957 "three regulations on changes in the system of industrial, commercial and financial administration."43 Schurmann describes the major changes:

> First, on industry. The most important change was the transfer to provincial governments of a broad range of industries. This included: almost all light industry, nonstrategic heavy industrial enterprises, the timber industry, ports, some enterprises under the jurisdiction of the Ministry of Communications, and many construction enterprises. The principle of dual rule was to be universally implemented in industry. Enterprises still subject to central jurisdiction were henceforth to be linked to regional authorities through dual rule. Regional authorities acquired greater powers over allocation of materials. They now got a greater share of above-target production, as well as a share of enterprise profits. Regional authorities also acquired greater control over personnel, including those working in central state-owned enterprises. The planning system was greatly simplified with greater leeway given factory managers to practice flexibility. A system of profit-sharing made it possible for enterprises to derive some of their investment funds directly from enterprise profit.
> Second, on commerce. As in industry, a broad range of commercial agencies and enterprises were placed under provincial control. The big "specialized commercial corporations," which earlier had acquired needed goods for central government agencies, were abolished. Wholesale trading stations, formerly entirely

under central control, now came partly under provincial control. The planning system was greatly simplified. A profit-sharing system was introduced, and provincial authorities were given greater control over enterprise profits (this to be done "gradually" and "experimentally"). Provincial authorities were given the right to set some prices in their areas of jurisdiction, although here too the regulations indicated that great care had to be exercised, and all efforts made to achieve coordination in price-setting between the center and the provinces. Again, as in industry, the principle of dual rule was universally introduced into the commercial network.

Third, on finance. Unlike in the other two sectors, no structural rearrangements were indicated, and no mention was made of dual rule. The regulations on finance laid down general lines of revenue division between the center and the regions, with the latter given a greatly increased share of budgetary revenue.44

The organizational changes Schurmann discusses led to severe economic disruption from 1958 until 1961. For example, Nicholas Lardy examines the effects of the decisions from an economic perspective and suggests that decentralization was more cosmetic than real.45 He points out that the Center continued to control the fiscal system even after the 1958 attempts to decentralize, and he concludes that in the early 1970's "the fiscal system remains highly centralized. This evidence bears on the nature of the revenue collection and sharing system, Center-provincial revenue sharing rates, and central government control of provincial expenditures."46 He also suggests that actual results of the decentralization attempts led to a highly differentiated system in which "more developed provinces give up substantial portions of the revenues they collect while poorer provinces retain all of their revenues and receive subsidies from the central government as well."47 This is an indication of central control.

It is clear that decentralization is a relative term. While some decisionmaking authority was undoubtedly transferred to the provinces in 1957, the central government retained the power to make the most crucial economic decisions resulting in relatively centralized control. This result supports a finding of this book, which will be discussed in greater detail in later sections, that there has been a general movement toward national integration.

By January 1961 a party rectification movement in the aftermath of the disastrous Great Leap Forward, reduced the power of the party committees and increased the influence of professionals, managers, and intellectuals.48 There was also some movement toward recentralization in early 1962. However, as the PRC headed into the Cultural Revolution a new balance of decisionmaking power began to emerge between the center, provinces, and production units.49

The Cultural Revolution can be characterized as another period of extreme decentralization even though some of the major policy guidelines came from the Center. The province level party committees were destroyed by local red guards units. During the height of the Cultural Revolution three-in-one committees were formed to manage political and economic decisionmaking at almost every level from province to workshop. These committees consisted of representatives of the PLA, the government and the masses. The period of three-in-one revolutionary committees restored some of the power to the provincial level authorities, but it was not until the rebuilding of the province party committees in the early 1970's that the center-province relationship was brought into a degree of equilibrium.

The relationship between the Center and provinces has been particularly complicated by political style in China. Consensus decisionmaking stimulates much political maneuvering in order for any individual or group to prevail or achieve a consensus with a minimum of compromise. A conflict which reaches an impasse at any given level, or a conflict in which one individual perceives he will lose too much, causes him to expand the forum of debate to reinforce his position.50 For example, when Mao wanted to push the decentralization issue in 1957, he went beyond the Central Committee and elicited the support of provincial party secretaries who were concerned with implementing policy. This added some weight to his opinions.51 There are natural limits to which Mao's arguments could be extended effectively and the most likely limit probably included key elites in the provinces, especially military region commanders and party first secretaries. The Cultural Revolution was an example of extending the debate beyond the maximum possible limits, and the end result was chaos. It is likely, however, that party first secretaries will be included in important policy debates, but this no longer requires the debate to be extended beyond the Central Committee since most party first secretaries are currently members of the Central Committee.

After the downfall of the Gang-of-Four, and more particularly since the Third Plenum of the Eleventh Central Committee (December 1978), the PRC leadership has begun again to experiment with policies aimed at refining the center-province balance. They are in a way debating issues similar to those in the late 1950's described above by Schurmann. While the outcome of this evolutionary process is still not complete it is clear that a form of centralized planning and decentralized execution of commerce and industry is likely. The 1983 decentralization efforts differed from those of 1957 in that they moved key decisionmaking to the enterprise/ factory level rather than to the provincial level. But like the late 1950's general fiscal policies are likely to remain highly centralized.

Intraregion

Institutional relationships in the People's Republic of China are basically competitive. In center-province relations local interests conflict with national interests and at the province level parochial interests create tensions between institutions. The remainder of this chapter will describe some of the forces at work which contribute to competitive relationships between institutions. The foundation will then be prepared for a more detailed analysis of the nature and scope of institutional linkages and attempts by PRC elites to reduce the degree of competition in the relationships.

Chairman Mao considered the relationship between center and province to be one of "contradiction," a schism which poses a severe problem to national unity. He officially labeled the relationship a contradiction in his 25 April 1956 speech on the "Ten Great Relationships."52 The earlier campaign against "independent kingdoms," which was publicized when Rao Shushi and Gao Gang were purged in 1955, was another indication of Mao's strong concern about the potential for the development of regionalism.53

The center-province schism cannot be explained in simple institutional interest terms. There are extremely complex forces at work which create natural tendencies toward provincial self-interest, and these forces cross institutional boundaries. They are a significant factor in pushing institutions (party-army-government) within a province closer together in cooperative activities directed against the Center. Whether these forces are the result of competition for national resources or some combination of expression of interests by province interest groups is beyond the scope of this work, but it is important to note their existence and the fact that they have contributed to a real center-province schism.

The relationships between party, army, and government leadership groups at the province level reflect institutional viewpoints but probably not to the extent most literature on party-army or party-government relations would suggest. The literature focuses primarily on party-army relations and often begins the analysis with Mao's dictum that the "party commands the gun, and the gun will never be allowed to command the party."**54** Chairman Mao never officially labeled these relationships as contradictions as he did the center-region relationships, but he did discuss at length the central role of the party.55 Certainly the fact that the key decisionmaking role is reserved for party leaders, yet the tools of force are in the hands of the army, sets up a potential conflict. The leadership of a civilian party which operates under the principle of democratic centralism and maintains effective control over the entire population must recognize that since popular revolution is not probable, the only means by which they are likely to lose power is some type of military coup at the top of the authority structure. Consequently, the military is a source of concern.

The party-army-government trichotomy is in turn made up of three dichotomies: party-army, party-government, and army-government. The party-army relationship is clearly the most important and potentially a source of serious conflict. The party-government relationship is also important but not for the same reasons. Conflict results when alternate means for accomplishing party goals emerge. The challenge to the party is not in the potential use of force, as with the army, but in the expertise of government/enterprise officials as the implementors of policy. The army-government relationship is important primarily as an indicator of the degree of army involvement in the affairs of the nation. If the army becomes too involved in government operations, as it did toward the end of the Cultural Revolution, it becomes a potential challenge to party leadership.

These dichotomies exist at two levels. First, conflict as a result of pragmatic institutional interests. The red-expert debate is often a manifestation. The second level is in the values and attitudes of individual elites or interest groups within the institutional hierarchies. These groups tend to reinforce or mitigate conflict based on institutional interests.

Institutional interests are based upon the organizational task. The task of the party is to define goals and direction and to provide the leadership for all aspects and levels of social, political and economic change. This all-pervasive task by definition creates a new elite class in the Djilas sense.56 It creates psychological attitudes of confidence and superiority in the minds of party cadre who have been "certified" by the party as being enlightened. It also makes the party, as an institution, almost sacred and immune from criticism or attack. Hence, the tasks which drive the party are: to maintain party discipline internally; and to assure that party members are located strategically throughout the society to serve as communicators of policy goals, arbiters of disputes over methods, and monitors of policy implementation. In an idealistic sense individual party members are also expected to set the example of a model self-sacrificing citizen.

The nature of these party tasks generates a number of interests which affect relations with other institutions. The need to assure compliance with party doctrine and to maintain its leading role motivates the party to find structural as well as doctrinal solutions to the tasks. The structural solution is to assign party members to key positions in the hierarchy of other institutions, thus challenging the autonomy of those institutions. Doctrinal solutions include, but are not limited to, the promulgation of ideal-type models or rules and regulations for behavior of elites and institutions. They also include the establishment of selection and advancement criteria and the approval of appointments for most institutions. These party activities are prone to abuse and when perceived by non-party cadre as such, are likely to create conflict within institutions.

The army and government have also developed institutional interests based upon tasks. The army was charged with three missions in the 1973 constitution: to be prepared for combat, to engage in labor for the people, and to be a production force in society.57 It is not simply a user of national resources. The accomplishment of the first task requires the army leadership to examine the capabilities of potential adversaries. At two points, the Korean War and the Sino-Vietnam "Lesson", it tested its capability through actual combat. The results of their analyses caused some military elites to see a need for a modernized army.58 It is easy for army leaders to perceive their job as the most critical for Chinese society. They recognize that a strong disciplined army should not only have modern weaponry, but it should also be managed rationally which means making key appointments based on merit and not just on political factors.

The second and third tasks outlined in the constitution were imposed on the army by the party. Leaders within the armed forces recognized that the time spent in nonmilitary activity reduces military combat effectiveness. The party also imposes egalitarian principles in the military which professional military leaders perceive as a threat to discipline. The confrontation between party and army is manifested in the constant struggle between the commander of the military unit and his political commissar, the party representative who runs the powerful unit party committee.59 This dichotomy is often labeled expert versus red and can easily be equated to the organizational theory debate between rational managers and human relations advocates.60 In practice the two sides usually reach an accomodation, but there are strong tendencies toward conflict. This relationship will be discussed in more detail in Chapter Four.

The government encounters the same problem as does the military, except that their task is generally economic rather than military. In their concern for modernization, the same tendencies toward rational management emerge and conflict with party ideals and doctrine. Government/enterprise leaders generally perceive a pragmatic value in providing material incentives for production and that also runs counter to party doctrine. They, as do the army leaders, resent the penetration of party representatives, especially when they perceive party policies as reducing the effectiveness of the institution.

The above descriptions of roles and attitudes are pure types. They suggest forces which are likely to influence the behavior patterns of elites who fill particular roles. They provide some background for understanding the nature of institutional schisms.

The nature of the relationships between party, army and government clearly demands more research. It is sufficient for present purposes, however, to note that conflict exists, and that the party leadership is aware of that conflict and has been taking structural and doctrinal measures to reduce it.

By focusing on elites and elite career patterns within these institutions it is possible to shed light on the changing formal relationships and informal linkages between center and regional institutions and between party, army and government institutions at the province level. One of these career patterns, the political commissar, stands out as critical, particularly in the all-important party-army relationship which is central to the question of political stability.

NOTES

1. A useful source on the party congresses is found in James Pinckney Harrison, The Long March to Power: A History of the Chinese Communist Party, 1921-1972 (New York: Praeger, 1972).
2. United States Department of State, Bureau of Intelligence and Research, Directory of Party and Government Officials of Communist China, vol. I, BD 271, (Wash DC: 20 July 1960): pp. 2-3.
3. United States Government Printing Office, Reference Aid, Directory of Chinese Communist Officials: Party, Provincial, Municipal and Military, (Wash DC: US Govt Printing Office, May 1970 A70-13).
4. Union Research Institute, Hierarchies of the People's Republic of China -- March 1975 (Hong Kong: Union Research Institute, 1975), pp. 1-4.
5. National Foreign Assessment Center, Directory of Officials of the People's Republic of China, (Wash DC: US Govt Printing Office, Oct. 1977).
6. Zhongguo Gongchandang Di Shierce Quanguo Daibiao Dahui Wenjian (Documents of the 12th Party Congress of the Chinese Communist Party), (Hong Kong: Joint Publishing Co., September 1982).
7. Eighth CC data from US Department of State, Directory, p.4. Tenth CC data from Union Research Institute, Hierarchies, p. 5. Twelfth CC data from National Foreign Assessment Center, Directory of Officials, Nov. 1978.
8. Franz Schurmann, Ideology and Organization in Communist China, 2d ed. (Berkeley: University of California Press, 1968), p. 150.
9. For a description of the MAC prior to 1983 see Ibid., pp. 150-151.
10. Chang, Power and Policy in China, p. 186.
11. See The Constitution of the People's Republic of China, (Adopted on December 4, 1982 by the Fifth National People's Congress of the People's Republic of China at its Fifth Session), Beijing: Foreign Languages Press, 1983.
12. Bureau of Intelligence, Ministry of National Defense, Republic of China, pamphlet Fei Hsienhsing Kuofang Tzuchih Tihsi (Current National Defense Organization System in Communist China) (Taipei, Taiwan, 1976), p. 3.
13. See Yu-shen Chien, China's Fading Revolution, 1967-1968 (Hong Kong: Centre of Contemporary Chinese Studies, 1969) for an analysis of the potential for regionalism based on the military region after the Wuhan Incident.
14. Schurmann, Ideology and Organization, p. 149.
15. Ibid., pp. 183-186, 211.
16. Ibid., pp. 175-178.

17. Kenneth Jowitt, "An Organizational Approach to the Study of Political Culture in Marxist-Leninist Systems," The American Political Science Review 68 (September 1974): p. 1173.
18. Ibid.
19. See Hierarchies of the People's Republic of China -- March 1975 for complete listings.
20. Schurmann, Ideology and Organization, p. 149.
21. Liaoning, Shandong, Jiangsu, Anhui, and Hubei listed no first secretary and Liaoning, Shandong and Hubei listed second secretaries.
22. All information on 1973 Central Committee and Politburo memberships and region or province positions comes from Union Research Institute, Hierarchies in the People's Republic of China.
23. Documents of the 12th Party Congress of the Chinese Communist Party (See footnote 6).
24. Tianjin, Hebei, Liaoning, Heilongjiang, Ningxia, Qinghai, Xinjiang, Shandong, Shanghai, Hubei, Hunan, Guizhou and Yunnan.
25. Hebei
26. Xinjiang
27. Hebei and Qinghai
28. Hebei had eight
29. Anhui, Gansu, Heilongjiang, Hubei, Jiangsu, Qinghai, Shanghai, Shanxi, Sichuan, and Zhejiang
30. Hebei, Shaanxi, Ningxia, Jiangsu, Zhejiang, Henan, Guizhou, Yunnan and Qinghai
31. Beijing
32. Research on behavior patterns might begin with John Starr and Nancy Dyer, Post-Liberation Works of Mao Zedong: A Bibliography and Index (Berkeley: Center for Chinese Studies, 1976), pp. 101-106.
33. William W. Whitson, The Chinese High Command: A History of Communist Military Politics, 1927-1971 (New York: Praeger, 1973), p. 438.
34. For explanations about the government role see Schurmann, Ideology and Organization, chapter III; John Starr, Ideology and Culture: An Introduction to the Dialectic of Contemporary Chinese Politics (New York: Harper and Row, 1973), chapter 8; and A. Doak Barnett, Cadre, Bureaucracy, and Political Power in Communist China (New York: Columbia University Press, 1967), part II.
35. Schurmann, Ideology and Organization, p. 86.
36. Ibid., pp. 196-197.
37. Ibid., pp. 188-194.
38. Described as Decentralization I by Schurmann. This is an extremely important distinction since it is key to understanding the economic reforms of 1983 and 1984. It seems clear at the end of 1984 that critical reforms are being made and that those reforms are in the

direction of Decentralization I; that is, decentralizing the key decisionmaking to the economic enterprise level as opposed to the political province level. The major difference in the 1984 reform effort is that the commune is being phased out. As a result the key level for the decentralization effort will include factories, enterprises, research institutes, and other similar level institutions. In the rural areas some production brigades may remain but the old village organizations are likely to play an important role.

39. Described as Decentralization II by Schurmann.
40. Schurmann, Ideology and Organization, p. 195.
41. Ibid., p. 196.
42. Ibid., p. 197.
43. Ibid., p. 206-207.
44. Ibid., p. 207-208.
45. Nicholas Lardy, "Centralization and Decentralization in China's Fiscal Management," China Quarterly 61 (January-March 1975), pp. 25-60.
46. Ibid., p. 58.
47. Ibid., p. 58.
48. Schurmann, Ideology and Organization, p. 218.
49. Ibid., p. 219.
50. Chang, Power and Policy in China, pp. 51-55.
51. Ibid., p. 219.
52. Survey of China Mainland Press, 4000, 14 August 1967, p. 16.
53. Harrison, pp. 467-469. While the fear of regionalism has always been strong there have also been a number of serious discussions about establishing regional economic zones. It is a debate which is likely to continue.
54. See for example Ralph Powell, "The Power of the Chinese Military," Current History 59 (September 1970:p. 129. The actual quote comes from Mao Tse-tung, Selected Works, vol. II (New York: International Publishers, 1954), p. 272.
55. See "On the Correct Handling of Contradictions Among the People," Peking Review (23 June 1967), pp, 1-36.
56. Milovan Djilas, The New Class (New York: Praeger, 1957.
57. Article 15, "Revised Constitution of the People's Republic of China," found in John Starr, Ideology and Culture, p. 283.
58. Alice Langley Hsieh, Communist China's Strategy in the Nuclear Era (Englewood Cliffs, New Jersey: Prentice-Hall, Inc., 1962), chapter 2.
59. Whitson, The Chinese High Command, chapter 10.
60. For an important discussion of the rational or scientific management school see Frederick Taylor, Scientific Management, (New York: Harper and Row Publishers, Inc., 1911). For an important analysis of

the human relations approach see Philip Selznick, *Leadership in Administration* (Evanston, Ill.: Row, Peterson, 1957). For the most recent solid academic discussion of these concepts see Thomas J. Peters and Robert H. Waterman, Jr., *In Search of Excellence: Lessons from America's Best-Run Companies,* (New York: Harper and Row Publishers, 1982).

4
The Political Commissar System: Evolution, Structure, and Functions

OVERVIEW

The civilian communist party and the military communist party in China are separate and distinct organizations. The military party is known collectively as the political commissar system and that system is the most important linkage point in the relationships between the army and party or government organizations.1 The military and civilian parties are separate in that their organizational allegiances are different. Civilian party cadre owe primary loyalty to the party or government organizations in which they work. Military party cadre, on the other hand, owe loyalty primarily to the PLA. The two bodies are distinct in that many of their identity-forming experiences and daily activities are different. Military political commissars are educated totally within the PLA's political commissar school system and generally serve their entire career within the military. There are two exceptions, at the military district and subdistrict levels, which will be discussed below. Military party cadre are also distinct in that they work within a social group, the PLA, which permits more discipline or control over the daily activities of its members than groups managed by civilian cadre. While PLA political commissars should not be considered an extension of the civilian party system, neither should they be considered equivalent to professional military officers. They are sui generis and they are the key to the political-military relationship. For these reasons this chapter was included in this study.

CONCEPT ORIGIN

Although the commissar system has been employed by various combatants in international warfare, it has evolved primarily in civil or revolutionary war environments. Internal strife generates unique military problems which do not exist in wars between nations. The single most important of these problems is that of loyalty. In international wars it is generally easy to distinguish the enemy by language or race. In a civil war, however, where citizens are forced to choose sides against fellow citizens, the problem of detecting the enemy becomes much more difficult. A second major problem which emerges in a civil war is the decision which confronts commanders of military units who must destroy an opponent's forces or put down an uprising which may include friends, relatives, and citizens of the commander's own country. Under these conditions, the question of loyalty to a cause or political group becomes all important. General Wang Sheng of the Chinese Nationalist Army made the following remarks concerning this problem:

> During the civil war in China it was impossible to distinguish friends from foes. At every level our forces had been infiltrated by communist sympathizers. In many cases previously loyal officers either defected or remained in our armed forces to do as much damage as possible from within. The fact that we were all Chinese made it impossible to distinguish the loyal from the disloyal.2

The first traceable institutional solution for loyalty problems occurred in 1793 during the French Revolution. During the course of the revolution, the army of the Monarchy changed its loyalty to the revolutionary side, the First Republic. In the process of change, 593 generals were replaced and there were a number of key defections.3 The question of loyalty to the First Republic was of supreme importance. On 30 April 1793, the Convention (France's governing power) decreed a system of "Representants en Mission." Four Representatives were sent to each of the eleven armies "to exercise the most active supervision on the conduct of the generals, officers and soldiers."4 Article 16 of the decree spelled out their responsibilities:

> They shall take every measure to discover, to have the Generals arrested, and to have arrested and brought before the 'Tribunal revolutionnaire,' every military man, civil agent and other citizen who may have aided, favoured, or counselled a plot against the liberty and safety of the Republic or who may have engineered the disorganization of the armies and fleets, and robbed the public funds.5

Article 18 of the decree stated, "The Representatives of the people sent with the armies are invested with unlimited powers for the exercise of the functions delegated to them."6 The "Representants en Mission" lasted only a short time in France, but their activities were fairly well documented.7 The important point is that they provided an institutional mechanism for civilian checks on military power and were the forerunner of the modern day political commissars.

POLITICAL COMMISSAR CONCEPT BROUGHT TO RUSSIA

Although forms of direct political control over the military were used in France and Russia on a number of occasions by Louis Philippe, Louis Napoleon, Nicholas I, and Nicholas II, it was not until July 1917 that a recognizable commissar system emerged. At that time "The provisional government under Alexandre Kerensky appointed several front commissars to the armed forces."8 The Russian commissars focused their activities on improving the morale and discipline of the troops.

Both the Mensheviks and the Bolsheviks were serious students of the French Revolution and their analyses of the activities of the "Representants en Mission" may have provided them with the idea for commissars in their respective military organizations.

On 5 November 1917, the Bolshevik Military Revolutionary Committee issued a "proclamation explaining that commissars were being appointed in the military units of Petrograd and its environs."9 Although the role of Bolshevik commissars was initially not well-defined, by 15 January 1918 they were regularized in the Red Army. The Bolshevik commissar system was at first directed primarily at the political loyalty of the leaders and troops in the Red Army. Eventually the role of the commissar was clearly articulated. His duties were:

1. To check on officers' loyalty and honesty.
2. To maintain high morale by explaining to the troops what they are fighting for.
3. To organize study classes, discussion groups, lectures, and dramatic circles.
4. To assist unit commanders to make tactical decisions.10

Immediately after the commissar system was implemented the most controversial aspect of the concept became evident: the duality of command which created the classic conflict between commissars and commanders.

Soviet political commissars have been alternately strong and weak compared to commanders in the Red Army and in 1941 they were completely abolished for a short period.11 One of the factors which contributed to the eventual longevity of the political commissar system was the inclusion of the notion of a "positive appeal" through mass indoctrination and political training."12 This concept will be explained in more detail later in the chapter. Positive appeal, in contrast with the more well-known negative aspects of a political commissar system (surveillance, purge, etc.), became a significant element of the doctrine which was passed on to the political commissar systems of other nations.

THE CHINESE SETTING

When the political commissar concept was introduced to China it found a suitable environment. Historical, military, social, economic, and political conditions were ideal for the acceptance of such a system. Chinese history is often analyzed using the "Dynastic Cycle" theory.13 This theory explains that a dynasty usually begins with a strong central government supported by a powerful army. Eventually the centralized power dissipates into several autonomous powers. The personal armies of leaders away from the capital become larger and stronger until they can challenge the authority of the emperor. At times there were hundreds of independent armies all over China with no recognized central authority.14 Eventually one of these armies becomes stronger than the rest and, after defeating each in turn, reestablishes a central authority; a new dynasty with a new army as the central power. The cycle thus begins again.

The period from 1911 to 1927 in China is known as the "Warlord Period."15 It was one of the periods of disunity in which hundreds of warlords throughout China maintained autonomy over their own geographical jurisdictions. Conflict among and between warlords and the central government was the rule, not the exception. It was in this period of extreme disunity that the concept of political commissars entered China.

The entry of a political commissar system into China could not have been timed better. The sociopolitical conditions in China demanded answers to deep-rooted military problems which had plagued Chinese armies for centuries.16 These problems, byproducts of the conditions, were of every type and description, from discipline to morale, and included corruption, despotism, desertion, mutiny, and defection. All of these stemmed from two central questions: how to obtain the **loyalty** of men to their leaders, nation, or ideology and how to establish effective **political-military relations**. The first requires the instilling and maintaining of the loyalty within an army to one's own cause concurrently destroying the loyalty of the enemy's forces to their leaders. The solution to the second problem requires obtaining and maintaining civilian popular support and concurrently convincing the civilian populace not to support the enemy.

SOCIOLOGICAL, POLITICAL, AND ECONOMIC FACTORS CONTRIBUTING TO THE ACCEPTANCE OF POLITICAL COMMISSARS IN CHINA

There is no tradition in China of loyalty to a nation-state or ideology.17 Loyalty has first and foremost been to individuals and family. The leaders of China had the monumental task of transferring this loyalty object to the nation-state or their particular ideology.18 The political commissar system was a vehicle for this transfer.

China also has no tradition of democracy or individual rights. Even under the future democracy of China, as envisioned in the "Three People's Principles" by Sun Yat-sen, the individual was to be subordinated to the needs of the state rather than, as in the United States, the state existing for the general benefit of the people.19 It was true that the people (masses) came first in everything, political and economic, but the term people always referred to people as a whole, not as individuals. When this concept is combined with the authoritarian tradition, the notion of standing up for one's individual rights is lost. As a result, a type of passive submission to authority existed among the people, especially in the army.20 This situation meant that if a military commander were to take advantage of his position to oppress or abuse his soldiers or even the civilians in his area of jurisdiction, traditionally, there was no peaceful recourse for the mistreated. There was no one to mediate differences between the soldier and his commander or between civil and military authorities. There were few checks on the power of the commander.21 If a commander were well-read, and understood the humanitarian principles of Confucius, he might be a benevolent leader and there would be fewer problems. The majority of commanders, however, were not well-educated.22

A second problem endemic to the system was that the pay of officers as well as soldiers in China was always low in comparison to other elements of the society. Additionally, the fringe benefits often found in Western armies were lacking. Consequently, the unit commander, who received only a nominal salary, certainly not enough to support a family, often took advantage of his position for economic gain. If he were given money to buy food for his troops, he embezzled a portion of it and as a result the troops ate less. If he had an opportunity to confiscate some of the produce of local civilians, he would. He would send soldiers to confiscate the farmers' rice. But the soldiers also saw an opportunity for themselves. They confiscated more than the commander asked for and kept the surplus for themselves. The entire system was pervaded by a feeling that one was entitled to his share regardless of the means, and the individual rights of others were ignored.23

Another condition which existed in China was the lack of regard for the civilian populace by the military. The armies of China have maltreated, robbed and abused the civilian population for centuries and this caused a deep-rooted enmity of historic proportions. This is reflected in the Chinese saying, "One does not use good steel to make nails nor does one use good men to make soldiers."

The People's Liberation Army under Mao Zedong saw the necessity for overcoming this hostility and gaining the support of the populace.24 Its political commissar system served it well in this respect, and proved to be a major factor in their victory on the Mainland. The Republic of China under Chiang Kai-shek realized too late the need for obtaining the support of civilians.

A very important sociological reason for the quick acceptance of the political commissar concept into China concerned basic family relationships. Individual and group relationships in China were strictly governed by tradition. In family relationships authority and responsibility were vested in the eldest member. The problems of livelihood and protection of the family members were his responsibility. In order to make this system function, strict rules governed individual behavior and discipline, and all members of the family were expected to be completely responsive to the wishes of the group leader.25

The individual derived a strong sense of security from this complex system of relationships. He knew he could depend on his family to help him solve his personal problems, especially those with people outside the family group.

When a youth in traditional China was taken from the relative security of his family group he experienced much more of a traumatic shock than his American counterpart. He was completely lost when he found that he must accept full responsibility for his own actions and had no one to provide him with guidance and support. The political commissar concept was an effective solution to this problem. If the concept is carried out as intended, the military unit replaces the family, the political commissar provides assistance in solving personal problems, and the commander represents parental and supreme authority.26

The concept of the military commander and the political commissar acting in loco parentis is not explicit in the various handbooks or instructions for commissars, but it is known that the commander of a unit represents the father (disciplinarian) of the unit family and the political commissar represents the mother (sympathetic listener).27 This idea is communicated to soldiers by means of military magazines, radio and television, usually in the form of fictional stories which dramatize the role of the unit commissar.28

However, the role of a unit political commissar goes beyond serving <u>in loco parentis</u>. He is also responsible for personalizing relationships within a unit. His goal is to make the unit into the soldier's new primary group, i.e., a surrogate family. The assumption is that if the military unit becomes a <u>de facto</u> primary group, favorable patterns of behavior can be stimulated more easily and new values can be formulated. The organizational techniques of a political commissar system were designed to accomplish this task and the Chinese recognized this as a possible solution for remoulding attitudes and forming new values which could transfer the loyalty of soldiers from their real family to their new military family and beyond that to the nation.29

A second sociological reason for the ready acceptance of the political commissar concept was directly related to the first. This reason had to do with low level personal relationships. Asian culture had virtually codified the nature of relationships between individuals. Relationships were for the most part based upon the teachings of Confucius, but other philosophies have had some influence.30 Custom dictated how one individual dealt with another. There were acceptable and unacceptable behavior patterns. When a conflict between two persons arose, the means of resolving it were especially limited by the "code of conduct". Conflict could not be solved by direct confrontation. The traditional way to resolve conflict between two individuals was to use a "go-between."31 The dictum which disallowed direct confrontation was magnified in the military hierarchy where the commander of a unit had to maintain a special image. As a result, if a soldier had a grievance which might reflect adversely on the capabilities of the unit commander, he could not seek redress because the commander could not recognize the fact that something was wrong with his own unit. Traditionally, the commander was always the final authority. He was always correct in his actions and the subordinate who disagreed was considered a troublemaker who did not understand his place or the circumstances. Consequently, to personalize the relationships within a military unit, provisions had to be made to resolve problems which were caused by the commander's actions. It was necessary, however, that no culpability be attributed to the commander. He had to appear as the champion of his troops striving to protect them from grievances brought about by "the faults of the time." The means selected to bring authentic problems to the attention of the commander, was through a mediator. Political commissars served this purpose as grievances could be aired before him without attacking the dignity of the commander.32

Whether or not the Chinese, from the outset, recognized the sociological value of political commissars is debatable; it is certain, however, that once the political commissar system was functioning, the favorable results it produced in providing an outlet for troop grievances were not overlooked. The political commissar had in fact become the conscience of the unit commander; he actively sought out problem areas and tried to resolve them for the commander.

POLITICAL COMMISSAR CONCEPT BROUGHT TO CHINA

In 1923 General Chiang Kai-shek was sent to the Soviet Union for the purpose of determining the applicability of Soviet Communist Party (CPSU) military and political operations to Kuomintang (KMT) needs.33 Chiang spent three months in Russia studying political and military organizations. He was able to observe first-hand the Party's political training program within the Red Army. Chiang noted that the Russian unit commander's responsibility was strictly limited to military affairs. General education, morale building, and political training were the purview of the CPSU political commissar.34

Chiang returned to China in 1924 to assume command of the Whampoa Military Academy. This institution, created by the Kuomintang with considerable Soviet financial (three million rubles) and advisory assistance, was designed to forge a loyal officer corps that in turn would build a politically reliable army.35

The Soviets, aided by Chinese Communists who were then in coalition with the Kuomintang (KMT), must be given credit for inspiring the basic organizational structure, doctrine, and the ideological orientation of the political commissar system which was superimposed on the Chinese Army.36 With the passage of time, the Russian political commissar system was sinicized as Soviet methods were adapted to the Chinese situation.

When the KMT and the Communist forces split in 1927, so did the political organization within the army. The political system within the PLA was steadily nurtured along classic communist ideological and organizational lines and in later years became the model for the North Vietnamese military's political structure.37

By comparison, the political system in the Republic of China's (ROC) Army faced many difficulties and evolved slowly. Germans replaced the Russians as advisors to the ROC Army after 1927.38 The Germans were strong proponents of "unity of command," and saw in the ROC Army's political organization, with its authority over all nonmilitary aspects of soldiering, a distinct threat to a commander's prerogatives which would adversely affect his ability to lead troops. Upon German insistence, Chiang formally disbanded the political organization within ROC Army ranks; however, many national level political activities were retained.39

In 1938 a "second united front" was established between the KMT and the Chinese Communists and with it a reactivated political organization in the ROC Army. The political organization functioned until 1945, when Chiang bowed to US pressures to remove Kuomintang influence from the ROC Army on the grounds that it jeopardized the formation of a ROC/Communist coalition government.40 Many ROC officers attribute the rapid disintegration of their armed forces after World War II, and their eventual defeat by the Communists to the 1945 decision to disestablish the military-political cadre organization.41

In fact, one of the first acts taken by the ROC Government after withdrawing to Taiwan was to reorganize the political commissar system within the remnant forces. They have maintained the system to the present and it is now called the political warfare system. This is despite consistent American Military Assistance Advisory Group attempts during the 1950's and 1960's to convince them to abandon it.42

Since 1950 the ROC has concentrated on the refinement of its military political system and doctrine. As a result, a unique political organization within the ROC Armed Forces has evolved, somewhat different in nature than its Soviet predecessor. The ROC political commissar model was adopted by the South Vietnamese Army and has been studied by other Asian nations.43 (See Table 4-1: Evolution of the Political Commissar Concept.) The PLA took a different path in developing its political commissar system and was instrumental in the building of a similar system within the North Vietnamese army. The remainder of this chapter will describe the PLA political commissar system.

PLA POLITICAL COMMISSAR SYSTEM: ORGANIZATION AND FUNCTIONS

The primary mission of the PLA's political commissar system is to ensure "unity of thought" throughout the Chinese military. This statement assumes that the original source of the thought which must be unified is the Communist Party. As a result, a concomitant mission of the political commissar system is to ensure that the PLA understands party policy and that it implements that policy properly. This is often stated in terms of "the Party controlling the gun."44

TABLE 4-1

EVOLUTION OF THE POLITICAL COMMISSAR CONCEPT

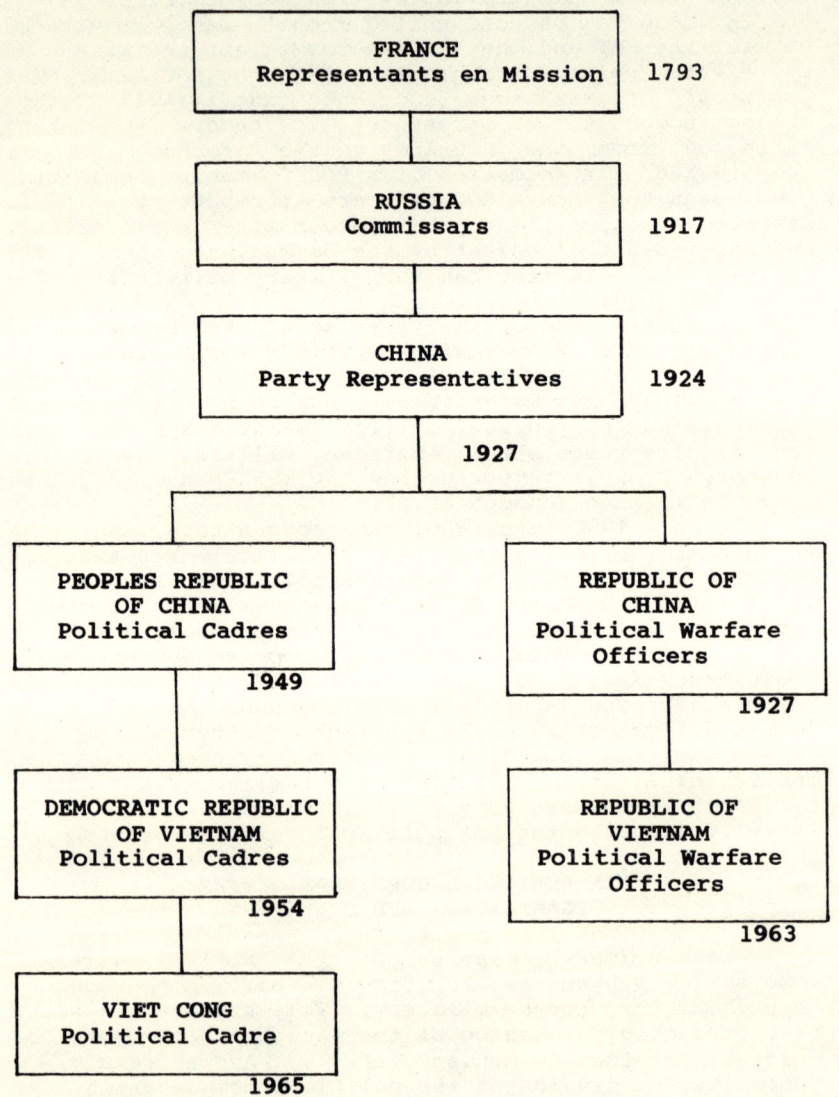

The political commissar's job, however, goes far beyond this task. He is responsible for the morale of soldiers and nearly all personnel actions to include promotions and assignments. The political commissar makes sure the troops are happy; i.e., receptive to indoctrination. He then indoctrinates them, tests them to see that they understand the substance of indoctrination and he monitors compliance. He is a sounding board for troop complaints. Once becomes aware of a grievance he, with the commander, must either fix the problem or explain to the soldier why he/she must "sacrifice" for the good of the country.

The political commissar must identify individuals who do not accept the ideology or whose thoughts are not unified. He then attempts to persuade that person to repent and accept the system. If the recalcitrant refuses to go along he is forced out of the military.

The political commissar is also responsible for civil-military relations. Every PLA action, in peacetime or wartime, that causes the military to come into direct or indirect contact with civilians must be considered to assure good civil-military relations. In other words, he must consider explicitly all potential political consequences of any military activity; combat or noncombat.

The political commissar, when used properly, can be an extremely important officer who contributes to the efficiency of the military unit in an environment like that of China. When he and the commander cooperate well they make an effective team. The methods by which commissars accomplish these tasks are relatively standardized and carried out by a well-defined structure. The rest of this chapter will explain that system.

The underlying philosophy of Chinese political commissar doctrine is similar to that of the Soviet Union; that is, it is based on the idea of a positive appeal. Mao first articulated this theory with respect to guerrillas, but he has extended the idea to the PLA. He stated:

> A revolutionary army must have discipline that is established on a limited democratic basis. In all armies, obedience of the subordinates to their superiors must be exacted. This is true in the case of guerrilla discipline, but the basis for guerrilla discipline must be the individual conscience. With guerrillas, a discipline of compulsion is ineffective.... (It) must be self-imposed, because only when it is, is the soldier able to understand completely why he fights and how he must obey. This type of discipline becomes a tower of strength within the army, and it is the one type that can truly harmonize the relationship that exists between officers and soldiers.45

Alexander George succinctly describes the idea:

> An army fights best when discipline and the performance of military duties rest at least in part on genuinely voluntaristic motives (emphasis added) and are not extracted solely through fear of punishment for disobedience.46

There appears to be a conflict in the Chinese Communist approach to the political commissar system. On the one hand, there is the requirement to "control" by traditional methods of surveillance, punishment, purge, etc. On the other hand, there is the requirement to motivate by assuring voluntary action thus creating a "New Communist Man" by inculcating "in the individual the basic moral and ethical standards of Chinese Communism: anti-individualist, dedication of self to the interests of the 'people,' acceptance of the leadership of the party...."47 The diverse elements and activities of the political commissar system were merged to overcome this apparent conflict. These concepts help to explain why the PLA political commissar system includes the seemingly contradictory activities described below.

The organizational structure of the commissar system begins with the General Political Department which is subordinate to the Military Affairs Commission of the Central Committee at the national level. At each level in the military chain-of-command there is a "political co-commander" or "commissar" who is equal in rank and responsibility to the commander.48 Unit commissars have their own staffs, with staff sizes increasing at higher echelons. All levels of the PLA from regiment to military district and military region are organized similarly to the division political staff.

Divisions, corps and army groups are considered independent units. They are, however, more contingency planning than operational headquarters in peacetime, when the regiment is the key actor allowed a high degree of autonomy and given independent missions. Division and Corps headquarters do plan and supervise some forms of integrated (combined arms) training exercises. The company can also be given independent missions, but never the battalion.

The political commissar at division or corps levels is called "zhengwei". He has a staff element headed by a director called "zhengzhibu zhuren". The director usually has two or three assistants and a staff of four sections (called "ke" at the division level and "qu" at the corps level). The first or organization (zuzhi) section is responsible for all personnel actions such as nominations for promotions, assignments or schooling within the division. It also supervises the activities of the China Youth League at lower levels. The second section is the propaganda (xuanchuan) section. It is responsible for assuring that the troops understand "why" they do what they do. If they are required to sacrifice for the good of the motherland, this section will prepare explanations of the official rationale in terms understandable to the troops. The third or security (baowei) section performs a counter-intelligence function. It is concerned with enemy infiltration or personnel security as opposed to physical security (camouflage, etc.) which is handled by a similarly named section on the military staff. The fourth section is the cultural (wenhua) section which prepares materials and programs to assure the development of proper attitudes and behavior patterns not only for relationships within the army but for the period after release from the army. This section is also charged with instilling a sense of nationalism in each soldier. In other words the PLA plays a critical role as a school of citizenship. During the last few years this effort has been manifested in the attempts to create a "socialist spiritual civilization."

The political commissar system at division and corps level also includes two specialized units directly responsible to the political commissar: a headquarters (housekeeping) company headed by a political assistant (xielijun) and a cultural affairs unit (wengongdui). The headquarters unit has no formal name but includes: an accountant (kuaiji), field sanitation personnel (weishengyuan), a quartermaster (siwuzhang), a communications clerk (tongxinyuan), a clerk (wenshu), a cultural affairs instructor (wenhua jiaoyuan), and a mess squad (chuishiban). The cultural affairs unit produces politically-oriented literature (under the staff supervision of the division culture section described above) and provides organized entertainment and recreation/athletic programs for the soldiers.

The regimental level political office (qu) is headed by a political commissar (zhengwei) who usually has one or two assistants. At this level there are only three sections (gu): organization, propaganda and security. The head of the organization section is concurrently the secretary of the Regimental Youth League.

The Youth League (qingniantuan) is particularly important to PLA leaders. It provides the means by which the commissar can identify and cultivate future leaders for the Communist Party. All soldiers between the ages of 18 and 25 are encouraged, but not required, to join. If someone in this group meets set standards (mostly based on attitude criteria) he/she can be nominated for full party membership. The Secretary of the Youth League is concurrently the head of the organization section at each level and is the one person in the Youth League who can be over age 25.

There are many more Youth League members than party

members because of the much stricter lifestyle expected of party members. Joining the Youth League provides the benefits of implied loyalty to the system without too much sacrifice. There are many special recreational activities organized for Youth League members so many young people join solely for those opportunities.

The battalion level political officer in independent battalions is also called "zhengwei". Most battalion political officers, however, are called "zhiaodaoyuan". The political officer in militia battalions are officially called "zhidaoyuan." There are frequently deputy political officers but there are no political staff elements at the battalion level.

The company level political officer, called "zhidaoyuan," is perhaps the most important commissar in the system because it is at this level that the system meets the average soldier. The zhidaoyuan is responsible for the political life of the unit which includes: political indoctrination, welfare, entertainment/recreation, general education and counterintelligence. All orders in peacetime must be countersigned by the political officer to be valid. This rule is now in the process of being changed to reflect a functional differentiation between the commander's military responsibilities and the commissar's political responsibilities. Many of the functions handled by the political officer are similar to those handled by noncommissioned officers in other armies.

The company political officer is appointed by the regimental level organization section of the political staff. He is sometimes given an assistant but usually works alone. He does cooperate with the company commander and work with the party committee (branch) which is the key organization for political work to include party control. Some political commissars develop secret informants within the company to assure he knows what is going on among the troops.

Party committees are found at all levels from the company up and in effect provide a second and distinct political chain-of-command, although membership overlaps significantly with the political commissar chain-of-command. The committees are perceived by the Chinese as the critical means by which the Party assures control over the Army. At the company level the party committee is elected by the company's "zhengzhibu" or political branch, the organization to which all party members belong. It usually consists of five or seven members; always an odd number to assure a majority vote in decisionmaking. The committee members are elected under the guidelines of democratic centralism. That is, nominations are made from below after a considerable amount of advanced "political work." The term "political work" is a euphemism used to describe the manipulation exercised to develop "unanimous" consensus in decisionmaking or the nominations in the election process. Nominations are approved by the regimental party committee prior to the vote. There is, however, a genuine attempt to identify natural leaders during the political work phase and to coopt them into the system during the election.

The party committee has four subelements: the secretary (usually the political commissar, but sometimes the commander), an organization subcommittee, a propaganda subcommittee and two or three members who belong to no special subcommittee. The secretary is appointed by the regimental party committee and the organization and propaganda subcommittee members are appointed by the secretary after they have been elected to the party committee. The secretary is responsible for convening and serving as chairman of the political committee and branch meetings. The organizational subcommittee (one or two members) is responsible for recruitment of new party members, usually through personal contact and persuasion. The propaganda subcommittee (also one or two members) assures the party message is disseminated to the troops through various means (newspaper reading sessions, posters, etc.).

The political commissar also organizes informal subcommittees on occasion to assure he has appropriate feedback from the troops. He might form a "welfare" subcommittee which could include representatives from each of the squads. The purpose of the committee would be to communicate troop complaints to the commissar. The commissar would then have the task of changing the conditions which caused the complaint or developing an indoctrination program to explain to the troops why the condition cannot be changed and why they must sacrifice for the good of their motherland. This process provides an effective feedback mechanism to ensure the commissar is in a position to alleviate any discontent within the unit at an early stage.

The exact role of the party branch varies depending upon the strength of the unit commissar. There are times when the party branch (or committee at higher levels) is the key force in the decisionmaking process. This is accomplished by a principle known as "command by consensus." If the commissar is adept he can control the consensus, but on many occasions it is actually the party branch's consensus which controls or directs the activities of the unit.49 This contrasts with the USSR where subordination of the political commissar to the unit commander is an attempt to adhere to the concept of "unity of command." The PLA does not consider the notion of "unity of command" as critical as many Western armies do.50 "Command by consensus" could be considered a mechanism to assure the primacy of the political commissar over the commander. The political commissar is often the key figure in determining the consensus which gives him ascendancy over the unit commander. The "command by consensus" system was described by a former political commissar as follows:

> The political commissar calls a meeting of the party committee of the unit. The commissar, responding to instructions from above or to a problem which has come up in the unit, presents the problem to the committee. Since the commissar is the committee secretary, he can influence the solution. He establishes a consensus within the committee. The committee members then serve as activists among the troops to create a general consensus. The unit commander is then obligated to go along with the consensus. This procedure makes the troops feel like they have participated in the decision and have a stake in carrying out the solution.51

The struggle between commander and commissar, in the Soviet Union, went through many cycles in which the commander, at times, had more relative power than the political commissar and vice versa. The relationship in China has been much more stable and political commissars have often held the greatest authority. In the last few years, however, with the PLA movement to regularize and professionalize its force there have been significant changes in the relationship resulting from a more careful definition of functions; a functional specialization which has the effect of taking the commissar out of the decisionmaking process for purely military operational decisions. He continues to have the strongest voice, however, in personnel matters such as promotions and assignments.52

The five or seven members of the company level political committee implement party instructions at the basic levels in the PLA. When there are disagreements within the committee on how to interpret party policy, the first step is to label the disagreement as "minor" or "major" - based upon perceived importance. "Major" disagreements are those which involve matters of principle while those concerned with selecting among alternate means to accomplish an objective are usually considered "minor." If the problem is labeled "minor", decisions are made by simple majority vote after the appropriate "political work" or lobbying has been accomplished. If the problem is "major" it is referred to the next higher level party committee for resolution. Thus, when the company's party committee cannot reach agreement on a major issue the problem is referred to the battalion party general branch (zong zhibu) for resolution.53

There are 21 to 27 members on the battalion party

committee: five members from each of the company party committees (to include the machine gun and mortar companies if they exist) and the secretary who is usually the battalion political officer. Sometimes the battalion commander and/or another cadre from the battalion staff is included in the battalion party committee, but the total number of members must be odd. The battalion party committee also has two or three man organization and propaganda subcommittees appointed from among the members of the branch. Major problems which cannot be resolved at the battalion level are referred to the regimental party committee.54

The regimental party committee (dangweihui) is selected in the same way as the battalion committee. The number of members varies based upon the number of battalions. Each battalion elects five members to the regimental party committee. An independent company would elect one member. There are also an unspecified number of members from the regimental staff. The principle that the total number must be odd remains. One of the key roles of the regimental party committee is the review of personnel files to approve promotions, schooling and reassignments within the regiment. It also attempts to solve problems which affect the regiment as a whole. Again, "major" problems of principle which cannot be resolved by the regimental party committee are referred to the division party committee.55

Division and corps party committees, also called "dangwei hui", are formed in the same manner as those of regiments. Major problems which cannot be resolved at the corps level are referred to the military region party committee in the case of main force units and the military district party committees for reserve (houbei budui) and militia (minbing) corps, divisions or independent regiments.56

The military districts and subdistricts are the only points in the PLA party system where the civilian party can influence the PLA other than at the central level (Central Committee's Military Affairs Commission). The influence is exercised usually by only one person: the first political commissar who is concurrently the first party secretary of the province or prefecture level party committee. Since military districts and subdistricts have no operational or administrative control over main force units, this point of control does not affect the PLA's main forces. The military district political commissars and party committees report to their counterpart organizations at the military region level. However, the first political commissar, by virtue of his concurrent position as first party secretary can report directly to the Communist Party Central Committee at the national level without going through the Military Region. This is sometimes viewed as a check against the accumulation of too much power by military regions (sometimes called "mountain-topism").57

Military regions are principally contingency planning headquarters and problems of principle which cannot be solved at that level are referred directly to the PLA General Political Department in the case of commissar system problems and to the Military Affairs Commission in the case of party committee problems.58

In sum, the spheres of authority or functional areas of interest between the political commissar system and party committee system are clearly delineated. Generally, the political commissar system chain-of-command handles routine indoctrination, organization, psychological operations and counterintelligence functions. The party committees deal with questions of implementation of party policies, provide feedback to higher levels on successes or failures in party policies, approve personnel assignments and promotions and conduct special investigations. It is important to note that there is a separate military party organization within the PLA manned completely by PLA commissars except for the two points at the military district and subdistrict level. The political commissar system is relatively well-disciplined and unified. Generalizations about party-army relations or party control over the army must be refined to include these facts.

SUMMARY

The political commissar is perhaps the most powerful single position at any level of military organization. His access to information about all members of the unit, control over personnel assignments and promotions; responsibility for counterintelligence, indoctrination, cultural and entertainment activities; and concurrent position in the parallel party structure and direct contact with the next higher level political commissar, all serve to make him a powerful individual.

If one assumes that the political commissar is assigned by the party to control the army, there is no doubt that he could do it with the organizational structure and techniques available. On the other hand, the nature of the tasks with which he deals on a daily basis is more likely to develop idealistic and humanistic behavior and attitude patterns in him.

An important result of the political commissar's daily responsibilities is that he ends up playing the mediator role. Whether mediating conflicts between the commander and his troops or between party policy and army professionalism, the political commissar must develop an ethic and workstyle which is perceptive and sensitive to different viewpoints. It is **not** primarily a style of patronizing elitist indoctrination of others or controlling for power purposes, although some commissars do fall into that trap. The commissar who does his job properly would develop an approach to interpersonal relationships and institutional problems which relies on a positive appeal, not negative sanctions. The commissar learns to persuade others and avoid commandism to resolve conflict. His primary activities, in the ideal, are not, as often described, negative and nefarious control activities. Rather they are supposed to be positive morale-building activities using methods of persuasion, consensus-building, and mediation between conflicting viewpoints. As with other aspects of the Chinese Communist approach, the degree to which political commissars have become "New Maoist Men" and carry out their work according to these ideal principles is open to question. Nonetheless, the constant training in these techniques is likely to influence attitudes and behavior patterns in an idealistic direction.

Political commissar training and experience then is likely to produce elites who are particularly suited to institution-building by mediating opinion, interest, or personal power conflicts. They are one of the few elite categories in the bureaucracies of China who are more concerned with conflict resolution in itself than advocacy of a particular line or institutional interest. They seek to preserve a system rather than becoming advocates for one side or the other in conflicting issues. Those elites who have extensive experience in the political commissar role are likely to emerge as key leaders in the movement to rationalize the bureaucracy by bringing the various institutions closer together and reducing schisms.

NOTES

1. See conclusions, Chapter Five.
2. General Wang Sheng was the Director, General Political Warfare Department, Ministry of National Defense (MND), Government of the Republic of China. He was the Commandant of the Political Warfare Staff College prior to transferring to MND. He is considered a leading theoretician on political warfare in the Republic of China and is the author of numerous books and articles on the subject. This quote resulted from an interview with General Wang in March 1968. I owe a great debt to General Wang for the insights into political warfare concepts that he has provided to me over the past 15 years.
3. Colonel Ramsay Weston Phipps, The Armies of the First French Republic (London: Oxford University Press, 1926), p. 20.
4. Ibid., p. 21.
5. Ibid., p. 21.
6. Ibid., p. 21.
7. Henri Wallon, Les Representents du Peuple en Mission et la Justice Revolutionnaire dans les Departements in L'an II (1793-1794), 5 volumes (Paris: Hachette, 1889-1890.
8. Littleton B. Atkinson, Dual Command in the Red Army (Air University Document Research Study, Maxwell Air Force Base, Alabama, 1950): p. 1.
9. Ibid., pp. 2-4.
10. Ibid., p. 5.
11. Roman Kolkowicz, The Soviet Military and the Communist Party (Princeton, New Jersey: Princeton University Press, 1967), pp. 63-74; and Zbigniew Brzezinski, ed., Political Controls in the Soviet Army (Research Program on the USSR, New York: 1954), p. 5.
12. Brzezinski, Political Controls, p. 85.
13. Edwin O. Reischauer and John K. Fairbank, East Asia: The Great Tradition (Boston: Houghton-Mifflin, 1960).
14. William Whitson with Chen-hsia Huang, The Chinese High Command: A History of Communist Military Politics, 1927-1971 (New York: Praeger, 1973), pp. 7-8.
15. Excellent references on the "warlord period" which explain the warlord system include: James E. Sheridan, Chinese Warlord, The Career of Feng Yu-hsiang (Stanford, California: Stanford University Press, 1966); Donald Gillin, Warlord, Yen Hsi-shan in Shansi Province 1911-1949 (Princeton, New Jersey: Princeton University Press, 1967), and Hsi-sheng Chi, Warlord Politics in China, 1916-1928 (Stanford, California: Stanford University Press, 1976).

16. For an excellent historical account from a military perspective see Sun Chin-ming, *Chungkuo Ping Chih Shih* (A History of Chinese Military Systems)(Taipei: United Press Center, 1960).

17. There was, of course, a commitment to Confucianism which contributed to national unity but it still allowed for passive rather than active citizenship and it promoted strong identification with family and clan.

18. This was identified as a significant problem in a major work by Sun Yat-sen, *San Min Chu I* (The Three People's Principles)(Taipei: China Publishing Co., n.d.).

19. Ibid.

20. Richard Solomon, *Mao's Revolution and the Chinese Political Culture* (Berkeley: University of California Press, 1971), pp. 105-122.

21. Notes from lectures on the "History of the Political Commissar System," at the Political Warfare College, Fuhsingkang, Taiwan, 1968.

22. Ibid.

23. Ibid.

24. John Gittings, *The Role of the Chinese Army* (London: Oxford University Press, 1967), p. 102. Also see Chalmers Johnson, *Peasant Nationalism and Communist Power: The Emergence of Revolutionary China 1937-1945* (Stanford, California: Stanford University Press, 1962).

25. Solomon, pp. 105-109.

26. Ying-mao Kau et al., *The Political Work System of the Chinese Communist Military: Analysis and Documents* (Province: East Asia Language and Area Center, Brown University, 1971), pp. 142-215.

27. From an interview in March 1968 with an major in the Republic of China Army who had served as a political commissar in the PLA until 1951 when he was captured in Korea. He was later repatriated to Taiwan.

28. Ibid.

29. Notes from a lecture on "Political Warfare and the Chinese Political Culture," at the Political Warfare Staff College, Fuhsingkang, Taiwan, 1968.

30. See Feng Yu-lan, *A Short History of Chinese Philosophy*, Derk Bodde, ed. (New York: MacMillan, 1948). Also see Francis L.K. Hsu, *Americans and Chinese: Two Ways of Life* (New York: Henry Schuman, 1953).

31. Solomon, *Mao's Revolution*, p. 128.

32. These conclusions are not explicit in writings about the political commissar system. They represent my conclusions after examining commander-commissar relationships at the company level.

33. Chiang Kai-shek, *Soviet Russia in China* (New York: Ferrar, Straus, and Cudahy, 1967), pp. 21-22.

34. S.I. Hsiung, *The Life of Chiang Kai-shek* (Shanghai: China Publishing Co., 1937), pp. 177-178.

35. Zhou Enlai was an assistant in the political department of the Whampoa Academy. See Roderick L. Macfarquhar, "The Whampoa Military Academy" (Harvard Papers on China, August 1955): pp. 1-25.
36. Ibid.
37. George K. Tanham, Communist Revolutionary Warfare (New York: Praeger, 1961), p. 39.
38. Joseph J. Heinlein, "The Political Establishment in the Army of the Republic of China," Thesis, Command and General Staff College, Ft. Leavenworth, Kansas, 1967, pp. 28-29.
39. Ibid., pp. 28-29.
40. Ibid., pp. 55-57.
41. From informal conversations with several general officers in the ROC Army to include: Gen. Kao Kuei-yuan, Lt. Gen. Chou Chung-feng, and Lt. Gen. Ning Chun-hsing in June 1963 and with Gen. Wang Sheng in May 1968. Gen. Gao Kuei-yuan later became Minister of Defense; Lt. Gen. Chou Chung-feng became the Director of the Public Security Bureau and Lt. Gen. Ning Chun-hsing became the Director of the Political Department of the Taiwan Garrison Command. Wang Sheng was the Director of the General Political Warfare Department of the Ministry of National Defense. This is the senior political commissar job in the Chinese Nationalist Army.
42. Charles H. Barber, "China's Political Officer System," Military Review 33 (July 1953): pp. 11, 20-21.
43. Monte R. Bullard, "Political Warfare in Vietnam," Military Review 49 (October 1969): p. 56.
44. Mao Tse-tung, Selected Works, Vol. II, p. 272.
45. Mao Tse-tung, quoted in Alexander George, The Chinese Communist Army in Action (New York: Columbia University Press, 1967), p. 25.
46. Ibid., p. 25.
47. Ibid., p. 32.
48. From interviews of numerous political commissars in the People's Republic of China from July 1980 to June 1982. The interviews included those from the Military Region Headquarters and Military District Headquarters levels, various depots and military bases and the senior political commissars in three divisions. In each case the commissars were eager to explain the role of the political commissar in the PLA.
49. George, The Chinese Communist Army in Action, p. 128. Also see Joffe, Party and Army, pp. 58-67.
50. George, The Chinese Communist Army in Action, p. 113.
51. See footnote #27 above.
52. From interviews of numerous political commissars in the PRC from July 1980 to June 1982.

53. Ibid.
54. Ibid.
55. Ibid.
56. Ibid.
57. Ibid.
58. Ibid.

5
The Interlocking Directorate—Nature and Scope

PART I: OVERVIEW

Political evolution in the People's Republic of China has been characterized by instability. During the first decade of rule, after major purges of rural gentry and Kuomintang remnants, the Chinese Communist Party initiated a number of rectification campaigns which imposed small quotas for elites to be purged **within** the party. It was generally a period of consolidation in which charismatic revolutionary-type leaders were replaced by rational administrators or those more loyal to communist doctrine. Many elites were purged during that period but not on as large a scale as during the second decade.

The second decade of Communist rule began with the Great Leap Forward which was the beginning of a different political environment -- political revolution rather than evolution. During the GLF elites were polarized within institutions on the basis of whether they believed the correct approach to nation-building was to give priority to economic development based on some type of rational administrative procedure, or whether it was to first create the "new socialist man" and perfect social institutions and only then concentrate on economic progress. Those who opted for the former have been labeled "moderates", "experts", or "pragmatists", and those who believed in the latter have been called "radicals", "reds", or "party conservatives".

The polarization came to a head during the Great Proletarian Cultural Revolution when large numbers of elites were purged or at least involved in serious confrontations. While this simple dichotomy is not sufficient to explain events in China, for purposes here it does provide an important explanation for why some elites were purged. Many of those purged during the Cultural Revolution were reinstated after 1970 and the rehabilitation process was accelerated in 1973. For the most part it was the moderates who were purged during the Cultural Revolution, but after 1970 they gradually worked their way back into key positions in the provinces and to some degree at the Center. While this moderate-radical conflict was going on throughout China, there were also some important structural changes taking place which began to reduce the significance of the dichotomy.

For purposes of this chapter the PRC structure in 1960, 1973 and 1982 will be compared.1 Center and region institutions and roles within institutions will be analyzed by matching elites to roles. The comparison is concerned primarily with changes in role linkages. Changes in role linkages are manifested in changes in the scope of dual/triple positions -- the interlocking directorate -- within the provinces and in province representation at the Center.

Part 2 of this chapter deals with a relatively narrow data base: those elites who were full or alternate members of the Politburo or Central Committee in 1960, 1973 and 1982, and also held positions outside the Center. The purpose is to examine the extent of general changes in regional representation (military region and province elites) at the Center.

Part 3 focuses on military region elites in order to determine the scope and type of linkages to the Center and to the provinces. Seven general categories of elites are examined: those who held party, government, or army positions only; those who held dual party-army, party-government, or army-government positions; and those who held triple party-army-government positions. The army category is further divided, based on whether the individual elite member was a commander or commissar or whether he was at the military region or military district level. In some cases, the level of the elite role in an institution hierarchy is considered (such as first secretary versus secretary and deputy secretary), but generally the institutional affiliation is the principal focus.

It is important to note that these categories are based upon current role affiliation and not on background, identity-forming experience or issue orientation. For example, a political commissar is categorized on the basis of holding a political commissar job at a particular time. No attempt is made to label him as a professional or life-long political commissar.

Part 4 expands the data base to include province level elites to determine changes in the interlocking directorate. It also examines roles and linkages from the perspective of each of the three institutions: province party committee, military district and province people's government (called province revolutionary committees in 1973).

Part 5 summarizes changes in the nature and scope

of the interlocking directorate phenomenon.

PART 2: REGIONAL REPRESENTATION AT THE CENTER

The center-region relationship has often been identified as a major problem for China because of the sheer size of the country and it's population. The degree of centralization or decentralization seems to run in cycles since 1949. It is also possible to see a form of movement between centralized and decentralized control from a political perspective as reflected in regional representation at the Center; an apparent method used by PRC leaders to reduce center-region schisms by making key leaders from the provinces feel they are part of the central policymaking process. It is an important way of improving national integration and it has been relatively successful over the past 30 years. This section will attempt to clarify political change in this area by examining the scope and type of regional elites who have been elected to the Central Committee at different points in time: 1960, 1973 and 1982.

The total scope of regional representation in the Central Committee by military region, province party, military district and province government elites fluctuated widely between 1960 and 1982. Furthermore, the number of representatives from each of these four organizations has varied significantly. This section will break down the representation by province and by organizational affiliation. It will also briefly examine regional representation in the Politburo.

Central Committee

The Eighth Central Committee, elected in 1956 and 1958, consisted of 190 members; 96 full members and 94 alternates.2 Only 14 (15%) of the full and 37 (39%) of the alternate members were listed as holding concurrent positions in the provinces or military regions. The Tenth Central Committee, elected in 1973, included 195 full and 124 alternate members.3 One-hundred and five (54%) full and 64 (52%) alternate members held positions in the provinces or military regions.

The Twelfth Central Committee, elected in 1982, included 210 full members and 138 alternates.4 Eighty-one (39%) of the full and 43 (31%) of the alternate members held positions in the provinces or military regions (see Table 5-1 for a comparison of these three central committees).

Thus, based upon statistics alone, it can be seen that between 1956 and 1973 there was a great increase in the number of provincial representatives at the Center;

an apparent effort to strengthen center-province ties by coopting key provincial leaders and making them a part of the process at the Center. Between 1973 and 1982 the process was reversed. The reversal, however, probably reflects a refining of the system by focusing on the quality of representatives rather than the quantity. It also reflects an uneven retirement policy which dismissed more from the provinces than the Center. It appears to be a normal evolution or rationalization of the bureaucracy.

TABLE 5-1

PRC CENTRAL COMMITTEE COMPOSITION

Central Committee	Total Members	Center Jobs Only	Jobs Outside Center
8th Full	96	82	14 (15%)
8th Alt	94	57	37 (39%)
10th Full	195	90	105 (54%)
10th Alt	124	59	65 (52%)
12th Full	210	129	81 (39%)
12th Alt	138	95	43 (31%)

Hierarchy of Province Representation

Some provinces have been better represented at the Center at different times than others. Table 5-2 provides a weighted hierarchy which compares representation in the Eighth, Tenth and Twelfth Central Committees and breaks down province elite positions by party, army and government positions. The values were assigned arbitrarily to give more weight to provinces which are better represented.

The province-level units which were best represented by 1973 were Shanghai, Beijing, Guangdong, Henan, and Liaoning. The period from 1973 to 1982 showed a leveling of provincial representation consistent with a general trend of structural refinements. In 1982 all the province-level party committees elected at least one full member to the Central Committee and only two provinces stand out as having slightly more representation at the Center: Sichuan and Xinjiang. Sichuan elected four full and two alternate members to the Twelfth Central Committee. The mean was one alternate and two full members. The provinces with the least representation were Qinghai, Anhui and surprisingly Beijing.

TABLE 5-2

WEIGHTED HIERARCHY OF PROVINCE
REPRESENTATION AT THE CENTER

PROVINCE	PARTY 8TH CC(a)	PARTY 10TH CC	PARTY 12TH CC	GOVT 8TH CC	GOVT 10TH CC	GOVT 12TH CC	ARMY 8TH CC(b)	ARMY 10TH CC	ARMY 12TH CC	TOTAL 8TH CC	TOTAL 10TH CC	TOTAL 12TH CC
ANHUI	2	8	2	0	5	0	0	2	2	2	8	2
BEIJING (c)	8	18	2	5	14	2	2	11	0	10	25	2
FUJIAN (c)	1	4	7	0	4	1	0	4	2	1	9	7
GANSU (c)	1	6	2	0	8	1	1	4	2	2	10	3
GUANGDONG (c)	5	14	6	2	16	2	2	12	4	5	25	8
GUANGXI	2	7	5	2	10	0	1	5	3	0	10	6
GUIZHOU	0	5	7	0	4	5	0	2	2	0	5	8
HEBEI	3	8	7	1	9	3	0	2	0	3	9	7
HEILONGJIANG	3	7	6	1	3	2	0	2	4	3	6	6
HENAN	2	15	1	2	14	1	2	4	0	2	15	6
HUBEI (c)	1	10	7	0	10	2	0	4	1	1	12	7
HUNAN	1	12	4	0	11	0	1	8	2	1	12	4
JIANGSU (c)	1	8	4	0	6	2	3	4	2	3	8	4
JIANGXI	1	6	5	1	5	0	0	1	2	1	7	5
JILIN	1	4	5	0	4	1	1	2	4	1	4	6
LIAONING (c)	3	5	9	1	14	2	3	6	0	4	23	9
NEI MONGGOL	5	4	6	5	6	2	5	4	2	6	6	6
NINGXIA	3	1	4	3	1	2	0	1	2	3	1	4
QINGHAI	0	4	2	0	4	0	0	1	2	0	4	2
SHAANXI	2	7	5	1	7	0	1	4	2	2	7	5
SHANDONG (c)	4	2	6	4	2	2	3	4	2	4	4	6
SHANGHAI	6	28	6	5	27	0	5	14	2	5	31	6
SHANXI	1	11	6	0	11	0	1	1	2	1	12	6
SICHUAN (c)	7	9	10	4	14	2	5	8	4	10	16	10
TIANJIN	0	8	6	0	8	2	0	3	2	0	8	6
XINJIANG (c)	3	7	10	3	9	2	3	7	6	3	10	10
XIZANG	1	5	7	0	6	0	0	3	2	1	6	7
YUNNAN (c)	1	7	3	0	7	0	1	6	2	1	7	3
ZHEJIANG	1	8	5	0	8	2	1	3	2	1	8	5
TOTALS	69	238	161	40	247	38	41	132	62	76	310	166

```
POLITBURO              =5
ALT POLITBURO          =4
CENTRAL COMMITTEE      =2
ALT CENTRAL COMMITTEE  =1
```

a. Each single column includes elites who hold dual or triple positions so that the total column is less than the sum of the three institutional columns.
b. Includes military region and military district elites. Those who held positions at both military region and military district levels are counted only in the province of the military district.
c. Provinces in which military region headquarters is located.

Perhaps more striking, however, was the drastic reduction by 1982 in people's government and province-level military (military district) representation at the Center. The vast majority of the government and army representatives who were elected were those in interlocking roles who were elected by virtue of their party position. For example, military district first political commissars were concurrently first secretaries in the party. If this group is subtracted from the army column only six individuals would remain and two (full CC members) of those were from Xinjiang; of the remaining three, one was a military district commander (Guangxi) and an alternate CC member, one was a military district political commissar (Hubei) and an alternate member, and two were political commissars (Heilongjiang and Jilin) and were full CC members.

Hierarchy of Military Region Representation

Representation from the military regions has also varied. Table 5-3 shows a weighted hierarchy of representation with and without elites from military districts. The only anomalies in 1973 were the numbers for Nanjing and Wuhan, both of which would be expected to be higher if compared with the province hierarchies (Table 5-2). The implication is that there was a slightly more civilian or party-government character to the Nanjing (including Shanghai, Jiangsu, Zhejiang, and Anhui) and Wuhan (Hubei and Henan) Military Regions. The Beijing, Guangzhou, Chengdu, Shenyang, Lanzhou, Fujian, Kunming and Urumqi Military Regions were relatively evenly balanced between military and civilian representatives in 1973. Only the Jinan Military Region (which includes only Shandong Province) had a slightly more military character in the Central Committee representation: i.e., of the 2 Central Committee members, 1 held only a military position (commander of Jinan Military Region) and the other held a triple party-army (political commissar)-government position.

In 1982 the Shenyang Military Region stands out. It elected seven representatives to the 12th Central Committee; two alternate and five full members. One of the full members, the military region commander, was reelected to the Politburo. The Kunming, Lanzhou and Urumqi military regions had slightly more than average representation. Wuhan Military Region had the least representation with only two alternate members.

The most significant change in military region representation in the Central Committee was the total increase from the Eighth to the Tenth Central Committees and then a leveling by the Twelfth Central Committee. In 1960 a total of 26 (14%) members or alternate members of the Central Committee came from the military regions or military districts. During the unique period of the

TABLE 5-3

WEIGHTED HIERARCHY OF
MILITARY REGION REPRESENTATION AT THE CENTER

MILITARY REGION	8TH CC (MR)	8TH CC (W/MD)(a)	10TH CC (MR)	10TH CC (W/MD)	12TH CC (MR)	12TH CC (W/MD)
BEIJING MR	1	2	22	31	5	11
CHENGDU MR	2	2	8	11	5	9
FUZHOU MR	1	1	5	5	5	9
GUANGZHOU MR	2	2	22	25	2	6
JINAN MR	3	3	4	4	4	6
KUNMING MR	1	1	8	8	7	11
LANZHOU MR	1	1	8	9	0	8
NANJING MR	2	3	13	23	3	6
NEI MONGGOL(b)	4	4	0	0	0	0
SHENYANG MR	1	2	12	13	15	21
WUHAN MR	0	0	6	8	4	5
URUMQI MR	3	3	8	8	6	6
XIZANG (c)	0	0	0	0	0	0
TOTALS	21	24	116	145	56	98

WEIGHTING KEY: POLITBURO   - 5
                ALT POLITBURO   - 4
                CENTRAL COMMITTEE   - 2
                ALT CENTRAL COMMITTEE - 1

a. Total for military region plus military districts within the military region.
b. Became a military district in the Beijing Military Region.
c. Became a military district in the Chengdu Military Region.

Cultural Revolution military representation reached a peak. In 1969 there were 97 central committee members (35%) who held positions in the military regions or military districts; by 1973 the number was reduced to 64 (20%), but this figure still represented a significant increase over 1960. In 1982 there were only 55 (16%) alternate and full central committee members who held positions in the military regions and districts. This represents a slightly lesser percentage than in 1972 but the difference is not significant.

If the military district elites were removed from the statistics there is a slight increase in military region representation from the Tenth to the Twelfth Central Committee. As we shall see later this is consistent with the pattern of separating institutions and assuring adequate representation in the Central Committee from each. From this perspective the military regions were still well-represented at the Center. All had at least two representatives except Guangzhou which had only one full member. Shenyang topped the list, as mentioned above, with five full members and two alternates.

By 1982 almost all of the military region-provincial interlocking roles had been eliminated, but the military regions had been given representation on the Central Committee (See Appendix F). This is a strong indicator that the PLA has generally "returned to the barracks" and the principal military region role as a wartime contingency headquarters has been resumed. Generally speaking, the focus of military region attention in peacetime is on main force units while that of the military districts is on local forces and militia. These relationships were possibly undergoing revision in 1982 but for purposes of this discussion it can be said that military regions have withdrawn from provincial politics.

Politburo

In 1960 only 3 of 19 full and 1 of 6 alternate members of the Politburo held positions in the provinces. One held a triple party (first secretary) - army (political commissar) - government (mayor) position in Shanghai; 1 held a dual party (first secretary) - army (deputy political commissar) position in Sichuan; and the last one held a dual party (first secretary) - government (mayor) position in Beijing. The alternate held a triple party (first secretary) - army (commander) - government position in Nei Monggol.

In 1973, 11 of 22 full and 3 of 4 alternate members of the Politburo held positions outside of the Center. Six of the 11 full members held triple party-army (political commissar)-government positions, 2 held dual party-government positions and 3 were commanders of military regions. One of the alternate members held a triple party-army (political commissar)-government position and 2 held dual party-government positions.

By 1982 the situation had changed significantly: only 1 of the 25 full and 1 of the three alternate members of the Politburo held positions outside the Center. One of those, the Beijing Military Region Commander, is actually located at the Center. The other, the Shenyang Military Region Commander, holds a center position in the party's Military Affairs Commission so is in reality the only representative from outside the Center. Thus, except for these two who hold positions at the Center, there is now no provincial party or government representation in the Politburo.

In 1960, none of the 7 Politburo standing committee members held positions outside the Center, whereas in 1973, 3 of 10 standing committee members did. Two held triple party-army (political commissar)-government positions in Shanghai and the third was the military region commander of the Shenyang Military Region. In 1982 none of the 5 standing committee members held positions outside the Center.

Summary

Regional representation at the Center increased from 15% of full and 39% of alternate members of the Central Committee in 1960 to 54% of the full and 52% of the alternate members in 1973. In 1982 the percentages decreased to 39% of the full and only 31% of the alternates holding positions in the provinces or military regions.

Although the decisionmaking process in China is not well-understood, especially the role of the Central Committee, it is clear that even with the reductions from 1973 to 1982, Center elites no longer monopolize policymaking. The reductions in 1982, particularly among new alternate members, indicate some movement toward recentralization, but there has been what appears to be a deliberate effort to ensure that each key institution outside the Center is represented and that the representation is relatively evenly distributed. The exceptions, of course, are the government elites who are not as well-represented as the party or army; but it must be remembered that the Central Committee is, after all, a party organization.

PART 3: MILITARY REGION-PROVINCE LINKAGES

The role of the military region in Chinese politics is one of the least understood of all institutions, even though its involvement in provincial politics was reported in detail during the Cultural Revolution. There is, therefore, a need to analyze its role in more depth.

Scope of Interlocking Roles--1960
(See Appendix D)

In 1960 there were 13 military regions5 and in only 7 MR's could there be found elites with party or government positions in the provinces.6 Those positions were in only 7 of the 29 provinces.7 All 7 provinces were considered strategic frontier areas in which active military participation could be justified at that time for purposes of national defense.

There were a total of 21 military region elites who held dual or triple positions in the provinces in 1960 (See Table 5-4). Twelve of the 21 held positions in only two military regions (Xinjiang and Xizang), both of which were considered strategic areas.

Four military region commanders held triple positions in the provinces in the provinces; one held the top party job (first secretary) and the top government job (governor); one held the top party job and a lower government job (vice-governor); and two held lower positions in the party and government.

One military region commander held a triple position and five held dual positions. The triple position was the top government job and a lower level in the party. Two of the dual positions were at lower levels in the party and three were lower levels in the government.

Three military region political commissars held triple and four held dual positions. Of the three who held triple positions, one held the top party and government jobs, one held the top party job and one held lower positions in the party and government. Of those in dual positions, three were first secretaries and one was a secretary.

Scope of Interlocking Roles -- 1973 and 1982
(See Appendixes E and F)

There were only 11 military regions in 1973 and all of them contained elites who held interlocking roles in the provinces.8 A total of 80 military region elites (as opposed to 19 in 1960) held concurrent (dual or triple) positions in the province party or government organizations. Table 5-5 shows a breakdown of the 1973 military region dual/triple positions.

Military region commander and political commissar elites in 1973 were involved in the government or party organizations of 24 of the 29 provinces (Table 5-7). The remaining 5 provinces (without military region representation) had military district elites in government and party positions (Anhui, Shaanxi, Shanxi, Xizang, and Zhejiang).

TABLE 5-4

DUAL/TRIPLE POSITIONS
HELD BY MILITARY REGION ELITES - 1960

POSITION	TRIPLE PARTY/ ARMY/ GOVT	DUAL PARTY/ ARMY	DUAL GOVT/ ARMY	NO DUAL OR TRIPLE JOB	TOTAL SAMPLE
Commanders	4	1	0	11	16(a)
First PC's (b)	3 (c)	4	0	3	10
Command System (d)	1	2	3	21	26
PC System (e)	0	3	1	10	14
Totals	8	10	4	45	66

a. One military region (Beijing) had two commanders during the 1958-1960 time frame. The only names listed in Appendix D are those with dual/triple positions or memberships in the central committee so the total sample numbers in this table will not equal the number of names in the appendix.
b. PC = political commissar. In 1960 the first PC was listed only as PC but was the equivalent to the first PC in 1973. Only 9 military regions (Guangzhou, Nei Monggol, Lanzhou, Shenyang, Nanjing, Beijing, Xinjiang, Xizang, Jinan) listed PC's in 1960; two of those (Nei Monggol and Xinjiang) listed the CO as his own PC, four (Chengdu, Fuzhou, Kunming, Wuhan) listed no PC and one (Shenyang) listed 2 PC's during the 1958-1960 time period but not at the same time.
c. Two of these (Ulanfu and Wang Enmao) were CO and PC at the same time.
d. Includes chiefs-of-staff.
e. Includes second political commissars, directors, and deputy directors of military region political departments.

TABLE 5-5

DUAL/TRIPLE POSITIONS HELD BY MILITARY REGION ELITES
1973

TITLE	TRIPLE PARTY/ARMY/ GOVERNMENT	DUAL PARTY/ ARMY	DUAL GOVT/ ARMY	NO DUAL OR TRIPLE POSITIONS	TOTAL SAMPLE
Commanders	2	0	0	9	11
First PC	8	0	0	1	9
CO System	16	2	17	79	114
PC System	20	5	12	39	76
Totals	46	7	29	128	210

Command System--1973

The commanders of military regions were not significantly involved in provincial politics in 1960. Although they were drawn into the revolutionary committees which governed the provinces during the Cultural Revolution, by 1973 they had withdrawn almost totally. Only two commanders of military regions held triple positions in 1973 and both held important (but not the top positions) in party and government organs. Both were second secretaries in the province party organizations and both were full members of the Tenth Central Committee. One was the first vice-chairman of the government organization, and the other was the first-listed of 14 vice-chairmen of the government organization.

Deputy commanders did not follow the same pattern. Unlike the commanders, linkages between military region deputy commanders and provincial party and government organizations increased by 1973 (See Appendix E).

In 1960 only 6 (all 6 were in Xinjiang and Xizang) deputy commanders held dual or triple positions in the provinces, whereas in 1973, 16 held triple positions, 2 held dual party-army positions and 17 held dual army-government positions. The dual and triple positions held by deputy commanders in 1973 were not insignificant. Three were first secretaries in the party, 6 others held secretary positions, and the remaining 9 were standing committee members of the party organization. On the government side, 3 were chairmen, 13 were vice-chairmen, and 17 were standing committee members. This represents a significant increase in military influence within the government organization compared with 1960 when commanders who held government positions were either powerful local leaders being accomodated or were officers heading activities indirectly related to the military, such as the Physical Culture and Sports Commissions.

None of the three deputy commanders who held the top party and government positions were in provinces in which the military region were located. Two of the three provinces (Heilongjiang and Nei Monggol) can be considered strategic areas. Most of those who held lesser party and government jobs in 1973, however, were in provinces in which the military region headquarters were located (See Appendix E).

Command System -- 1982

By 1982 all but 3 elites in the military region command system had been withdrawn from interlocking positions. There were no triple positions (Table 5-6). Two commanders and one deputy commander held dual party-army positions. All three were at the standing committee member level in the province party organization (Appendix F).

Political Commissar System--1973

Political commissar linkages with party and government organizations are more important than commander and deputy commander linkages. Of the 11 first or first-listed political commissars in the military regions in 1973 (See Appendix E), 9 held triple positions and 6 of those held the top party (first secretary) and government (chairman) positions in the provinces. Two of the 9 held second secretary positions in the party where there was no first secretary and one other was a secretary. All three of those who held second secretary or secretary positions in the party also held vice-chairman positions in the government organization. Two military region first political commissars held no triple positions (Shenyang and Fuzhou) and both were in military regions which had no designated first political commissar so the first-listed political commissars were counted in the first political commissar statistics.

There were two additional second political commissars in 1973. One of those held the top party (first secretary) and government (chairman) positions in Beijing. The Beijing Military Region Second Political Commissar was second to a first political commissar who held a triple position outside the military region. The other second political commissar (Chengdu MR) held a

TABLE 5-6

DUAL/TRIPLE POSITIONS HELD BY MILITARY REGION ELITES
1982

POSITION	TRIPLE PARTY/ ARMY/ GOVT	DUAL PARTY/ ARMY	DUAL GOVT/ ARMY	NO DUAL OR TRIPLE JOB	TOTAL SAMPLE
Commanders	0	2	0	9	11 (a)
First PC's	0	1	0	2	3 (b)
Dep Commanders	0	1	0	69	70
PC's	1	3	0	6	10
Command System	0	0	0	79	79
PC System	0	0	0	125	125
Totals	1	7	0	290	298

a. Total sample included those listed in Directory of PRC Military Personalities, published by the US Defense Liaison Office, US Consulate, Hong Kong in July 1983.
b. Six military regions listed no first political commissar but did list political commissars. The trend seems to be to eliminate the first political commissar title.

secretary job in the party and was a vice-chairman in the government organization.
 The next level in the political commissar system in 1973 was the political commissar. Of the 8 with this title, 6 held triple positions, 1 held a dual party-army position and 1 held a dual army-government position. Three of the 6 with triple positions held the top province party (first secretary) and government (chairman) job, 1 was a third secretary, and 2 were secretaries. The one who held a dual party-army position was a second secretary in the party and the one who held a dual army-government position was a standing committee member in the government organization.

In 1960 only Xizang and Xinjiang listed elites in the political commissar system below the political commissar level (i.e., deputy political commissar and members of the military region political departments). In 1973, 14 deputy political commissars and lower level political commissar system elites held triple positions, 4 held dual party-army positions and 10 held dual party-government positions. Of those with triple positions, two held the top party (first secretary) and government (chairman) job and one held the second position in the party (second secretary) and the government organization (first vice-chairman), 7 held secretary or deputy secretary and vice-chairman jobs, and 4 held party jobs at the standing committee level with vice-chairman or standing committee jobs in the government. Of the 4 who held dual party-army positions, one was a second secretary, 2 were secretaries and one was a standing committee member. Four of the dual army-government positions were vice-chairmen, and the others were standing committee members or members in the government organization.

Eight of the 11 first or second political commissars who held triple positions in 1973 held them in provinces in which the military region headquarters was located. One held a position in Shanghai, one moved (in 1976) to the province in which the military region headquarters was located (from Guangxi to Guangdong) and assumed the first secretary and chairman duties there, and one held a position outside the military region.

At the lower political commissar and deputy political commissar levels, none (of 5) of those who held first secretary and chairman positions in 1973 held them in provinces in which the military region headquarters was located. These positions were indications of the expanding involvement of military regions in provincial politics in 1973.

Political Commissar System -- 1982

By 1982 the number of elites in the military region political commissar system who held interlocking roles was reduced to five. Only one of the five held a triple position (Xinjiang). It was a case of the governor of the province maintaining a secretary position in the party and a lesser political commissar position in the military region. The first secretary of Xinjiang also held the military region first political commissar job. Xinjiang is a special case since it is a frontier area and the military region covers only one province. The first secretary of another frontier area, Xizang, also held a deputy political commissar position in the Chengdu Military Region. Finally, a secretary in Heilongjiang held a political commissar position in the Shenyang Military Region and a Beijing party standing committee member held a political commissar position in the Beijing Military Region.

Summary

Military region involvement in provincial politics was considerably greater in 1973 than in 1960 (Table 5-7), but by 1982 was reduced to a level below that of 1960. Interlocking directorate patterns existed in 1960, but compared to 1973 the scope and significance were at a much reduced level. Military region elites who were involved in interlocking roles were found primarily in strategic frontier provinces and mostly in Xinjiang and Xizang (12 of 21). By 1973, however, all military regions had elites in interlocking roles and the elites in these roles were found in all except five of the provinces. The remaining five, however, had elites with interlocking roles at the military district level.

The total number of military region elites in the command system who held interlocking roles jumped from 11 in 1960 to 33 in 1973 and then declined to 3 in 1982. The number in the political commissar system increased from 11 in 1960 to 48 in 1973 and then decreased to 5 in 1982.

A noteworthy change between 1960 and 1973 involved the quality of the linkage roles. In 1960 only two of the military region elites involved in interlocking roles held the top army (first political commissar or commander), party (first secretary) and government (governor/mayor) positions. There were some who held the top party and army positions, but in each case they were at a lower level in the government organization. In 1973, 19 military region elites (3 in the command system and 16 in the political commissar system) were involved in the top party and government positions. Several were in the next to the highest roles in all three organizations. In 1982 only 3 were involved in the top party or government roles; two first secretaries and one governor. All 3 were assigned to strategic frontier areas.

In 1973 political commissars held positions in provinces beyond those in which the military region headquarters were located. By 1973, the interlocking role had also appeared at much lower levels in the military region structure and those roles were not insignificant.

Some of the elites who were listed in the top three levels (first and second political commissars and political commissars) of the political commissar system in 1973, held no military job in 1960. This is an important indication of civilian lateral entry into the political commissar system at high levels which could have an adverse effect on the morale of professional

TABLE 5-7

MILITARY REGION COMMANDER AND POLITICAL COMMISSAR
INVOLVEMENT IN THE PROVINCES IN 1973 AND 1982

PROVINCE	CO 1973	CO 1982	PC 1973	PC 1982	TOTAL 1973	TOTAL 1982
ANHUI	0	0	0	0	0	0
BEIJING (a)	0	0	3	1	3	1
FUJIAN (a)	3	0	2	0	5	0
GANSU (a)	4	0	2	0	6	0
GUANGDONG (a)	3	0	2	0	5	1
GUANGXI	0	0	1	0	1	0
GUIZHOU	2	0	0	0	2	0
HEBEI	1	0	0	0	1	0
HEILONGJIANG	2	0	0	1	2	1
HENAN	0	0	2	0	2	0
HUBEI (a)	3	0	4	0	7	0
HUNAN	0	0	1	0	1	0
JIANGSU (a)	1	0	3	0	4	0
JIANGXI	0	0	1	0	1	0
JILIN	0	0	1	0	1	0
LIAONING (a)	1	0	5	0	6	0
NEI MONGGOL	1	0	0	0	1	0
NINGXIA	0	0	1	0	1	0
QINGHAI	0	1	0	0	0	1
SHAANXI	2	0	1	0	3	0
SHANDONG (a)	3	0	4	0	7	0
SHANGHAI	1	0	1	0	2	0
SHANXI	0	0	0	0	0	0
SICHUAN (a)	2	1	3	0	5	1
TIANJIN	0	0	1	0	1	0
XINJIANG (a)	4	1	6	2	10	3
XIZANG	0	0	0	1	0	1
YUNNAN (a)	4	0	3	0	7	0
ZHEJIANG	0	0	0	0	0	0
TOTALS	37	3	47	5	84	8

a. Provinces in which military region headquarters are located.
b. The data for 1960 was not sufficiently reliable to be included in this table.

political commissars. This is also an indication of party control over the military. The lateral entry phenomenon seems to have disappeared at the military region level in the last decade, but is still prevalent at the military district level.

PART 4: PROVINCE LEVEL PARTY, GOVERNMENT, AND MILITARY DISTRICT LINKAGES

Province Level Party Linkages

Linkages between province party elites and other key institutions (army, government, Central Committee) increased significantly from 1960 to 1973, but decreased by 1982. Furthermore, the ties have increased and decreased with identifiable patterns.

The first secretary is the top party job in the province party organization. In 1960 all provinces except Xizang listed a first secretary. In Xizang there was a single secretary listed and he has been counted as a first secretary for purposes of this analysis. In 1973, five provinces (Anhui, Hubei, Jiangsu, Liaoning, and Shandong) listed no first secretary, but three of those listed second secretaries which will be counted with first secretaries as the highest party job in the province (Hubei, Liaoning, and Shandong). One province promoted a deputy secretary and another promoted a secretary to first secretary in 1975 so they will be considered as first secretaries in this analysis.9 By 1982 eleven provinces listed no first secretary.10 Seven of the ten listed only one secretary followed by assistant or deputy secretaries.11 One of those (Hubei) was titled the senior secretary as "Secretary in Overall Charge of the Provincial Party Committee". One province (Shandong) listed two secretaries, one (Qinghai) listed three and one (Heilongjiang) listed four. The first listed in each of these is considered the first secretary in this analysis.

Scope of Interlocking Roles: 1960-1982
(Appendixes D, E and F)

In 1960 22 of 29 first party secretaries held interlocking roles (Table 5-8). Seven of the 22 held triple positions, 12 held dual party-army positions, and 3 held dual party-government positions. In 1973, 28 of 29 (all except Jiangxi) first party secretaries held dual or triple positions (Table 5-9). Twenty-four of the 28 held triple positions, 3 held dual party-government positions and one held a dual party-army position.

By 1982 a uniform pattern had emerged (Table 5-10). All 29 first party secretaries held dual party-army (first political commissar) positions while none held

TABLE 5-8

PROVINCE LEVEL FIRST PARTY SECRETARIES - 1960

PROVINCE	PC	CO	GOVT ARMY GOVT	PARTY MBR CC	ALT MBR CC	FULL MBR PB	ALT MBR PB	MBR PB
ANHUI					X			
BEIJING			X(e)		X			X
FUJIAN	X(a)			X				
GANSU				X				
GUANGDONG	X(a)				X			
GUANGXI				X				
GUIZHOU	X(b)		X(e) X					
HEBEI	X				X			
HEILONGJIANG					X			
HENAN	X(b)		X(e) X		X			
HUBEI				X				
HUNAN	X			X				
JIANGSU	X(b)			X				
JIANGXI	X(b)		X X					
JILIN	X(b)				X			
LIAONING	X				X			
NEI MONGGOL	X(a)	X(c)	X(e) X		X	X		
NINGXIA			X(e)	X				
QINGHAI								
SHAANXI	X(b)			X				
SHANDONG	X(a)		X X		X			
SHANGHAI	X(a)		X(e) X		X			X
SHANXI	X(b)			X				
SICHUAN	X				X			X
TIANJIN								
XINJIANG	X(a)	X(c)	X X		X			
XIZANG				X				
YUNNAN	X(a)			X				
ZHEJIANG	X(b)			X				
TOTALS	19	2	9 7	14	11	1		3

a. Highest ranking political commissar - military region.
b. Highest ranking political commissar - military district.
c. Highest ranking commander - military region.
d. Highest ranking commander - military district.
e. Highest ranking government official (governor/mayor).

TABLE 5-9

PROVINCE LEVEL FIRST PARTY SECRETARIES - 1973

PROVINCE	PC	CO	GOVT	PARTY ARMY GOVT	ALT MBR CC	MBR CC	ALT MBR PB	MBR PB
ANHUI	X(b)		X(e)	X		X		
BEIJING	X(b)		X(e)	X		X		X
FUJIAN			X(e)		X			
GANSU	X(a)		X(e)	X		X		
GUANGDONG			X(e)			X		
GUANGXI	X(ab)		X(e)	X		X		X
GUIZHOU		X	X(e)	X		X		
HEBEI	X(b)		X(e)	X		X		
HEILONGJIANG		X(d)	X(e)	X	X			
HENAN	X(b)		X(e)	X		X		
HUBEI	X(a)		X(e)	X	X			
HUNAN	X(b)		X(e)	X		X		X
JIANGSU			X(e)		X			
JIANGXI					X			
JILIN	X(b)		X(e)	X		X		
LIAONING	X(a)					X		
NEI MONGGOL		X(d)	X(e)	X		X		
NINGXIA	X(b)		X(e)	X	X			
QINGHAI	X(b)		X(e)	X				
SHAANXI	X(b)		X(e)	X		X		
SHANDONG	X(a)		X(e)	X		X		
SHANGHAI	X(ab)		X(e)	X		X		X
SHANXI		X(d)	X(e)	X	X			
SICHUAN	X(a)		X(e)	X		X		
TIANJIN	X(b)		X(e)	X		X		
XINJIANG	X(a)		X(e)	X		X	X	
XIZANG	X(b)		X(e)	X	X			
YUNNAN	X(a)		X(e)	X		X		
ZHEJIANG	X(b)		X(e)	X		X		
TOTALS	21	4	27	24	8	20	1	4

a. Highest ranking political commissar - military region.
b. Highest ranking political commissar - military district.
c. Highest ranking commander - military region.
d. Highest ranking commander - military district.
e. Highest ranking government official (chairman).

TABLE 5-10

PROVINCE LEVEL FIRST PARTY SECRETARIES - 1982

PROVINCE	PC	CO GOVT	PARTY ARMY GOVT	ALT MBR CC	FULL MBR CC	ALT MBR PB	MBR PB
ANHUI	X(b)						
BEIJING	X(b)				X(c)		
FUJIAN	X(b)				X		
GANSU	X(b)				X		
GUANGDONG	X(b)				X		
GUANGXI	X(b)				X		
GUIZHOU	X(b)				X		
HEBEI	X(b)				X(c)		
HEILONGJIANG	X(b)				X		
HENAN	X(b)				X(c)		
HUBEI	X(b)						
HUNAN	X(b)				X		
JIANGSU	X(b)				X		
JIANGXI	X(b)				X		
JILIN	X(b)				X		
LIAONING	X(b)				X(c)		
NEI MONGGOL	X(b)				X		
NINGXIA	X(b)				X		
QINGHAI	X(b)				X		
SHAANXI	X(b)				X		
SHANDONG	X(b)				X		
SHANGHAI	X(b)				X		
SHANXI	X(b)				X		
SICHUAN	X(b)				X		
TIANJIN	X(b)				X		
XINJIANG	X(a)				X		
XIZANG	X(b)				X		
YUNNAN	X(b)				X		
ZHEJIANG	X(b)				X		
TOTALS	29	0 0	0 0	0	23	0	0

a. Highest ranking political commissar - military region.
b. Highest ranking political commissar - military district.
c. Elected to Central Advisory Commission - not included in totals.

triple positions. The army position was the first political commissar of the military district except in the case of Xinjiang where the position was at the military region level.

In 1960 two first secretaries were commanders of military regions. Both were concurrently military region first political commissars. In 1973 there were 4 first secretaries who held command positions in the PLA. Three were military district commanders and the fourth was a deputy commander at the military region level. In 1982 no first secretaries held command positions.

In 1960, only 9 first secretaries held government jobs. Six of those held the top position. In 1973, 27 of the 29 first secretaries held government positions and all of those were governor/mayor positions. By 1982 the party-government roles were separated completely and no first secretary held a government position.

Linkages between first secretaries and the Central Committee also increased between 1960 and 1973, but more in quality than quantity. In 1960, 14 of the first secretaries were alternate members and 11 were full members of the Eighth Central Committee. In 1973, 8 were alternate members and 20 were full members of the Tenth Central Committee. Only the first secretary of Qinghai held no membership in the Tenth Central Committee.

By 1982 there was a general pattern of first party secretaries being full members of the Central Committee. Twenty-three were full members of the Twelfth Central Committee. Four were elected to the Central Advisory Commission of the CCP and must be considered transition leaders who were destined to retire in the near future. The remaining two held no central committee membership. None of the first party secretaries were alternate members of the Central Committee in 1982.

In 1960, only 1 first secretary was an alternate member of the Politburo and 3 were full members. In 1973, one was an alternate member and 4 were full members. By 1982 none of the first secretaries were members of the Politburo.

When all secretaries (first, second, third, deputy, alternate, acting secretaries and secretaries) were examined the direction of the changes in organizational linkages was even more apparent. In 1960, of 222 elites considered, 11 held triple positions, 100 held dual positions and 111 held positions in the party only (Table 5-11). In 1973, of the 184 listed, 73 held triple positions and 88 held dual positions. Only 22 held positions only in the party (Table 5-12). In 1982 the party structure was streamlined and the number of secretaries was reduced significantly to a total of 145 (Table 5-13). Only one of those held a triple position, 68 held dual positions and 80 held positions in the party only. Thus, in 1960, 44% of the party

TABLE 5-11

PROVINCE LEVEL PARTY COMMITTEE MEMBERS (a)
1960

PROVINCE MUNICIPALITY	TOTAL SAMPLE	PC	PC GOVT	CO	CO GOVT	GOVT	PARTY ARMY GOVT	ALT MBR CC	MBR CC	ALT MBR PB	MBR PB	NO MULTI-ROLE
ANHUI	10	0	0	0	0	5	0	0	1	0	0	5
BEIJING	9	0	0	0	0	2	0	1	1	0	1	7
FUJIAN	9	1	0	0	0	4	0	1	0	0	0	4
GANSU	9	0	0	0	0	4	0	1	0	0	0	5
GUANGDONG	8	1	0	0	0	1	0	1	2	0	0	6
GUANGXI	6	0	0	0	0	3	0	2	0	0	0	3
GUIZHOU	7	0	1	0	0	0	1	0	0	0	0	6
HEBEI	9	1	0	0	0	4	0	1	1	0	0	4
HEILONGJIANG	8	0	0	1	0	4	0	1	1	0	0	3
HENAN	7	0	1	1	0	4	1	0	1	0	0	1
HUBEI	8	0	0	0	0	3	0	1	0	0	0	5
HUNAN	9	1	0	0	0	3	0	1	0	0	0	5
JIANGSU	6	1	0	0	0	3	0	1	0	0	0	2
JIANGXI	7	1	1	1	0	4	1	1	0	0	0	0
JILIN	7	1	0	0	0	3	0	1	0	0	0	3
LIAONING	7	2	0	0	0	1	0	3	0	0	0	4
NEI MONGGOL (b)	6	0	1	0	1	3	1	1	1	1	0	2
NINGXIA	6	0	0	0	0	3	0	1	1	0	0	3
QINGHAI	7	0	0	0	0	1	0	0	0	0	0	6
SHAANXI	8	1	0	0	0	1	0	2	0	0	0	6
SHANDONG	10	0	1	0	1	5	2	2	0	0	0	3
SHANGHAI	7	0	1	0	0	2	1	1	1	0	1	4
SHANXI	9	1	0	0	0	2	0	1	0	0	0	6
SICHUAN	8	1	0	1	0	2	0	2	1	0	1	4
TIANJIN	6	0	0	0	0	1	0	0	0	0	0	5
XINJIANG (b)	8	1	1	0	2	0	2	1	1	0	0	5
XIZANG	6	1	1	2	1	1	2	1	0	0	0	0
YUNNAN	8	1	0	0	0	5	0	1	0	0	0	2
ZHEJIANG	7	1	0	0	0	4	0	1	0	0	0	2
TOTALS	222	16	8	6	5	78	11	30	12	1	3	111

a. Includes first, second, third, deputy, alternate and acting secretaries and secretaries.
b. Same individual holds commander and commissar positions.

TABLE 5-12

PROVINCE LEVEL PARTY COMMITTEE MEMBERS (a)
1973

PROVINCE MUNICIPALITY	TOTAL SAMPLE	PC	PC GOVT	CO	CO GOVT	GOVT	PARTY ARMY GOVT	ALT MBR CC	MBR CC	ALT MBR PB	MBR PB	NO MULTI-ROLE
ANHUI	5	1	1	0	0	2	1	0	3	0	0	1
BEIJING	9	0	3	0	1	4	4	2	4	1	1	1
FUJIAN	5	0	1	0	1	3	2	1	0	0	0	0
GANSU	4	0	1	0	1	2	2	0	2	0	0	0
GUANGDONG	4	0	1	0	0	3	1	1	3	0	0	0
GUANGXI	5	0	2	0	0	3	2	0	1	0	1	0
GUIZHOU	7	0	0	0	3	3	3	1	2	0	0	1
HEBEI	5	0	1	0	1	3	2	0	2	0	0	0
HEILONGJIANG	9	0	1	0	1	4	2	3	1	0	0	3
HENAN	7	0	2	0	2	3	4	0	4	0	1	0
HUBEI	9	1	2	1	0	4	2	1	0	0	0	1
HUNAN	9	0	4	0	1	2	5	2	2	0	1	2
JIANGSU	4	0	2	0	0	2	2	1	2	0	0	0
JIANGXI	6	0	2	0	1	1	3	4	0	0	0	2
JILIN	6	1	1	0	1	3	2	0	1	0	0	0
LIAONING	5	1	1	0	0	1	1	0	1	0	0	2
NEI MONGGOL	3	0	1	0	1	1	2	0	2	0	0	0
NINGXIA	6	0	1	1	0	2	1	1	0	0	0	2
QINGHAI	7	1	1	0	1	3	2	2	0	0	0	1
SHAANXI	6	0	1	0	2	3	3	1	2	1	0	0
SHANDONG	3	0	1	0	0	2	1	0	1	0	0	0
SHANGHAI	7	0	2	0	1	4	3	0	7	0	3	0
SHANXI	9	1	1	0	1	5	2	3	2	0	1	1
SICHUAN	8	0	3	0	1	3	4	1	4	0	0	1
TIANJIN	7	0	3	0	1	2	4	0	1	0	0	1
XINJIANG	8	1	2	0	1	2	3	0	3	1	0	1
XIZANG	8	0	2	0	2	3	4	1	2	0	0	1
YUNNAN	7	0	2	0	2	2	4	0	3	0	0	1
ZHEJIANG	6	0	2	0	0	4	2	1	1	0	0	0
TOTALS	184	7	47	2	26	79	73	26	56	3	8	22

a. Includes first, second, third, alternate, deputy and acting secretaries and secretaries. Does not include standing committee members or members - see Table 5-14.

TABLE 5-13

PROVINCE LEVEL PARTY COMMITTEE MEMBERS (a)
1982

PROVINCE MUNICIPALITY	TOTAL SAMPLE	PC	PC GOVT	CO	CO GOVT	GOVT	PARTY ARMY GOVT	ALT MBR CC	MBR CC	ALT MBR PB	MBR PB	NO MULTI-ROLE
ANHUI	6	1	0	0	0	1	0	0	1	0	0	4
BEIJING	4	1	0	0	0	1	0	0	1	0	0	2
FUJIAN	5	1	0	0	0	1	0	1	3	0	0	3
GANSU	4	1	0	0	0	1	0	0	1	0	0	2
GUANGDONG	6	1	0	0	0	1	0	0	3	0	0	4
GUANGXI	6	1	0	0	0	3	0	1	2	0	0	4
GUIZHOU	4	1	0	0	0	2	0	1	3	0	0	2
HEBEI	5	1	0	0	0	1	0	2	2	0	0	3
HEILONGJIANG	4	1	0	0	0	1	0	0	2	0	0	2
HENAN	5	1	0	0	0	1	0	2	2	0	0	3
HUBEI	6	2	0	0	0	1	0	1	3	0	0	3
HUNAN	4	1	0	0	0	1	0	0	2	0	0	2
JIANGSU	5	1	0	0	0	1	0	0	2	0	0	3
JIANGXI	4	1	0	0	0	1	0	1	1	0	0	2
JILIN	6	2	0	0	0	1	0	1	2	0	0	4
LIAONING	6	1	0	0	0	1	0	2	2	0	0	4
NEI MONGGOL	5	1	0	0	0	1	0	2	2	0	0	3
NINGXIA	5	1	0	0	0	2	0	1	1	0	0	2
QINGHAI	5	1	0	0	0	1	0	0	1	0	0	3
SHAANXI	6	1	0	0	0	1	0	1	2	0	0	4
SHANDONG	6	1	0	0	0	2	0	2	2	0	0	3
SHANGHAI	5	1	0	0	0	2	0	0	3	0	0	2
SHANXI	4	1	0	0	0	1	0	0	2	0	0	2
SICHUAN	5	1	0	0	0	2	0	2	1	0	0	2
TIANJIN	5	1	0	0	0	2	0	0	3	0	0	2
XINJIANG	6	1	1	0	0	0	1	1	3	0	0	4
XIZANG	5	1	0	0	0	1	0	1	3	0	0	3
YUNNAN	4	1	0	0	0	1	0	1	1	0	0	2
ZHEJIANG	4	1	0	0	0	2	0	0	2	0	0	1
TOTALS	145	31	1	0	0	37	1	23	58	0	0	80

a. Includes first, second and deputy secretaries and secretaries. Does not include standing committee members - see Table 5-15.

secretaries were involved in interlocking roles compared with 88% in 1973 and 45% in 1982.

In 1960, 16 secretaries held dual party-army (political commissar) positions, 8 held triple party-army (political commissar)-government positions, 6 held dual party-army (commander) positions and 5 held triple party-army (commander)-government positions (Table 5-11).

In 1973, 7 secretaries held dual party-army (political commissar) positions, 47 held triple party-army (political commissar)-government positions, 2 held dual party-army (commander) positions, and 26 held triple party-army (commander)-government positions (Table 5-12).

In 1982 there was only one triple party-army (political commissar)-government position (Xinjiang). Hubei Province (Table 5-13).

In 1960, 78 secretaries held dual party-government positions as compared to 79 in 1973 and 34 in 1982. Twenty-eight of the 34 in 1982 were secretaries who held the governor or mayor positions. The twenty-ninth governor, in Xinjiang, held the triple position. Six other secretaries held vice-governor or vice-mayor positions.

In 1960, 30 party secretaries were alternate members of the Central Committee compared with 26 in 1973 and 23 in 1982. Only 12 party secretaries were full members of the Central Committee in 1960 whereas in 1973 there were 56, but by 1982 there were only 34. Party secretary membership in the Politburo increased from 3 full and 1 alternate in 1960 to 8 full and 3 alternate positions in 1973. No party secretaries were no full or alternate politburo members in 1982.

In 1960 province party lists did not include standing committee members and members of the province party committees. In 1973, 362 elites were listed in those positions (Table 5-14). It was clear that the interlocking directorate phenomenon extended deep into the institutional structures. There were 24 triple party-army (political commissar)-government positions, 23 triple party-army (commander)-government positions, 5 dual party-army (political commissar) positions, 8 dual party-army (commander) positions, and 144 dual party-government interlocking roles among the standing committee members and members which were all below the secretary level in the party committees. This means that 57% of these lower level elites were involved in interlocking roles in 1973. There were 17 alternate and 26 full members of the Tenth Central Committee among this group of lower level party committee members.

By 1982 the significant reduction of standing committee members who held interlocking roles followed the general pattern of separating party-army-government roles (Table 5-15). There were 177 elites elected as

TABLE 5-14

PROVINCE LEVEL PARTY COMMITTEE MEMBERS
(Standing committee members and members)
1973

PROVINCE MUNICIPALITY	TOTAL SAMPLE	PC	PC GOVT	CO	CO GOVT	GOVT	PARTY ARMY GOVT	ALT MBR CC	MBR CC	ALT MBR PB	MBR PB	NO MULTI-ROLE
ANHUI	16	0	0	0	1	11	1	2	0	0	0	4
BEIJING	70	0	0	0	0	9	0	1	1	0	0	61
FUJIAN	13	2	1	0	2	5	3	1	1	0	0	3
GANSU	7	0	0	0	1	5	1	0	1	0	0	1
GUANGDONG	15	0	1	0	2	10	3	1	3	0	0	2
GUANGXI	16	0	1	1	4	3	5	0	0	0	0	7
GUIZHOU	3	0	0	0	0	2	0	0	0	0	0	1
HEBEI	13	0	2	0	1	6	3	0	2	0	0	4
HEILONGJIANG	13	0	2	0	0	4	2	0	1	0	0	7
HENAN	13	0	2	0	1	5	3	2	1	0	0	5
HUBEI	19	1	2	0	2	9	4	2	3	0	0	5
HUNAN	23	0	3	2	3	6	6	1	1	0	0	9
JIANGSU	7	0	0	1	0	6	0	1	1	0	0	0
JIANGXI	14	1	1	3	0	9	1	0	1	0	0	0
JILIN	5	0	2	0	0	3	1	0	1	0	0	0
LIAONING	5	0	0	0	0	2	0	1	1	0	0	3
NEI MONGGOL	10	0	1	0	1	2	2	0	0	0	0	6
NINGXIA	2	0	0	0	1	0	1	0	0	0	0	1
QINGHAI	10	0	0	0	1	4	1	2	0	0	0	5
SHAANXI	8	0	2	0	0	4	2	0	0	0	0	2
SHANDONG	11	0	2	0	0	5	2	0	0	0	0	4
SHANGHAI	13	0	0	0	1	9	1	1	2	0	0	3
SHANXI	8	0	0	0	0	6	0	0	1	0	0	2
SICHUAN	3	0	0	0	0	1	0	0	0	0	0	2
TIANJIN	5	0	1	0	0	4	1	0	3	0	0	0
XINJIANG	6	0	1	0	0	1	1	0	0	0	0	4
XIZANG	10	0	0	0	0	2	0	0	0	0	0	8
YUNNAN	11	0	0	0	1	2	1	1	0	0	0	8
ZHEJIANG	13	1	0	1	1	9	1	1	2	0	0	1
TOTALS	362	5	24	8	23	144	46	17	26	0	0	158

TABLE 5-15

PROVINCE LEVEL PARTY COMMITTEE MEMBERS
(Standing committee members only)
1982

PROVINCE MUNICIPALITY	TOTAL SAMPLE	PC	PC GOVT	CO	CO GOVT	GOVT	PARTY ARMY GOVT	ALT MBR CC	MBR CC	ALT MBR PB	MBR PB	NO MULTI-ROLE
ANHUI	3	0	0	0	0	1	0	0	0	0	0	2
BEIJING	9	1	0	0	0	1	0	0	0	0	0	7
FUJIAN	7	0	0	0	0	0	0	0	0	0	0	7
GANSU	7	0	0	1	0	1	0	0	0	0	0	5
GUANGDONG	7	0	0	0	0	1	0	0	0	0	0	6
GUANGXI	4	0	0	0	0	2	9	0	1	0	0	2
GUIZHOU	6	0	0	0	0	1	0	0	0	0	0	5
HEBEI	8	0	0	0	0	1	0	1	0	0	0	7
HEILONGJIANG	8	1	0	0	0	0	0	0	1	0	0	7
HENAN	6	0	0	0	0	0	0	0	0	0	0	6
HUBEI	7	0	0	0	0	1	0	0	0	0	0	6
HUNAN	0	0	0	0	0	0	0	0	0	0	0	0
JIANGSU	5	0	0	0	0	1	0	0	0	0	0	4
JIANGXI	7	0	0	1	0	1	0	0	1	0	0	5
JILIN	5	0	0	0	0	1	0	0	0	0	0	4
LIAONING	6	0	0	0	0	2	0	1	1	0	0	4
NEI MONGGOL	7	0	0	0	0	0	0	0	0	0	0	7
NINGXIA	3	0	0	0	0	1	0	1	0	0	0	2
QINGHAI	5	0	0	1	0	1	0	0	0	0	0	2
SHAANXI	6	0	0	0	0	1	0	0	0	0	0	5
SHANDONG	6	0	0	0	0	0	0	0	0	0	0	6
SHANGHAI	4	0	0	0	0	0	0	0	0	0	0	4
SHANXI	6	0	0	0	0	0	0	2	0	0	0	6
SICHUAN	11	0	0	1	0	1	0	0	3	0	0	9
TIANJIN	7	0	0	0	0	1	0	0	0	0	0	6
XINJIANG	8	1	0	1	0	0	0	1	1	0	0	6
XIZANG	6	0	0	0	0	1	0	0	0	0	0	5
YUNNAN	6	0	0	0	0	0	0	0	0	0	0	6
ZHEJIANG	7	0	0	0	0	1	0	1	0	0	0	6
TOTALS	177	3	0	5	0	21	9	7	8	0	0	147

standing committee members by 1982. Among them there were no triple positions, 21 dual party-government positions, 5 dual party-army (commander) positions, and 3 dual party-army (political commissar) positions. Thus, the percentage of elites at the standing committee member level who held interlocking roles was reduced from 57% in 1973 to 16% in 1982. There were only 7 alternate and 8 full members of the Twelfth Central Committee in this group.

Summary

It is clear that both vertical and horizontal linkages increased significantly between 1960 and 1973 and then decreased by 1982. The total number of province party committee members who were alternate members of the Central Committee decreased from 30 in the Eighth Central Committee to 26 in the Tenth Central Committee and then to 23 in the Twelfth Central Committee. The number who were full members increased from 12 in the Eighth Central Committee to 56 in the Tenth Central Committee and then to 57 in the Twelfth Central Committee. When standing committee members and members are included the totals change from 43 alternates in 1973 to 30 in 1982 and from 82 full in 1973 to 65 in 1982.

The total number and percentage of party committee members involved in interlocking roles fluctuated widely between 1960 and 1982. In 1960 there were only 11 (5%) who held triple positions and 100 (45%) who held dual positions. By 1973, 119 (22%) province party elites occupied triple positions and 245 (45%) dual positions (including standing committee members and members). In 1982 the numbers decreased to 1 triple position and only 94 dual positions. The quality of the interlocking roles also increased between 1960 and 1973 as was reflected in the number (27 of 29) of first secretaries who held top army and government positions (Tables 5-8 and 5-9). But by 1982 the dual party (first secretary)-army (first political commissar) interlocking roles were dominant. It is important to note that elites who held positions only in the party at the secretary level decreased considerably from 111 in 1960 to 22 in 1973 and then increased again to 80 in 1982.

Province Level Government Linkages

The highest position in the government hierarchy is the governor or mayor (chairman in 1973). Below the governor or mayor are vice-governors or vice-mayors, standing committee members and members.

Since five of the provinces listed no chairman in 1973, for purposes of this study, the first listed vice-chairman is included (Liaoning, Shandong, Anhui,

Jiangxi, Hubei). In addition, one province only listed an acting chairman in 1973 (Hua Guofeng/Hunan), and he is treated as a chairman in the analysis below.

Scope of Interlocking Roles: 1960-1982
(Appendixes D, E, and F)

Only 5 of 29 governors/mayors of provincial government organizations in 1960 held triple positions, none held dual army-government positions and 14 held dual party-government positions (Table 5-16). Ten governors/mayors held no party or army job.12 Of the 5 who held triple positions, 4 were government-party-army (political commissar) and 1 was government-party-army (commander). One of the commanders was also the first political commissar of a military region so he is counted in both categories. Two of the political commissars were first political commissars of military districts. The other commander was a deputy commander of a military region. Six of the governors/mayors with interlocking roles held first secretary positions in the party.

In 1973, 26 of the 29 chairmen were involved in triple positions (Table 5-17). Twenty-two held government-party-army (political commissar) positions and 4 held government-party-army (commander) positions. As in 1960, there were no chairmen who held dual army-government positions, but there were 3 who held dual party-government positions.

Six who held political commissar positions in 1973 were military region first political commissars. Two others were first political commissars of both military regions and military districts. Thirteen were first political commissars of military districts. One of the chairmen held a lesser political commissar position in a military region. Three of the commanders were military district commanders and one was a deputy commander of a military region.

Twenty-seven of the 29 chairman positions in 1973 were held by elites who were concurrently first secretaries in the party while only 3 were lesser secretaries, both involved in triple positions.

By 1982 a clear pattern had emerged (Table 5-18). All 29 governors/mayors held secretary positions in the party but none of them held the first secretary position nor any position in the army, except the Governor of Xinjiang who held the only triple position - government-party (secretary)-army (political commissar). The key government position was completely separated from the army but maintained a lesser connection with the party.

In 1960, 9 governors/mayors were alternate members of the Central Committee and in 1973 there were also 8. By 1982, only 4 chairmen were alternate members. In

TABLE 5-16

PROVINCE LEVEL GOVERNORS/MAYORS (GOVERNMENT)
1960

PROVINCE MUNICIPALITY	PC	CO	PARTY ARMY GOVT	PARTY MBR CC	ALT MBR CC	MBR CC	ALT MBR PB	MBR PB
ANHUI			X					
BEIJING			X(e)			X		X
FUJIAN			X					
GANSU								
GUANGDONG			X			X		
GUANGXI			X		X			
GUIZHOU	X(b)		X(e)	X				
HEBEI			X		X			
HEILONGJIANG								
HENAN	X(b)		X(e)	X		X		
HUBEI			X					
HUNAN								
JIANGSU								
JIANGXI			X		X			
JILIN								
LIAONING			X		X			
NEI MONGGOL	X(a)	X(c)	X(e)	X		X	X	
NINGXIA			X(e)		X			
QINGHAI								
SHAANXI			X		X			
SHANDONG			X		X			
SHANGHAI	X(a)		X(e)	X		X		X
SHANXI								
SICHUAN			X		X			
TIANJIN								
XINJIANG		X	X	X	X			
XIZANG								
YUNNAN			X					
ZHEJIANG								
TOTALS	4	2	19	5	9	5	1	2

a. Highest ranking political commissar - military region.
b. Highest ranking political commissar - military district.
c. Highest ranking commander - military region.
d. Highest ranking commander - military district.
e. Highest ranking party official (first secretary).

TABLE 5-17

PROVINCE LEVEL CHAIRMEN (GOVERNMENT)
1973

PROVINCE MUNICIPALITY	PC	CO	PARTY	PARTY ARMY GOVT	ALT MBR CC	MBR CC	ALT MBR PB	MBR PB
ANHUI	X(b)		X(e)	X		X		
BEIJING	X(b)		X(e)	X		X		X
FUJIAN			X(e)		X			
GANSU	X(a)		X(e)	X		X		
GUANGDONG			X(e)			X		
GUANGXI	X(ab)		X(e)	X		X		X
GUIZHOU		X	X(e)	X		X		
HEBEI	X(b)		X(e)	X		X		
HEILONGJIANG		X(d)	X(e)	X	X			
HENAN	X(b)		X(e)	X		X		
HUBEI	X(a)		X	X	X			
HUNAN	X(b)		X(e)	X		X		X
JIANGSU			X(e)		X			
JIANGXI	X(b)		X	X	X			
JILIN	X(b)		X(e)	X		X		
LIAONING	X		X(e)	X				
NEI MONGGOL		X(d)	X(e)	X		X		
NINGXIA	X(b)		X(e)	X	X			
QINGHAI	X(b)		X(e)	X				
SHAANXI	X(b)		X(e)	X		X		
SHANDONG	X(a)		X	X		X		
SHANGHAI	X(ab)		X(e)	X		X		X
SHANXI		X(d)	X(e)	X	X			
SICHUAN	X(a)		X(e)	X		X		
TIANJIN	X(b)		X(e)	X		X		
XINJIANG	X(a)		X(e)	X		X	X	
XIZANG	X(b)		X(e)	X	X			
YUNNAN	X(a)		X(e)	X		X		
ZHEJIANG	X(b)		X(e)	X		X		
TOTALS	22	4	29	26	8	19	1	4

a. Highest ranking political commissar - military region.
b. Highest ranking political commissar - military district.
c. Highest ranking commander - military region.
d. Highest ranking commander - military district.
e. Highest ranking party official (first or first-listed secretary).

TABLE 5-18

PROVINCE LEVEL GOVERNORS/MAYORS (GOVERNMENT)
1982

PROVINCE MUNICIPALITY	PC	CO	PARTY	PARTY ARMY GOVT	ALT MBR CC	MBR CC	ALT MBR PB	MBR PB
ANHUI			X					
BEIJING			X			X		
FUJIAN			X		X			
GANSU			X					
GUANGDONG			X			X		
GUANGXI			X					
GUIZHOU			X			X		
HEBEI			X			X		
HEILONGJIANG			X			X		
HENAN			X		X			
HUBEI			X			X		
HUNAN			X					
JIANGSU			X			X		
JIANGXI			X					
JILIN			X					
LIAONING			X					
NEI MONGGOL			X			X		
NINGXIA			X		X			
QINGHAI			X					
SHAANXI			X					
SHANDONG			X			X		
SHANGHAI			X					
SHANXI			X					
SICHUAN			X		X			
TIANJIN			X			X		
XINJIANG	X		X	X		X		
XIZANG			X					
YUNNAN			X					
ZHEJIANG			X			X		
TOTALS	1	0	29	1	4	12	0	0

a. Highest ranking political commissar - military region.
b. Highest ranking political commissar - military district.
c. Highest ranking commander - military region.
d. Highest ranking commander - military district.
e. Highest ranking party official (first or first-listed secretary).

1960, 5 governors/mayors were full members of the Eighth Central Committee and by 1973 the number had increased to 19. But by 1982 the number was reduced to 12. It is significant that 13 chairmen were neither full nor alternate members of the Central Committee in 1982.

In 1960 one alternate and 2 full members of the Politburo were governors/mayors and in 1973 there was one alternate and 4 full members. In 1982 there were none.

When the sample of government elites is expanded to include vice-governors/mayors, standing committee members and members, the pattern of changing vertical linkages as well as horizontal interlocking roles becomes even more distinct (Tables 5-19, 5-20, and 5-21). The total sample size was 901 for 1960 and 1202 for 1973. In 1982 standing committee members and members were not listed, so only governors and vice-governors were included and the total sample was only 176.

In 1960 government elites occupied only 10 triple positions. Seven of the 9 had government-party-army (political commissar) roles and 2 had government-party-army (commander) roles. Two individuals held both political commissar and commander positions. In 1973, there were 119 triple positions: 67 were government-party-army (political commissar) positions and 51 were government-party-army (commander) positions. By 1982 there was only 1 triple position which was in Xinjiang.

In 1960 there were 102 government elites involved in dual positions. There were 9 dual government-army (political commissar) roles, 15 dual government-army (commander) roles, and 78 dual government-party roles. In 1973, government elites were involved in 306 dual positions of which 33 were government-army (political commissar) roles, 48 were dual government-army (commander) roles, and 225 were dual government-party roles. By 1982 there were only 55 government elites involved in dual positions and these were all party-government. The army was removed totally from interlocking roles with the government. It can be assumed that this separation of government roles from party and army roles was generally true at the lower levels.

Provincial government elite linkages with the Central Committee also showed significant changes over time. Among governmental elites in 1960, eight were full members of the Central Committee, while 12 were alternates. In 1973 these numbers increased to 87 and 52 respectively. However, by 1982 the number of members decreased to 13 full and 10 alternates. Provincial government representation in the Politburo followed a similar trend. In 1960 there were 2 full members and 1 alternate; in 1973 there were 8 full members and 3 alternates. However, by 1982 no provincial government elites held Politburo membership.

TABLE 5-19

PROVINCE LEVEL GOVERNMENT ORGANIZATION (a)
1960

PROVINCE MUNICIPALITY	TOTAL SAMPLE	PC	PC PARTY	CO	CO PARTY	PARTY ARMY GOVT	PARTY MBR CC	ALT MBR CC	MBR PB	ALT MBR PB	NO MULTI-ROLE
ANHUI	56	1	0	1	0	5	0	0	0	0	49
BEIJING	8	0	0	0	0	2	0	0	1	0	1	6
FUJIAN	46	0	0	0	1	4	1	1	0	0	41
GANSU	38	0	0	0	0	4	0	0	0	0	34
GUANGDONG	15	0	0	0	0	1	0	0	1	0	14
GUANGXI	8	0	0	0	0	3	0	1	0	0	5
GUIZHOU	35	1	1	1	0	0	1	0	0	0	32
HEBEI	56	1	0	0	0	4	0	1	0	0	51
HEILONGJIANG	46	0	0	1	0	4	0	1	0	0	41
HENAN	60	0	1	1	0	4	1	0	1	0	54
HUBEI	13	0	0	0	0	3	0	0	0	0	10
HUNAN	11	0	0	1	0	3	0	0	0	0	7
JIANGSU	10	0	0	0	0	2	0	0	0	0	8
JIANGXI	56	1	1	1	0	5	1	1	0	0	48
JILIN	47	1	0	0	0	3	0	0	0	0	43
LIAONING	12	0	0	1	0	1	0	1	0	0	10
NEI MONGGOL (b)	10	0	1	0	1	3	1	1	1	1	0	6
NINGXIA	8	0	0	0	0	2	0	0	1	0	6
QINGHAI	15	0	0	0	0	1	0	0	0	0	14
SHAANXI	42	1	0	1	0	1	0	1	0	0	39
SHANDONG	59	0	1	1	0	5	1	1	1	0	52
SHANGHAI	10	0	0	0	0	3	0	0	1	0	1	7
SHANXI	10	0	0	0	0	2	0	0	0	0	8
SICHUAN	13	0	0	2	0	2	0	2	0	0	9
TIANJIN	8	0	0	0	0	1	0	0	0	0	7
XINJIANG (b)	51	0	1	0	2	0	2	1	1	0	49
XIZANG	64	2	1	3	1	1	2	0	0	0	56
YUNNAN	47	0	0	1	0	5	0	0	0	0	41
ZHEJIANG	47	1	0	0	0	4	0	0	0	0	42
TOTALS	901	9	7	15	5	78	10	12	8	1	2	788

a. Includes governors/mayors, vice governors/mayors, secretary-generals and members.
b. Same individual held commander and political commissar positions.

TABLE 5-20

PROVINCE LEVEL GOVERNMENT ORGANIZATION (a)
1973

PROVINCE MUNICIPALITY	TOTAL SAMPLE	PC	PC PARTY	CO	CO PARTY	PARTY	PARTY ARMY GOVT	ALT MBR CC	MBR CC	ALT MBR PB	MBR PB	NO MULTI-ROLE
ANHUI	30	1	1	3	1	14	2	1	2	0	0	10
BEIJING	99	3	3	1	1	13	4	3	5	1	1	78
FUJIAN	51	0	2	0	3	8	5	2	1	0	0	38
GANSU	36	3	1	3	2	7	3	0	4	0	0	20
GUANGDONG	65	2	2	1	2	13	4	2	7	0	0	45
GUANGXI	41	1	1	3	4	6	7	1	3	0	1	26
GUIZHOU	36	2	0	3	3	5	3	0	2	0	0	23
HEBEI	29	0	3	1	2	9	5	1	3	0	0	14
HEILONGJIANG	53	2	3	4	1	8	4	4	0	0	0	35
HENAN	33	0	4	1	3	8	7	1	5	0	1	17
HUBEI	43	0	4	3	2	13	6	4	3	0	0	21
HUNAN	43	0	7	2	4	8	11	2	3	0	1	22
JIANGSU	31	1	2	0	0	8	2	2	3	0	0	20
JIANGXI	35	0	3	1	1	10	4	3	1	0	0	20
JILIN	30	1	2	0	2	6	3	0	2	0	0	19
LIAONING	47	4	0	1	1	3	1	2	6	0	0	38
NEI MONGGOL	45	1	2	4	2	3	4	0	3	0	0	33
NINGXIA	13	0	1	0	1	2	2	2	0	0	0	9
QINGHAI	28	1	1	0	2	7	3	4	0	0	0	17
SHAANXI	34	1	3	2	2	7	5	1	2	1	0	19
SHANDONG	48	2	3	5	0	7	3	0	1	0	0	31
SHANGHAI	74	2	2	1	2	13	4	2	9	0	3	54
SHANXI	38	0	1	1	1	11	2	2	3	0	1	24
SICHUAN	33	0	3	2	1	4	4	6	4	0	0	23
TIANJIN	42	2	4	0	1	6	5	0	4	0	0	29
XINJIANG	31	2	3	3	1	4	4	2	3	1	0	18
XIZANG	50	1	2	0	2	5	4	2	2	0	0	40
YUNNAN	32	1	2	3	3	4	5	1	3	0	0	19
ZHEJIANG	32	0	2	0	1	13	3	2	3	0	0	16
TOTALS	1212	33	67	48	51	225	119	52	87	3	8	778

a. Includes chairmen, vice-chairmen, standing committee members, and members.

TABLE 5-21

PROVINCE LEVEL GOVERNMENT ORGANIZATION (a)
1982

PROVINCE MUNICIPALITY	TOTAL SAMPLE	PC PARTY	PC PARTY	CO PARTY	CO PARTY	PARTY ARMY GOVT	PARTY MBR CC	ALT MBR CC	MBR PB	ALT MBR PB	NO MULTI-ROLE
ANHUI	6	0	0	0	0	2	0	0	0	0	4
BEIJING	7	0	0	0	0	2	0	0	1	0	5
FUJIAN	5	0	0	0	0	1	0	1	0	0	4
GANSU	6	0	0	0	0	2	0	1	0	0	4
GUANGDONG	8	0	0	0	0	2	0	0	1	0	6
GUANGXI	6	0	0	0	0	3	0	0	0	0	3
GUIZHOU	6	0	0	0	0	2	0	1	1	0	4
HEBEI	6	0	0	0	0	2	0	1	1	0	4
HEILONGJIANG	6	0	0	0	0	1	0	0	1	0	5
HENAN	5	0	0	0	0	1	0	1	0	0	4
HUBEI	6	0	0	0	0	2	0	0	1	0	4
HUNAN	5	0	0	0	0	1	0	0	0	0	4
JIANGSU	7	0	0	0	0	2	0	0	1	0	5
JIANGXI	4	0	0	0	0	2	0	0	0	0	2
JILIN	6	0	0	0	0	2	0	1	0	0	4
LIAONING	7	0	0	0	0	3	0	0	1	0	4
NEI MONGGOL	4	0	0	0	0	1	0	0	1	0	3
NINGXIA	7	0	0	0	0	3	0	2	0	0	4
QINGHAI	6	0	0	0	0	2	0	0	0	0	4
SHAANXI	7	0	0	0	0	2	0	0	0	0	5
SHANDONG	5	0	0	0	0	2	0	0	1	0	3
SHANGHAI	7	0	0	0	0	2	0	0	0	0	5
SHANXI	5	0	0	0	0	1	0	0	0	0	4
SICHUAN	7	0	0	0	0	3	0	2	0	0	4
TIANJIN	7	0	0	0	0	3	0	0	1	0	4
XINJIANG	7	0	1	0	0	0	1	0	1	0	6
XIZANG	6	0	0	0	0	2	0	0	0	0	4
YUNNAN	6	0	0	0	0	1	0	0	0	0	5
ZHEJIANG	6	0	0	0	0	3	0	0	1	0	3
TOTALS	176	0	1	0	0	55	1	10	13	0	120

a. Includes only governors, vice-governors, mayors and vice or deputy mayors. Although the sample is much smaller than Tables 5-19 and 5-20 the data still reflects the patterns.

In 1960 there were 788 (87%) elites in the government organization who held no interlocking role and in 1973 the number had decreased to 778 (64%). By 1982 the figure was 120 (68%), but standing committee members and ordinary members were not counted so the sample was much reduced.

Summary

In summary, interlocking roles which involve government positions increased between 1960 and 1973 as much as those involving party and army institutions, but decreased even more than the others by 1982. Vertical linkages were particularly noteworthy. The total number of elites who held government positions and alternate memberships in the Central Committee increased from 13 in 1960 to 52 in 1973, but decreased to 10 in 1982. Full memberships increased from 9 to 87 and then decreased to 13. The number involved in triple positions increased from 9 (1%) to 120 (10%) and then decreased to 1 (less than 1%); those in dual party-army roles increased from 9 (1%) to 79 (7%) then dropped to zero; and those involved in dual party-government positions increased from 78 (9%) to 225 (19%) and then decreased to 55 (31%) (due to the smaller sample). In 1973 the quality of interlocking roles also increased as is reflected in the number of chairmen (27 of 29) who were concurrently first party secretaries and first political commissars or commanders (25 of 28)(Tables 5-16, 5-17 and 5-18). However, by 1982 none of the governors or vice-governors held first political commissar or first party secretary roles.

Military District Linkages

The role of military district elites, like that of their military region counterparts is not clearly understood. Changes since 1960 in military district elite involvement in provincial and government activities were as significant as changes in other institutions. The top military district position is technically the commander, but the most powerful military district elite in the interface with the party and government organization is the political commissar. This section will include a description of the scope and changes in the military district elite involvement in party and government activities as measured by the interlocking directorate phenomenon.

The role and structure of military districts was still evolving in 1960. There were only 19 military districts in the provinces.13 In addition three of the garrison commands were treated as military district-level units in this analysis (Beijing, Shanghai, Tianjin). Within the 22 military district level units in 1960; only 17 listed commanders and 15 listed political commissars. The first political commissar designation was not used in 1960 so the political commissar at that time was the equivalent to the first political commissar in 1973. By 1982, however, the first political commissar designation was beginning to disappear. Deputy political commissars in 1960 were equivalent to political commissars in 1973.

In 1973 and 1982 there were 25 military districts and 3 garrison commands (Xinjiang was considered a military region). There are four other military districts,14 but they are not considered in this analysis because they are generally treated more as military subdistricts than military districts as manifested in the province level first secretary interlocking role with the military district first political commissar. In 1973 three (Anhui, Zhejiang, Fujian) of the 28 military district level units listed no commander and 10 listed no first political commissar.15 In six of those with no first political commissar, however, there were single political commissars listed and they are counted as first political commissars in this analysis (Liaoning, Hubei, Sichuan, Yunnan, Guizhou, Gansu). In four others, two political commissars were listed and the first listed are counted in the category of first political commissars (Shanxi, Heilongjiang, Shandong, Fujian). By 1982 unambiguous patterns had emerged. Commanders were listed for all the military districts and all the first political commissars were concurrently first secretaries.

Scope of Interlocking Roles: 1960 to 1982
(Appendixes D, E and F)

Command System -- In 1960 only 6 of the 17 commanders listed held interlocking roles in the provinces; 3 were low level dual army-government roles and 3 were low-level dual army-party roles. None held membership in the Central Committee (Table 5-22).

In 1973, 23 of 25 military district commanders listed were held interlocking roles (Table 5-23). Only 2 commanders occupied positions in the army only.16 Eighteen of the 23 involved in interlocking roles held triple positions, three held dual army-government positions, and two held dual party-army positions.

Three of the 18 commanders with triple positions in 1973 held first secretary and chairman positions, 2 were second secretaries and first (or first-listed) vice-chairmen, 12 held secretary positions in the party and vice-chairman jobs in the government, and the last one was a standing committee member in the party and a vice-chairman in the government.

In 1982, only 3 of the 28 military district commanders held interlocking roles and all three were dual

TABLE 5-22

MILITARY DISTRICT COMMANDERS
1960

MILITARY REGION/ DISTRICT	ARMY ONLY	PARTY	GOVT	PARTY ARMY GOVT CC	ALT MBR CC	MBR CC
BEIJING MR						
BEIJING GC(a)						
HEBEI MD (a)						
NEI MONGGOL(b)						
SHANXI MD	X					
TIANJIN GC	X					
CHENGDU MR						
SICHUAN MD(b)						
XIZANG MD(b)						
FUZHOU MR						
FUJIAN MD	X					
JIANGXI MD		X				
GUANGZHOU MR						
GUANGDONG MD	X					
GUANGXI MD	X					
HUNAN MD	X					
JINAN MR						
SHANDONG MD(b)						
KUNMING MR						
GUIZHOU MD			X			
YUNNAN MD(a)						
LANZHOU MR						
GANSU MD(b)						
NINGXIA MD(b)						
QINGHAI MD(a)						
SHAANXI MD			X			
NANJING MR						
ANHUI MD			X			
JIANGSU MD(a)						
SHANGHAI GC	X					
ZHEJIANG MD	X					
SHENYANG MR						
HEILONGJIANG MD		X				
JILIN MD	X					
LIAONING MD	X					
WUHAN MR						
HENAN MD		X				
HUBEI MD	X					
URUMQI MR						
TOTALS	11	3	3	0	0	0

a. No commander listed. GC = garrison command (for cities).
b. Not a military district in 1960.

TABLE 5-23

MILITARY DISTRICT COMMANDERS
1973

MILITARY REGION/ DISTRICT	ARMY ONLY	PARTY	GOVT	PARTY ARMY GOVT	ALT MBR CC	MBR CC
BEIJING MR						
BEIJING GC		X	X	X	X	
HEBEI MD		X	X	X		
NEI MONGGOL (a,b)		X	X	X		X
SHANXI MD(a,b)		X	X	X	X	
TIANJIN GC		X	X	X		
CHENGDU MR						
SICHUAN MD		X	X	X		
XIZANG MD		X	X	X		
FUZHOU MR						
FUJIAN MD(c)						
JIANGXI MD		X	X	X		
GUANGZHOU MR						
GUANGDONG MD	X					
GUANGXI MD		X				
HUNAN MD		X	X	X	X	
JINAN MR						
SHANDONG MD			X			
KUNMING MR						
GUIZHOU MD		X	X	X		
YUNNAN MD			X			
LANZHOU MR						
GANSU MD		X	X	X		
NINGXIA MD		X				
QINGHAI MD		X	X	X	X	
SHAANXI MD		X	X	X		
NANJING MR						
ANHUI MD(c)						
JIANGSU MD	X					
SHANGHAI GC		X	X	X		X
ZHEJIANG MD(c)						
SHENYANG MR						
HEILONGJIANG MD(a,b)		X	X	X	X	
JILIN MD		X	X	X		
LIAONING MD			X			
WUHAN MR						
HENAN MD		X	X	X		X
HUBEI MD		X	X	X		
URUMQI MR						
TOTALS	2	20	21	18	5	3

a. Party first secretary.
b. Government chairman.
c. No commander listed.

positions at the relatively low level of province party standing committee member (Table 5-24).

In 1960 no military district commanders held alternate or full memberships in the Central Committee, but by 1973, 5 commanders were alternate members and 3 were full members. In 1982 only one commander was elected to the Central Committee and he was an alternate member who held no position in the province party committee.

In 1960, only 6 of the command system elites at all levels (including the commanders) had interlocking roles (Table 5-25). By 1973, 36 held triple positions, 8 held dual army-party positions, and 30 held dual army-government positions (Table 5-26). Within the group below the commander level, party positions included one secretary, one deputy secretary, 18 standing committee members, and 4 members of party committees. Government positions included 11 vice-governors/mayors, 29 standing committee members, and one lesser member of the government organization. None of those below the commander level in 1973 held Central Committee membership. In 1982 none of those below the commander level held either an interlocking position or membership in the Central Committee.

<u>Political Commissar System</u> -- Political commissar system elites occupied more interlocking roles than command system elites even in 1960. At that time 9 of the 13 (first) political commissars listed held interlocking positions (Table 5-27). Three held triple positions, 5 held dual party-army positions, and 1 held dual army-government positions. Two of the three who held triple positions held the top party (first secretary) and government (governor/mayor) position. Five who held dual party-army positions were first secretaries. This group included 5 alternate and 1 full member of the Central Committee.

In 1973, 21 of the 28 military district first political commissars held triple positions, one held a dual army-party position, and 4 held dual army-government positions (Table 5-28). Two held no party or government jobs.

Fourteen of the 21 first (or first-listed) political commissars who held triple positions in 1973 were party first secretaries and government chairmen, one was a second secretary and first-listed vice-chairman, one was the second-listed secretary and first-listed vice chairman, three were secretaries and vice-chairmen, one was a secretary in the party and standing committee member in the government, and one was a standing committee member in the party and government.

The first political commissar who held a dual army-party position was a standing committee member in the party. Two of the 4 dual party-government positions were vice-chairmen and the other two were standing committee members.

TABLE 5-24

MILITARY DISTRICT COMMANDERS
1982

MILITARY REGION/ DISTRICT	ARMY ONLY	PARTY	GOVT	PARTY ARMY GOVT CC	ALT MBR	MBR CC
BEIJING MR						
BEIJING GC	X					
HEBEI MD	X					
NEI MONGGOL	X					
SHANXI MD	X					
TIANJIN GC	X					
CHENGDU MR						
SICHUAN MD	X					
XIZANG MD	X					
FUZHOU MR						
FUJIAN MD	X					
JIANGXI MD		X				
GUANGZHOU MR						
GUANGDONG MD	X					
GUANGXI MD	X				X	
HUNAN MD	X					
JINAN MR						
SHANDONG MD	X					
KUNMING MR						
GUIZHOU MD	X					
YUNNAN MD	X					
LANZHOU MR						
GANSU MD		X				
NINGXIA MD	X					
QINGHAI MD		X				
SHAANXI MD	X					
NANJING MR						
ANHUI MD	X					
JIANGSU MD	X					
SHANGHAI GC	X					
ZHEJIANG MD	X					
SHENYANG MR						
HEILONGJIANG MD	X					
JILIN MD	X					
LIAONING MD	X					
WUHAN MR						
HENAN MD	X					
HUBEI MD	X					
URUMQI MR						
TOTALS	25	3	0	0	1	0

TABLE 5-25

MILITARY DISTRICT COMMAND SYSTEM (a)
1960

MILITARY REGION/ DISTRICT	TOTAL SAMPLE	PARTY	GOVT	PARTY ARMY GOVT	ALT MBR CC	MBR CC	NO MULTI-ROLE
BEIJING MR							
BEIJING GC(b)	0	0	0	0	0	0	0
HEBEI MD	4	0	0	0	0	0	4
NEI MONGGOL (c)	4	0	0	0	0	0	4
SHANXI MD	4	0	0	0	0	0	4
TIANJIN GC	1	0	0	0	0	0	1
CHENGDU MR							
SICHUAN MD(b,c)							
XIZANG MD(c)							
FUZHOU MR							
FUJIAN MD(b)	4	0	0	0	0	0	4
JIANGXI MD	6	1	0	0	0	0	5
GUANGZHOU MR							
GUANGDONG MD(b)	5	0	0	0	0	0	5
GUANGXI MD	3	0	0	0	0	0	3
HUNAN MD	6	0	0	0	0	0	6
JINAN MR							
SHANDONG MD(b,c)							
KUNMING MR							
GUIZHOU MD	4	0	1	0	0	0	3
YUNNAN MD(b)	3	0	0	0	0	0	3
LANZHOU MR							
GANSU MD(b)	0	0	0	0	0	0	0
NINGXIA MD(c)							
QINGHAI MD	3	0	1	0	0	0	2
SHAANXI MD	4	0	1	0	0	0	3
NANJING MR							
ANHUI MD	4	0	0	0	0	0	4
JIANGSU MD(b)	0	0	0	0	0	0	0
SHANGHAI GC	5	0	0	0	0	0	5
ZHEJIANG MD	6	0	0	0	0	0	6
SHENYANG MR							
HEILONGJIANG MD	6	1	0	0	0	0	5
JILIN MD	5	0	0	0	0	0	5
LIAONING MD(b)	3	0	0	0	0	0	3
WUHAN MR							
HENAN MD	5	1	0	0	0	0	4
HUBEI MD(b)	4	0	0	0	0	0	4
URUMQI MR							
TOTALS	89	3	3	0	0	0	83

a. Includes commanders, deputy commanders and chiefs-of-staff.
b. Province in which military region headquarters was located.
c. Not a military district in 1960.

TABLE 5-26

MILITARY DISTRICT COMMAND SYSTEM (a)
1973

MILITARY REGION/ DISTRICT	TOTAL SAMPLE	PARTY	GOVT	PARTY ARMY GOVT	ALT MBR CC	MBR CC	NO MULTI-ROLE
BEIJING MR							
BEIJING GC(b)	10	0	1	1	1	0	8
HEBEI MD	3	0	0	2	0	0	1
NEI MONGGOL	6	0	4	2	0	1	1
SHANXI MD	6	0	1	1	1	0	4
TIANJIN GC	3	0	0	1	0	0	2
CHENGDU MR							
SICHUAN MD(b)	1	0	0	1	0	0	0
XIZANG MD	6	0	0	2	0	0	4
FUZHOU MR							
FUJIAN MD(b)	4	0	0	0	0	0	4
JIANGXI MD	10	3	1	1	0	0	5
GUANGZHOU MR							
GUANGDONG MD(b)	12	0	0	0	0	0	12
GUANGXI MD	11	1	1	4	0	0	5
HUNAN MD	14	2	2	4	1	0	6
JINAN MR							
SHANDONG MD(b)	6	0	2	0	0	0	4
KUNMING MR							
GUIZHOU MD	6	0	3	2	0	0	2
YUNNAN MD(b)	4	0	2	0	0	0	2
LANZHOU MR							
GANSU MD(b)	6	0	1	1	0	0	4
NINGXIA MD	3	1	0	1	0	0	1
QINGHAI MD	4	0	0	2	1	0	2
SHAANXI MD	4	0	1	1	0	0	2
NANJING MR							
ANHUI MD	8	0	3	1	0	0	5
JIANGSU MD(b)	6	0	0	0	0	0	6
SHANGHAI GC	6	0	1	1	0	1	4
ZHEJIANG MD	11	1	0	1	0	0	9
SHENYANG MR							
HEILONGJIANG MD	8	0	3	1	1	0	4
JILIN MD	6	0	0	2	0	0	4
LIAONING MD(b)	4	0	1	0	0	0	3
WUHAN MR							
HENAN MD	9	0	1	3	0	1	5
HUBEI MD(b)	10	0	2	1	0	0	7
URUMQI MR							
TOTALS	187	8	30	36	5	3	116

a. Includes commanders, deputy commanders, and chiefs-of staff.
b. Province in which military region headquarters was located.

TABLE 5-27

MILITARY DISTRICT POLITICAL COMMISSARS (a)
1960

MILITARY REGION/ DISTRICT	ARMY ONLY	PARTY	GOVT	PARTY ARMY GOVT CC	ALT ARMY MBR CC	MBR CC
BEIJING MR						
BEIJING GC(b)						
HEBEI MD		X				
NEI MONGGOL(d)						
SHANXI MD		X(c)		X		
TIANJIN GC(b)						
CHENGDU MR						
SICHUAN MD(d)						
XIZANG MD(d)						
FUZHOU MR						
FUJIAN MD	X					
JIANGXI MD		X	X	X		
GUANGZHOU MR						
GUANGDONG MD(b)						
GUANGXI MD	X					
HUNAN MD						
JINAN MR						
SHANDONG MD(d)						
KUNMING MR						
GUIZHOU MD		X(c)	X(e)	X		
YUNNAN MD(b)						
LANZHOU MR						
GANSU MD(d)						
NINGXIA MD(d)						
QINGHAI MD	X					
SHAANXI MD		X(c)		X		
NANJING MR						
ANHUI MD(b)						
JIANGSU MD		X(c)		X		
SHANGHAI GC(b)						
ZHEJIANG MD		X(c)		X		
SHENYANG MR						
HEILONGJIANG MD	X					
JILIN MD		X(c)		X		
LIAONING MD						
WUHAN MR						
HENAN MD		X(c)	X(e)	X	X	
HUBEI MD(b)						
URUMQI MR						
TOTALS	4	8	4	3	5	1

a. Equivalent to first political commissars in 1973.
b. No political commissar was listed.
c. Party first secretary.
d. Not a military district in 1960.
e. Government governors/mayors.

TABLE 5-28

MILITARY DISTRICT FIRST POLITICAL COMMISSARS
1973

MILITARY REGION/ DISTRICT	ARMY ONLY	PARTY	GOVT	PARTY ALT ARMY MBR GOVT CC	MBR CC	
BEIJING MR						
BEIJING GC		X(a)	X(b)	X		X(c)
HEBEI MD		X(a)	X(b)	X		X
NEI MONGGOL		X	X	X		X
SHANXI MD		X	X	X		
TIANJIN GC		X(a)	X(b)	X		X
CHENGDU MR						
SICHUAN MD	X					
XIZANG MD		X(a)	X(b)	X	X	
FUZHOU MR						
FUJIAN MD		X	X	X		
JIANGXI MD		X	X(b)	X		X
GUANGZHOU MR						
GUANGDONG MD			X			
GUANGXI MD		X(a)	X(b)	X		X(c)
HUNAN MD		X(a)	X(b)	X		X(c)
JINAN MR						
SHANDONG MD		X	X	X		
KUNMING MR						
GUIZHOU MD			X			
YUNNAN MD	X					
LANZHOU MR						
GANSU MD			X			
NINGXIA MD		X(a)	X(b)	X	X	
QINGHAI MD		X(a)	X(b)	X		
SHAANXI MD		X(a)	X(b)	X		X
NANJING MR						
ANHUI MD		X(a)	X(b)	X		X
JIANGSU MD		X	X	X		X
SHANGHAI GC		X(a)	X(b)	X		X(c)
ZHEJIANG MD		X(a)	X(b)	X	X	
SHENYANG MR						
HEILONGJIANG MD		X	X	X	X	
JILIN MD		X(a)	X(b)	X		X
LIAONING MD			X			
WUHAN MR						
HENAN MD		X(a)	X(b)	X		X
HUBEI MD		X				
URUMQI MR						
TOTALS	2	22	25	21	4	13

a. Party first secretary.
b. Government chairman.
c. Politburo member.

Military district first political commissars were well-represented in the Central Committee in 1973 compared to 1960. There were 13 full and 4 alternate members. Four of the first political commissars were Politburo members.

In 1982 all 28 of the military district first political commissar positions were held by first party secretaries; as opposed to professional PLA commissars (Table 5-29). None held positions in the government. Since the first political commissar is the most powerful figure in the military district, this is the key point at which the civilian party exercises direct control over the army.

Twenty-two of the military district first political commissars were full members of the Twelfth Central Committee. Four were elected to the Central Advisory Commission of the CCP and two held no central committee membership. There were no alternates and none were elected to the Politburo.

When all military district political commissar system elites are considered there are again large increases in interlocking role participation between 1960 and 1973, but decreases by 1982.

In 1960, 3 held triple positions, 9 held dual party-army positions and 3 held dual army-government positions (Table 5-30).

In 1973, political commissar system elites held 50 triple positions, 8 dual army-party positions, and 19 dual army-government positions (Table 5-31). This group included one second secretary, 30 secretaries, 2 deputy secretaries, 22 standing committee members, and 3 members of the party organizations. It also included 40 chairmen and vice-chairmen, 28 standing committee members, and one member of the government organization.

In 1973, in addition to the first political commissars who held central committee membership, there were 2 lower level political commissars who held alternate and 3 who held full membership in the Tenth Central Committee. All but one of the lower level political commissars were subordinate to full members of the Tenth Central Committee who were also Politburo members. The one exception seems to be a unique case in which a full member (second political commissar) of the Central Committee is subordinate to an alternate member (first political commissar).17

In 1982 there were only three elites in the political commissar system below the first political commissar level who held interlocking roles and they were both dual army-party roles. Two were standing committee members and one was a secretary. There were two lower level political commissars elected as members to the Twelfth Central Committee, one full and one alternate.

TABLE 5-29

MILITARY DISTRICT FIRST POLITICAL COMMISSARS
1982

MILITARY REGION/ DISTRICT	ARMY ONLY	PARTY	GOVT	PARTY ARMY GOVT	ALT MBR CC	MBR CC
BEIJING MR						
BEIJING GC		X(a)				X(b)
HEBEI MD		X(a)				X(b)
NEI MONGGOL		X(a)				X
SHANXI MD		X(a)				X
TIANJIN GC		X(a)				X
CHENGDU MR						
SICHUAN MD		X(a)				X
XIZANG MD		X(a)				X
FUZHOU MR						
FUJIAN MD		X(a)				X
JIANGXI MD		X(a)				X
GUANGZHOU MR						
GUANGDONG MD		X(a)				X
GUANGXI MD		X(a)				X
HUNAN MD		X(a)				X
JINAN MR						
SHANDONG MD		X(a)				X
KUNMING MR						
GUIZHOU MD		X(a)				X
YUNNAN MD		X(a)				X
LANZHOU MR						
GANSU MD		X(a)				X
NINGXIA MD		X(a)				X
QINGHAI MD		X(a)				X
SHAANXI MD		X(a)				X
NANJING MR						
ANHUI MD		X(a)				
JIANGSU MD		X(a)				X
SHANGHAI GC		X(a)				X
ZHEJIANG MD		X(a)				X
SHENYANG MR						
HEILONGJIANG MD		X(a)				X
JILIN MD		X(a)				X
LIAONING MD		X(a)				X(b)
WUHAN MR						
HENAN MD		X(a)				X(b)
HUBEI MD		X(a)				
URUMQI MR						
TOTALS	0	28	0	0	0	22

a. Party first secretary.
b. Elected to Central Advisory Council. Not included in totals.

TABLE 5-30

POLITICAL COMMISSAR SYSTEM
1960

MILITARY REGION/ DISTRICT	TOTAL SAMPLE	PARTY	GOVT	PARTY ARMY GOVT	ALT MBR CC	MBR CC	NO MULTI-ROLE
BEIJING MR							
BEIJING GC(a)	1	0	0	0	0	0	1
HEBEI MD	5	0	1	0	0	0	4
NEI MONGGOL(b)							
SHANXI MD	4	1	0	0	1	0	3
TIANJIN GC	0	0	0	0	0	0	0
CHENGDU MR							
SICHUAN MD(b)							
XIZANG MD(b)							
FUZHOU MR							
FUJIAN MD(a)	1	0	0	0	0	0	1
JIANGXI MD	4	1	0	1	0	0	2
GUANGZHOU MR							
GUANGDONG MD(a)	2	0	0	0	0	0	2
GUANGXI MD	2	0	0	0	0	0	2
HUNAN MD	4	1	0	0	1	0	3
JINAN MR							
SHANDONG MD(a,b)							
KUNMING MR							
GUIZHOU MD	4	0	0	1	0	0	3
YUNNAN MD(a)	1	0	0	0	0	0	1
LANZHOU MR							
GANSU MD(a)	0	0	0	0	0	0	0
NINGXIA MD(b)							
QINGHAI MD	1	0	0	0	0	0	1
SHAANXI MD	3	1	1	0	0	0	1
NANJING MR							
ANHUI MD	5	1	0	0	0	0	4
JIANGSU MD(a)	2	1	0	0	1	0	1
SHANGHAI GC	4	0	0	0	0	0	4
ZHEJIANG MD	5	1	0	0	0	0	4
SHENYANG MR							
HEILONGJIANG MD	3	0	0	0	0	0	3
JILIN MD	4	1	1	0	1	0	2
LIAONING MD(a)	4	1	0	0	1	0	3
WUHAN MR							
HENAN MD	4	0	0	1	0	1	3
HUBEI MD(a)	2	0	0	0	0	0	2
URUMQI MR							
TOTALS	65	9	3	3	5	1	50

a. Province in which military region was located.
b. Not a military district in 1960.

TABLE 5-31

POLITICAL COMMISSAR SYSTEM
1973

MILITARY REGION/ DISTRICT	TOTAL SAMPLE	PARTY	GOVT	PARTY ARMY GOVT	ALT MBR CC	MBR CC	NO MULTI ROLE
BEIJING MR							
BEIJING GC(a)	9	0	1	3	2	1(b)	5
HEBEI MD	4	0	0	3	0	1	1
NEI MONGGOL	4	0	1	2	0	1	1
SHANXI MD	2	1	0	1	0	0	0
TIANJIN GC	5	0	2	3	0	1	0
CHENGDU MR							
SICHUAN MD(a)	1	0	0	0	0	0	1
XIZANG MD	9	0	1	2	1	1	6
FUZHOU MR							
FUJIAN MD(a)	5	0	0	1	0	0	4
JIANGXI MD	5	1	0	3	1	0	1
GUANGZHOU MR							
GUANGDONG MD(a)	6	0	1	1	0	0	4
GUANGXI MD	6	0	1	3	0	1(b)	2
HUNAN MD	11	0	0	7	0	2(b)	4
JINAN MR							
SHANDONG MD(a)	3	0	0	1	0	0	2
KUNMING MR							
GUIZHOU MD	4	0	2	0	0	0	2
YUNNAN MD(a)	1	0	0	0	0	0	1
LANZHOU MR							
GANSU MD(a)	3	0	1	0	0	0	2
NINGXIA MD	2	0	0	1	1	0	1
QINGHAI MD	5	2	1	1	0	0	1
SHAANXI MD	6	0	1	3	0	1	2
NANJING MR							
ANHUI MD	7	1	1	1	0	1	4
JIANGSU MD(a)	2	0	0	1	0	1	1
SHANGHAI GC	7	0	2	2	0	2(b)	3
ZHEJIANG MD	8	1	0	2	1	1	5
SHENYANG MR							
HEILONGJIANG MD	5	0	2	3	1	0	0
JILIN MD	4	1	1	2	0	1	0
LIAONING MD(a)	3	0	1	0	0	0	2
WUHAN MR							
HENAN MD	5	0	0	3	0	1	2
HUBEI MD(a)	4	1	0	1	0	0	2
URUMQI MR							
TOTALS	136	8	19	50	7	16	59

a. Province in which military region was located.
b. Politburo member.

Summary

The number of military district elites holding interlocking positions increased nearly as much as party and government elites between 1960 and 1973, but the decrease to 1982 was even more pronounced than in the other organizations. The number of command system elites involved in triple positions increased from zero in 1960 to 36 (19%) in 1973 and then decreased to zero in 1982. Dual roles increased from 6 (7%) in 1960 to 38 (20%) in 1973 and then decreased to 3 (1%) in 1982. The number of military district political commissars holding multiple positions over this period of time varied to an even greater extent. The number of triple roles increased from 3 (5%) in 1960 to 50 (37%) in 1973 and then decreased to none in 1982. Dual roles increased slightly from 12 (18%) in 1960 to 27 (20%) in 1973 and 31 (20%) by 1982.

The most significant increase among all categories of interlocking roles between 1960 and 1973 was the triple role in which the political commissar was included. However, by 1982 military district commissars were no longer involved in government roles. At the same time the dual party (first secretary) - army (first political commissar) position seems to have been institutionalized. Furthermore, the individuals holding these positions gradually became civilian party cadre assigned as first political commissars rather than professional PLA commissars being assigned as first secretaries. Many of the first secretaries, however, do have extensive experience in the PLA political commissar system.

Only 2 of the military district elites (both political commissars) held the top party, army, and government position in 1960, whereas in 1973 fourteen political commissars and 3 commanders held all three key positions. By 1982, 28 political commissars held the top party (first secretary) position, but none held any other position in the government.

Military district vertical linkages also increased from 5 alternate and 1 full central committee member in 1960 to 12 alternate and 18 full members in 1973. In 1982 there were 2 alternate and 24 full memberships held by military district elites in the Twelfth Central Committee, but 23 of the full members were the first secretaries who concurrently held first political commissar jobs. In 1973, three Politburo members held military district first political commissar positions, whereas in 1960 and 1982 none did.

The increases in central committee membership by military district elites reflect the movement toward integration of institutions and consolidation of the first political commissar-first secretary pattern since most of the increases involved professional party cadre who were assigned to military district positions. In other words, the increases in Central Committee membership by military district elites were not really military cadre but were the first secretaries who concurrently held the first political commissar position.

PART 5: CONCLUSIONS

There is no doubt that between 1960 and 1973 the Chinese leadership made a special effort to increase linkages between institutions. The scope and quality of linkages increased greatly as indicated by the number of elites who became involved in interlocking roles at all levels. But by 1982 the trend toward increased linkages has been reversed and the linkage concept refined. The practical result was to separate government elites from party and army elites, to reduce significantly the number of PLA elites who held positions in civilian party committees and finally to assure party control of military districts (as opposed to regions) by regularizing the dual party (first secretary)- army (first political commissar) role.

The changing relationships between the provinces or military regions and the Center were particularly noteworthy. In 1960 policymaking was accomplished primarily at the Center; but by 1973 there was somewhat less distinction between Center and regions because the majority of the elites who served in the Central Committee were those who were at the Center as representatives of the provinces or military regions. It is clear that they were consulted more in 1973 than in the earlier period. By 1982 province representation was reduced slightly but it was regularized so there was relatively equal representation from each of the provinces and military regions.

One possible explanation of the increased involvement of province elites in the Central Committee is that the intent was to coopt local leaders and use them to promote national policy. It is a fact that a large number of province and military region elites have been given prestigious titles at the Center and it is inevitable that they have begun to identify with China as a nation to a greater degree than in the past. This does not imply an abandonment of working for local interests at the Center, but it does show a great potential for more input into national policymaking by elites who struggle with the realities of implementation outside the Center. On the other hand, increased provincial representation could set up an environment conducive to the formation of new competing interest groups at the Center.

It is likely that membership in the Central Committee adds a great deal of prestige to any given elite in his home area. The opportunity to mix with those elites at the Center who have been made legends by the Chinese press contributes to one's legitimacy or credibility in province or military region dealings.

On the other hand, the number of representatives from each province increased so much in 1973 that the significance of membership may have been diluted to some degree and that may be part of the reason for the slight decrease in 1982. It is clear that some provincial elites were given Central Committee membership for cooptation or honorific purposes only.

When all the data are considered, a continued reduction in center-region schisms can be predicted. The leadership has built a structural base which will aid in the resolution of conflict between national level and regional or provincial level interests. While there will be individual exceptions, the institutional environment created by increasing representation at the Center is bound to increase the number of key elites who identify with the nation first and the province or military region second. There are likely to be continued center-region conflicts in the future based on economic competition, but the conflict seems to have been routinized by these structural changes which have helped the national integration effort.

The military region played an increasingly important role in domestic politics between 1960 and 1973 but was removed from province level politics almost completely by 1982. In 1960 the elites of only six of thirteen military regions were involved in interlocking roles involving only six provinces. In 1973 elites from all eleven military regions had interlocking roles and they were located in all but five provinces. All five of those provinces, however, had interlocking roles with the army at the military district level. Military districts in general also became much more involved in interlocking roles with the party and government organizations between 1960 and 1973. But by 1982 the only significant provincial interlocking role pattern was the party (first secretary)- army (first political commissar) role.

There were also significant absolute and relative changes in the scope of interlocking roles involving elites in province party and government organizations. Table 5-32 summarizes these changes between 1960, 1973 and 1982. The number of political commissars involved in interlocking roles increased from 26 to 116 and then decreased to 34; the involvement of commanders increased from 17 to 105 and then decreased to 5. The number of dual party-government roles increased from 78 to 224 and then decreased to 34. The total number of elites involved in interlocking roles increased from 121 to 445 and then decreased to 73. The number of triple roles

TABLE 5-32

INTERLOCKING DIRECTORATE
IN THE PEOPLE'S REPUBLIC OF CHINA
(1960 - 1982)

	1960	1973	1982
Interlocking Roles			
Political Commissar/Party	16	12	33
Political Commissar/Govt	4	33	0
Political Commissar/Party/Govt	6	71	1
Commander/Party	6	10	5
Commander/Govt	6	46	0
Commander/Party/Govt	5	49	0
Party/Govt	78	224	34
Total Dual Positions	110	325	72
Total Triple Positions	11	120	1
Total Institutional Involvement in Interlocking Roles			
Party	111	366	73
Govt	99	423	35
Army	43	221	39

showed the greatest change from 11 to 120 and then to only 1. Seventy-one of those were political commissar roles in 1973 and the one in 1982 was a political commissar.

When one examines the increases from the perspectives of each of the three institutions, the results are similar. The total number of elites, without taking identity-forming background into account, who were involved in interlocking roles with the party increased from 111 to 366 and then decreased to only 73. Those involved in interlocking roles in the government increased from 99 to 423 and then decreased to only 35, and those involved in interlocking roles with the army increased from 43 to 221 and then decreased to only 39. Hence, the changes in the scope of interlocking roles are clear: there were three to five times as many elites involved in interlocking roles in 1973 as there were in 1960, depending on the institution; and by 1982 the interlocking role phenomenon was reduced to a point of even lesser scope than 1960. Based upon these figures it can be seen that the current leadership has been quite successful at separating party, army and government institutions. Whether this will result in a form of checks and balances system for internal politics remains to be seen. It is clear that the most significant interlocking role which persists is the involvement of the party in the political commissar system of the PLA, particularly at the military district level.

Obviously, there are weaknesses in the foregoing of statistical analysis. There are bound to be inaccuracies in the numbers and percentages. However, there is a large enough data base to validate the general patterns which have emerged. The figures in this chapter must be considered heuristic. They provide a base from which more research should be done to correlate the many categories discussed in Chapter One, such as identity-forming experience or current stands on issues, with interlocking roles. For example, critical questions which immediately arise are: Which categories of elites fill the critical roles? Do they have civilian or military backgrounds? What are their political philosophies?

In addition to the change in scope of interlocking roles there have been major changes in the quality and depth of linkages. For example one important pattern which emerged in 1973 was for the same elite member to serve as first secretary in the province party organization, first political commissar in the military region or district and chairman in the province government organization. By 1982 this pattern excluded the military region political commissars and the top government leaders. The interlocking role concept also penetrated to much lower levels in each of the institutions in 1973 but this pattern was reversed by 1982.

It can be concluded that since 1960, changes in the quantity and quality of interlocking roles between the five institutions under study (Central Committee, military region, province party committee, province government organization and military districts) have helped to shape the structural environment within which Chinese policymaking takes place and this must be taken into account in any comprehensive analysis of Chinese politics.

NOTES

1. All data for 1960 comes from United States Department of State, Bureau of Intelligence and Research, <u>Directory of Party and Government Officials of Communist China</u>, vol. 1, BD 271, (Washington DC: 20 July 1960). All data for 1973 comes from Union Research Institute, <u>Hierarchies of the People's Republic of China -- March 1975</u>, (Hong Kong: Union Research Institute, 1975). All data for 1982 comes from <u>The Twelfth National Congress of the CPC (September 1982)</u>, Beijing: Foreign Languages Press, 1982.

2. See Appendix D for a complete list of names, positions and locations of elites of the Eighth Central Committee who held concurrent positions outside the Center.

3. See Appendix E for a complete list of names, positions and locations of elites of the Tenth Central Committee who held concurrent positions outside the Center.

4. See Appendix F for a complete list of names, positions and locations of elites of the Twelfth Central Committee who held concurrent positions outside the Center.

5. Beijing, Chengdu, Fuzhou, Guangzhou, Jinan, Kunming, Lanzhou, Nanjing, Shenyang, Wuhan and Urumqi. Xizang and Nei Monggol were both military regions in 1960 but the former became a military district of Chengdu MR and the latter of Beijing MR by 1973.

6. Guangzhou MR, Fuzhou MR, Nei Monggol MR, Shenyang MR, Xinjiang MR, Jinan MR, and Xizang MR.

7. Fujian, Guangdong, Shandong, Liaoning, Nei Monggol, Xinjiang, and Xizang.

8. See Footnote 5.

9. Peng Chong/Jiangsu and Song Peizhang/Anhui respectively.

10. Anhui, Gansu, Heilongjiang, Hubei, Jiangsu, Ningxia, Qinghai, Shandong, Shanxi, Sichuan, Zhejiang.

11. Anhui, Gansu, Hubei, Jiangsu, Shanxi, Sichuan, Zhejiang.

12. Gansu, Heilongjiang, Hunan, Jiangsu, Jilin, Qinghai, Shanxi, Tianjin, Xizang and Zhejiang.

13. Nei Monggol and Xizang were considered military regions at that time but became military districts by 1973. There was no Shandong Military District since the area was the same as the Jinan Military Region. Other 1973 military districts not listed in 1960 include Sichuan, Gansu and Ningxia. Xinjiang was a military region in 1960 and is still considered so although some have listed it as a military district.

14. Hainan MD in Guangzhou MR and three MD's in Xinjiang: Nanjiang MD, Beijiang MD and Dongjiang MD.

15. Fujian, Gansu, Guizhou, Heilongjiang, Hubei, Liaoning, Shandong, Shanxi, Sichuan, and Yunnan.

16. Since these two commanders held no interlocking roles they are not listed in the appendixes.

17. Tian Bao subordinate to Ren Rong in the Xizang MD.

6
Conclusions

The study of political change in China is open to any number of methodologies or foci and while most of them contribute to post hoc explanations of change, very few provide predictive capacity. The methodology used in this book is different in emphasis from other approaches to elite analysis and despite its shortcomings allows prediction about the changing structure both of the Chinese bureaucracy and political-military relationships. Unlike most of the works outlined in Chapter One, this effort has shifted the focus within the field of elite studies from elite personalities to elite roles. Analysis of these roles and role linkages has provided some new perspectives which should contribute to explanation and prediction of political change in China. Hopefully it will also contribute to the efforts of others concerned with this topic. The methodology used here has proven useful in dealing with a topic about which there is incomplete data and as more data becomes available it should be even more valuable.

The most significant findings of this effort result from a juxtaposition of two factors. First, by focusing on roles it became apparent that there have been major changes in the structural underpinnings of the political system over the period from 1960 to 1982. That is, the nature and scope of role linkages between five key institutions (Central Committee, military region, military district, province party committee and province government organization) have changed in a patterned way to such a degree that those linkages are now such an important element of the political environment that they must be made explicit in any analysis of the Chinese political system. Second, at a more specific level, one particular role, the political commissar, has emerged as the most critical in the network of linkages at the province level. Furthermore, an understanding of that role reveals a great deal abut the nature of the key institutional linkages, especially in the general field of civil-military relations. Once these two factors are examined together it becomes possible to draw conclusions about bureaucratic change and to some extent, the stability of the Chinese political system.

An important finding of this book was that the scope and quality of elite linkages between institutions increased from 1960 to 1973 and then went through a process of rationalization and functional specialization from 1973 to 1982 when the process seemed to be nearly complete.

Membership in the Eighth Central Committee in 1960 was dominated (73%) by elites who held occupational positions only at the Center. By 1973 the pattern was reversed. The majority (52%) of the Tenth Central Committee members were elites who held positions outside the Center. By 1982 the pattern reversed again to the point that only 36% of the Twelfth Central Committee held positions outside the Center. This does not mean, however, that 64% hold positions at the Center because some were in a transition to retirement. Nonetheless, there has been a return to the pattern in which the majority of central committee members are employed at the Center, but a significant number of members come from the provinces and military regions. Moreover, the representation is relatively evenly distributed for the first time, so that each military region and province level unit (except the province government organization) is well-represented.

Whether these changes were to reduce the center-region differences in policy issues by establishing a more effective bureaucratic structure or whether they were merely an effort to coopt regional elites, it is likely that the effect was to cause more regional elites to identify with the Center. While some regional elites may feel they are advocates of local interests at the Center, by involving themselves in national problems they will begin to see themselves as part of the Chinese nation and place local interests into perspective. Another probable effect of membership in the Central Committee is an increase in the credibility and prestige of members when they return home. On the other hand, there is some evidence that the large increase in the number of regional elites has diluted the significance of central committee membership. It is clear that many members were elected for honorific or cooptation purposes and not because they held key party positions in the provinces. In fact, some were government leaders at relatively low levels with no party positions at all.

Another important finding was the major increase in military region involvement in provincial politics between 1960 and 1973 and then a near total withdrawal by 1982. In 1960 military region elites were involved in the governing of only six provinces. By 1973 they held interlocking roles in 24 of 29 provinces and in the remaining 5 there were a large number of interlocking roles involving the army at the military district level. By 1982, only 8 military region elites held positions in just 6 provinces.

Generally, there was a major increase in the number of interlocking roles held by elites in all three institutions (party, army and government) between 1960 (122) and 1973 (445) and then a dramatic decrease by 1982 (73). The greatest percentage increase in 1973 was in army involvement and much of that came after the Cultural Revolution began to wind down in 1969 and even after the 1971 Lin Biao Incident. Within the army the political commissar roles stood out as undergoing the greatest changes in interlocking role patterns.

The quality of the interlocking roles also changed between 1960 and 1982. In 1960 only one elite, Ulanfu in the strategic military region of Nei Monggol, held the top positions in the party, army and government. By 1973 the normal pattern (in 19 of 29 provinces) was for the first secretary of the province to also be the first political commissar of the military region or district and the chairman of the province government organization. By 1982 there was again only one individual holding a triple role: Ismail Aymat in Xinjiang. Two roles emerged in 1982 as routinized: (1) the dual party (first secretary)-army (military district and subdistrict first political commissars) position and (2) the dual government (governor/mayor)-party (secretary) position.

Interlocking roles were also found at the middle and lower levels of all three institutions in 1973 but this was not the case by 1982. In 1960 most of the roles were near the top, if not at the top, of each organization. By 1973 interlocking roles could be found at all levels listed. In 1982 the interlocking role phenomenon focused on the two patterns mentioned above and those at the lower levels seem to be holdovers destined to be phased out eventually.

A third important finding also concerns the nature of the political-military relationship at the province level. The most powerful position in each province has been the first party secretary from the time party committees were organized. Involving the first party secretary in an interlocking role has increased his power even more. The pattern by 1973 was for the first party secretary to hold top positions in the government organization and the army. The army role was usually a political commissar rather than a command system role. Individual elites who have assumed these top three positions have different backgrounds; some were professional party or government cadre and some were professional political commissars. This suggests that the nature of the triple interlocking role was not so much a mechanism to assure lateral party control of the army as it was a means by which all three organizations could be brought closer together and controlled from the Center. By 1982 the patterns indicate a separation of party-army-government institutions with the two exceptions discussed above. The fact that military regions control main force units and military districts control regional force and militia units is important. Since interlocking roles in military regions have been drastically reduced both in scope and quality it means an effective return to the barracks by PLA main force units, the professional part of the PLA. The meaning of the rationalization of the party (first secretary)-army (military district first political commissar) relationship is less certain, but the effect is likely to be the creation of a form of checks and balances and it clearly fits with Deng Xiaoping's efforts to separate centers of power. The separation of the government elites also fits this pattern and coincides with Deng's stated purpose of avoiding an overconcentration of power.

Those who focus on the "party control of the gun" concept are missing the main point. Certainly the party controls the army, but it does so from the top of the army structure, not at several levels through a parallel party structure as in the Soviet Union. The study of the political commissar system shows that political commissars can maintain effective control over the army, but they cannot be considered civilian party controllers at each level. They must be considered a military party organization wholly within the PLA, and when military interests conflict with civilian interests (as opposed to military versus party interests) they are likely to side with the military if there is no conflict with higher level party policy. The focus is downward, using the political commissar system for more effective control over subordinate units, not horizontal, using the political commissar system to control the commander of units, although that would be a byproduct in some cases. But from a Chinese perspective the commissar is a key element in the development of combat effectiveness. He works as a team with the commander and not in a watchdog role.

Furthermore, an understanding of the political commissar system helps one to understand the reason for the province level first secretaries being given the concurrent post of military district/garrison first political commissar. The effectiveness of the political commissar system as a means of social control is assured by the indoctrination system and the techniques used to develop feedback. It makes sense then, from the party perspective, to assure that province nonmobile military units are tied to the province party organization. Not only does it assure some degree of area stability and perceived security, it also provides the party secretary with a large group of citizens who are relatively more disciplined than others. For example, well-indoctrinated militia members, motivated by the positive appeal, are a powerful source of model citizens who will respond in their civilian jobs to guidance by the party.

The emphasis on positive appeal based upon maximum information about the behavior and attitudes of the members of an organization suggests that political commissars who are carefully chosen and armed with personnel information which can affect the selection and promotion of elites, are likely to be the most powerful elites in the provinces. This is especially true when the political commissar position is combined with the top policymaking (party) and policyimplementing (government) positions in the provinces. Thus it seems as though the Chinese have discovered that such a combination creates too much power in a single individual, so that by 1982 the pattern was changed to assure a reduction in the power that resulted from the pervasive interlocking roles, particularly the triple roles. By separating the military region elites and the key government jobs from the interlocking roles a new political environment was created, an environment in which the phenomena of "mountaintopism" or "independent kingdom creation" can be avoided.

Another weakness of the interlocking role which may hinder political progress is that it calls for generalists rather than specialists. Combining the leadership of diffuse institutions and placing general administrators in key positions in a period when the forces of modernization suggest a need for increased functional specialization is bound to create conflict and that may be a major cause of the pattern reversals between 1973 and 1982. On the personal level, specialists are likely to become disheartened when required to respond to a leadership made up of generalists with no technical expertise. At the organizational level, the understanding of the general need for increased functional specialization is likely to continue and cause some further evolution of the system. While this conflict is likely to emerge more strongly in the future it is a conflict which can be controlled. New criteria for promotion and advancement which favor specialists or technocrats is being developed and in time specialists could be coopted by promoting them into key positions.

In general it can be concluded that there was a major tightening of bureaucratic relationships between 1960 and 1982. The result was a streamlined structural environment with considerably less potential for schisms between the regions and the Center and between the province-level institutions.

The elites who are in dual roles should probably be characterized as mediators more than controllers. That is to say, whoever holds the role is likely to be one who can bring the two organizations together in some form of consensus through a positive appeal rather than by threat of sanction. In any case the political commissar system within the army is a critical institution in the linkage schemes for two reasons: it produces elites who understand and have experience in mediation as opposed to a commandism workstyle and it contains the structural mechanisms and organizational techniques to assure an effective supervision of the army. It will be more difficult in the future for competing individuals or factions at the Center to play one institution off against the other to consolidate their positions at the Center.

The most recent separation of interlocking roles suggests that in the future the Chinese bureaucracy will operate under an implicit set of checks and balances. Certainly there will still be some degree of interest group competition based upon institutional affiliation, but the interlocking directorate phenomenon which remains is likely to reduce the intensity of the conflict and place it into a national perspective. As the boundaries between institutions emerge again it is likely that the resultant larger bureaucratic form will resemble the Weberian ideal-type bureaucracy more closely. There is likely to be continued movement toward rational administration and all that this implies. Roles will become more important than personalities.

Whether the new bureaucracy can maintain a sensitivity to the needs of the common man is open to question. But as long as the political commissar concept remains operational and the political commissar retains a key role there will be a mechanism for grass roots feedback within the military. As more and more political commissars are laterally transferred to organizations outside the military the work style may benefit those organizations. The political commissar system could, however, be construed as a double-edged sword. That is to say, the positive appeal or sensitive feedback concepts could be converted quickly into stringent control mechanisms depending on the whims of whomever is in power at the top. The nature of the political commissar doctrine, however, makes that unlikely. The Chinese are victims, or one could say saved by, their own teachings. Benevolence and sensitivity are now a major part of the system. It would be possible for one individual to misuse the system for his own purposes by positing some form of higher ideal. Such an occurence is not unknown in China. But Deng Xiaoping has obviously opted for reinforcing this philosophical defense against misuse of power with some institutional or structural checks.

The effectiveness of a new rationalized and centrally controlled bureaucracy is open to question. Certainly many of the ills, described by Mao Zedong in his fight to avoid bureaucratism, are likely to emerge.

Nonetheless, the advantages are likely to outweigh the disadvantages. The principal advantage, one that seems to have been a major motivation for the original development of the interlocking directorate, will be the increase in environmental certainty. As elites learn what to expect in individual as well as institutional relationships they will be able to develop their own behavior patterns and personal potential to a much greater degree.

As the elite linkages between institutions become more routine and individual elites become more involved in the total political process and confident in their own positions they will be able to resume the tasks of nation-building begun in the 1950's and interrupted in the 1960's.

The prediction of increased certainty and **controlled conflict** in bureaucratic relationships can only be related to stability within a region or province. Any predictions about stability in China are hazardous at best, but it can be concluded from this study that events like the Great Proletarian Cultural Revolution are not likely to recur.

Appendix A: Party Cadre Levels

Grade	Central	Local
1	Politburo Standing Committee Members; General Secretary; Chairman, Central Advisory Council; Chairman, Military Affairs Commission; 1st Sec, Central Discipline Inspection Committee	
2/3	Central Secretariat Members, Vice-Chairmen, Military Affairs Commission; Vice-Chairmen, Central Advisory Council; 2d Sec, Central Discipline Inspection Committee	
3/4	Central Committee Dept Heads; Director, General Office; Secretary-General and Dep Sec-Gen, Military Affairs Commission	1st Sec, 2d Sec, Province, Municipal and Autonomous Region CCP Committees
5/6	Deputy Heads and Sec-Gen of Central Committee Depts; Dep Director, General Office	1st Sec, 2d Sec, Deputy Secs Province level CCP Committees
7/8	Heads of Offices and Bureaus of Various CC Departments	Secs, Dep Secs, and Sec Gen of Province Level Committees; 1st Sec, Sec, Province Capital Committees; Dept Heads, Province Party Committees; Party Sec

Grade	Central	Local
		of Various Province Commission, Offices and Debts; Secs of Prefectural and Municipal CCP Committees
9/10	Deputy Heads and Heads of Divisions (Chu) of CC Depts	Secs, Province Capital Committees; Heads Depts, Province Party Committees; Party Sec of Province Commissions, Offices, and Depts; Sec of Prefectural and Municipal CCP Committees; Party Sec of Prov Bureaus; Dep Sec of Prefectural and Municipal CCP Committees; Party Sec, Counties
11/12	Deputy Heads of Divisions under various CC Offices and Bureaus	Party Sec of Prov Bureaus; Dep Sec, Prefectural and Municipal CCP Committees, Party Sec, Counties
13-16	Heads of Sections under various Divisions	Party Secs, Province Bureaus; Dep Secs, Prefectural and Municipal CCP Committees, Party Sec, Counties
17		Party Secs, Communes
20		Sec of Party General Branch (Production Brigades).
23		Sec of Party Branch (Production Brigades)
27-30		Rural Cadres

Appendix B: Government Cadre Levels

Grade	Central	Local
1	State Chairman; National People's Congress Standing Committee Chairman; Premier, State Council	
2/3	Vice-Chairmen, Standing Committee, NPC; Vice Premiers; State Councilors	
4/5	Sec Gen, Standing Committee, NPC; Chairmen of Various NPC Committees; Ministers and Sec Gen of State Council	
5-7	Dep Sec Gen, Standing Committee NPC; Vice-Chairmen of various NPC Committees; General Office Director, Vice-Ministers and General Office Director of the State Council	Province Governors; Mayors of Municipalities directly subordinate to Central Govt; Vice-Governors, Vice-Mayors
7/8	Deputy Directors of NPC and State Council General offices; Assistants to State Council Ministers	Mayors of Province Capitals; Directors of Commissions and Offices under Province (Municipal) Govts
8-10	Directors of various NPC Offices; Directors of General Office and Heads of State Council Ministries	Prefectural Commissioners; City Mayors

Grade	Central	Local
11/12	Directors of Divisions (Chu) under various NPC Offices; Directors of Divisions under Depts of various ministries	Directors of Province Bureaus; Directors of Depts under Prefecture Commissioners; Heads of Counties, Towns
13-18	Staff Members of Sections under various organs of the NPC and State Council Ministries	Heads of Bureaus under County Govt; Heads of Communes; Staff Mbrs Sections under Prov, Prefecture, Municipal Govts; Section Chiefs of County Govts.
19/21		Staff Members of Sections under County Govts
22	Clerks	
23		Leaders of Production Brigades, Clerks of Province, Municipal and Prefecture Govts
24/25		Clerks of County Govts
26-30		Leaders of Production Teams

Appendix C:
Military Grade Levels

Grade	Level	Key Positions	Rank Prior to 1965
1	Defense Minister Grade	Minister of Defense	Marshal
2	Front Army Grade	Vice-Minister of Defense; Directors of General Depts and NDSTIC; Cdrs of Air Force and Navy; Commandants of Major Military Academies	
3	Deputy Front Army Grade	Cdrs of various Arms; Military Region Cdrs; Fleet Cdrs; Dep Chief of of General Staff; Dep Directors General Depts; Dep Cdrs, Air Force and Navy	General (Admiral); Lt General (Vice-Admiral)
4	Army Group Grade	Directors of GeneralDept Sub-Depts; Dep Cdrs of various Arms and Military Regions	Lt General (Vice-Admiral)
5	Deputy Army Group Grade	Chiefs of Staff of various Arms and Military Regions; Fleet Dep Cdrs	Lt General (Vice-Admiral); Major General (Rear Admiral)

161

Grade	Level	Key Positions	Rank Prior to 1965
6	Sub Army Group Grade	Military District Cdrs; Regional Military Academy Commandants; Regional Air Force Cdrs	Major General
7	Army Grade	Army Cdrs; Air Army Cdrs; Naval Flotilla Cdrs.	Major General (Rear Admiral)
8	Deputy Army Grade	Deputy Cdrs of of Grade 7	Major General (Rear Admiral); Senior Colonel (Senior Captain)
9	Sub Army Grade	Chiefs of Staff and Political Dept Directors of Grade 8	Senior Colonel (Senior Captain)
10	Division Grade	Division Cdrs and Equivalent	Senior Colonel
11	Deputy Division Grade	Division Dep Cdrs and Equivalent	Colonel
12	Sub Division Grade	Division Chiefs of Staff and Equivalent	Lt Colonel
13	Regiment Grade	Regimental Cdrs and Equivalent	Lt Colonel
14	Deputy Regiment Grade	Deputy Cdrs of Grade 13	Major
15	Sub Regt Grade	Chiefs of Staff of Grade 14	Major
16	Battalion Grade	Bn Cdrs and Equivalent	Major, Senior Senior Capt
17	Dep Bn Grade	Bn Dep Cdrs and Equivalent	Senior Capt, Capt
18	Dep Bn Grade	Bn Dep Cdrs and Equivalent	Capt

Grade	Level	Key Positions	Rank Prior to 1965
19	Company Grade	Company Cdrs and Equivalent	Capt, 1st Lt
20	Dep Co Grade	Dep Co Cdrs and Equivalent	1st Lt, 2d Lt
21	Dep Co Grade	Dep Co Cdrs and Equivalent	2d Lt
22	Platoon Grade	Platoon Leaders	2d Lt
23	Dep Pltn Grade	Dep Pltn Leaders	Warrant Officers
24	**		

---

* Political Commissars (and Battalion and Company Political Officers and Instructors) hold grades and ranks parallel to the Commanders at the corresponding level.

** Grade 24, formerly for Deputy Platoon Leaders with the rank of Master Sergeant, is believed to have been eliminated since 1965. The reinstitution was being reconsidered in 1984.

Appendix D: PRC Elites Holding Interlocking Positions (1960)

NAME	CC	PB	MIL REG POS	MILITARY REGION	MIL DIS POS	PARTY POS	GOVT POS	PROVINCE
APEIAWANGJINMEI	NO		DEP CO	XIZANG			GS	XIZANG
BAI DONGCAI	NO					PS	GS	JIANGXI
BAI RUBING	NO					PS	GS	SHANDONG
BI ZHANYUN	NO				CO	PS		HENAN
CAO DIQIU	NO					PS	GS	SHANGHAI
CHEN PEIXIAN	ALT					PS		SHANGHAI
CHEN WEIDA	NO					PS	GS	ZHEJIANG
CHEN XILIAN	ALT		CO	SHENYANG				
CHEN YU	FULL					PS	GOV	GUANGDONG
DENG CHENXI	NO					PS	GS	SHANDONG
DENG HUA	FULL						GS	SICHUAN
DENG KEMING	NO				CO	PS		JIANGXI
DENG SHAODONG	NO		DEP CO	XIZANG		PS		XIZANG
FANG ZHICHUN	NO					PS	GS	JIANGXI
FU ZHENSHENG	NO					PS	GS	JILIN
GUAN SHANFU	NO					PS	GS	JILIN
GUO CHAO	NO					PS	GS	YUNNAN
GUO GUANGZHOU	NO					PS	GS	JIANGSU
GUO PENG	NO		DEP CO	XINJIANG			GS	XINJIANG
HE BINGYAN	NO		CO	CHENGDU		PS		SICHUAN
HE CHENGHUA	NO					PS	GS	GANSU
HE XIMING	NO					PS	GS	GUANGXI
HUA GUOFENG	NO					PS	GS	HUNAN
HUANG HUOQING	ALT				DPC	1S		LIAONING
HUANG OUDONG	ALT					PS	GOV	LIAONING
HUANG YAN	NO					PS	GOV	ANHUI
HUI YOUYU	NO					PS	GS	JIANGSU
HUO SHILIAN	NO					PS	GS	ZHEJIANG
HUO WEIDE	NO					PS	GS	GANSU
JIANG HUA	ALT				PC	1S		ZHEJIANG
JIANG WEIQING	ALT				PC	1S		JIANGSU
JIANG YIZHEN	NO					PS	GOV	FUJIAN
KE QINGSHI	FULL	F	PC	NANJING		1S	MAY	SHANGHAI
KUI BI	ALT					PS	GS	NEI MONGGOL
LI DAZHANG	ALT					PS	GOV	SICHUAN
LI FANWU	NO					PS	GS	HEILONGJIANG
LI FENGPING	NO					PS	GS	ZHEJIANG
LI GENGTAO	NO					PS	GS	TIANJIN
LI JINGQUAN	FULL	F	DPC	CHENGDU		1S		SICHUAN
LI QUAN	NO		DPC	XINJIANG		PS		XINJIANG
LI SHIYAN	NO				DPC	PS		ANHUI
LI YOUWEN	NO					PS	GS	JILIN
LIANG LINGGUANG	NO					PS	GS	FUJIAN
LIAO RONGBIAO	NO				CO		GS	ANHUI
LIAO ZHIGAO	ALT					PS		SICHUAN
LIN TIE	FULL				DPC	1S		HEBEI
LIN ZHONGZHAO	NO				DPC	PS		JIANGXI

NAME	CC	PB	MIL REG POS	MILITARY REGION	MIL DIS POS	PARTY POS	GOVT POS	PROVINCE
LIU GEPING	FULL					1S	GS	NINGXIA
LIU JIANXUN	ALT					1S		GUANGXI
LIU JUNXIU	NO					PS	GS	JIANGXI
LIU MINGHUI	NO					PS	GS	YUNNAN
LIU REN	ALT					PS		BEIJING
LIU SHUZHOU	NO					PS	GS	SHANGHAI
LIU ZHUOFU	NO					PS	GS	YUNNAN
LIU ZIHOU	ALT					PS	GOV	HEBEI
MA GUORUI	NO					PS	GS	HEBEI
MA QIKONG	NO					PS	GS	YUNNAN
MA YUHUAI	NO					PS	GS	NINGXIA
MENG FUTANG	NO					PS	GS	HUBEI
NIU SHUSHEN	NO				DPC		GS	SHAANXI
OU MENGJUE	ALT					PS		GUANGDONG
OUYANG QIN	FULL					1S		HEILONGJIANG
PEI MENGFEI	NO					PS	GS	SHANDONG
PENG ZHEN	FULL	F				1S	MAY	BEIJING
QIANG XIAOCHU	NO					PS	GS	HEILONGJIANG
SAIFUDING	ALT		DEP CO	XINJIANG		PS	GOV	XINJIANG
SANGJIYUEXI	ALT						GS	SICHUAN
SANGPO CAIWANG	NO		DEP CO	XIZANG		PS		XIZANG
SHAO SHIPING	ALT					PS	GOV	JIANGXI
SHI XIANGSHENG	NO					PS	GS	HENAN
SHU TONG	FULL		PC	JINAN		1S	GS	SHANDONG
SONG MENGLIN	NO					PS	GS	ANHUI
SONG ZHIHE	NO					PS	GS	HENAN
SU QIANYI	NO					PS	GS	NEI MONGGOL
SU YIRAN	NO					PS	GS	ANHUI
TAN GUANSAN	NO		PC	XIZANG		PS	GS	XIZANG
TAN QILONG	ALT					PS	GOV	SHANDONG
TAN YINGJI	NO					PS	GS	GUANGXI
TAN YUBAO	NO					PS	GS	HUNAN
TANG LIANG	ALT		PC	NANJING				
TAO LUJIA	ALT				PC	1S		SHANXI
TAO ZHIYUE	NO		DEP CO	XINJIANG			GS	XINJIANG
TAO ZHU	FULL		PC	GUANGZHOU		1S		GUANGDONG
TENG JINGLU	NO					PS	GS	SHANDONG
TIAN WEIYANG	NO				CO		GS	GUIZHOU
WAN LI	NO					PS	GS	BEIJING
WANG ENMAO	FULL		CO, PC	XINJIANG		1S	GS	XINJIANG
WANG FENG	ALT					1S	GOV	NINGXIA
WANG GUANGLU	NO					PS	GS	ANHUI
WANG QICAI	NO				PC		GS	HEBEI
WANG QIMEI	NO		DPC	XIZANG		PS		XIZANG
WANG RENZHONG	ALT					1S		HUBEI
WANG YAOHUA	NO					PS	GS	GANSU
WANG YILUN	NO					PS	GS	HEILONGJIANG
WEI GUOQING	ALT					PS	GOV	GUANGXI
WEI HENG	NO					PS	GS	SHANXI
WEI JINSHUI	NO					PS	GS	FUJIAN
WU DE	ALT				PC	1S		JILIN
WU XIAN	NO					PS	GS	ZHEJIANG
WU ZHIPU	FULL				PC	1S	GOV	HENAN
WULANFU	FULL	A	CO, PC	NEI MONGGOL		1S	GOV	NEI MONGGOL
XU JIATUN	NO					PS	GS	JIANGSU
XU SHIYOU	ALT		CO	NANJING				
YAN DAKAI	NO					PS	GS	HEBEI
YAN HONGYAN	ALT		PC	KUNMING		1S		YUNNAN
YANG CHENGWU	ALT		CO	BEIJING				
YANG DEZHI	ALT		CO	JINAN		PS	GS	SHANDONG
YANG JIARUI	NO				CO		GS	SHAANXI
YANG SHANGKUI	NO				PC	1S	GS	JIANGXI
YANG WEIPING	NO					PS	GS	HENAN
YANG WENWEI	NO					PS	GS	FUJIAN
YANG YICHEN	ALT					PS	GS	HEILONGJIANG
YANG YONG	ALT		CO	BEIJING				
YANG ZHILIN	NO					PS	GS	NEI MONGGOL
YE FEI	ALT		PC	FUZHOU		1S		FUJIAN
YU YICHUAN	NO					PS	GOV	YUNNAN
YUAN RENYUAN	NO					PS	GS	QINGHAI

NAME	CC	PB	MIL REG POS	MILITARY REGION	MIL DIS POS	PARTY POS	GOVT POS	PROVINCE
ZENG XISHENG	FULL					1S		ANHUI
ZHAN HUAYU	NO		DPC	XIZANG			GS	XIZANG
ZHANG CHENGXIAN	NO					PS	GS	HEBEI
ZHANG DAZHI	ALT		CO	LANZHOU				
ZHANG DESHENG	ALT				PC	1S		SHAANXI
ZHANG GUOHUA	NO		CO	XIZANG		PS	GS	XIZANG
ZHANG JINGWU	ALT					1S		XIZANG
ZHANG KAIFAN	NO					PS	GS	ANHUI
ZHANG KAIJING	NO				CO	PS		HEILONGJIANG
ZHANG PENGTU	NO					PS	GS	GANSU
ZHANG PINGHUA	ALT				DPC	1S		HUNAN
ZHANG TIXUE	NO					PS	GOV	HUBEI
ZHANG ZHONGLIAN	ALT					1S		GANSU
ZHAO BOPING	ALT					PS	GOV	SHAANXI
ZHAO CANGBI	NO					PS	GS	SICHUAN
ZHAO WENFU	NO					PS	GS	HENAN
ZHAO XINCHU	NO					PS	GS	HUBEI
ZHENG LIN	NO					PS	GS	SHANXI
ZHOU HUAN	ALT		PC	SHENYANG		PS		LIAONING
ZHOU LI	NO					PS	GS	HUNAN
ZHOU LIN	NO				PC	1S	GOV	GUIZHOU
ZHOU RENSHAN	NO					PS	GS	XIZANG
ZHU SHIHUAN	NO				DPC		GS	JILIN

Appendix E: PRC Elites Holding Interlocking Positions (1973)

NAME	CC	PB	MIL REG POS	MILITARY REGION	MIL DIS POS	PARTY POS	GOVT POS	PROVINCE
A WAZIHAN	NO					MEM	MEM	XINJIANG
AN PINGSHENG	FULL					SEC	VC	GUANGXI
BA SANG	FULL					SEC	VC	XIZANG
BAI DONGCAI	ALT					SEC	VC	JIANGXI
BAI PING	NO				PC	SCM	SCM	GUANGDONG
BAI RUBING	FULL		(1) PC	JINAN		1S	CH	SHANDONG
BAORLEDAI	FULL						SCM	NEI MONGGOL
CAI SHUMEI	FULL					SCM	SCM	TIANJIN
CAO PUNAN	NO		PC	JINAN		SCM	VC	SHANDONG
CAO SIMING	NO		PC	URUMQI		3S	VC	XINJIANG
CAO YUQING	NO				DEP CO		SCM	SHANXI
CAO ZHONGNAN	NO				(1) PC	SEC	VC	SHANXI
CAODANUOFU	NO		PC	URUMQI		SCM	SCM	XINJIANG
CEN GUORONG	FULL						SCM	GUANGXI
CHAI QIKUN	NO					DS	VC	ZHEJIANG
CHEN BING	NO					SCM	SCM	ZHEJIANG
CHEN CHANGFENG	NO				CO	SEC	VC	JIANGXI
CHEN DE	NO				(1) PC		SCM	GUANGDONG
CHEN GUICHANG	NO				DEP CO		SCM	HENAN
CHEN HEFA	ALT					SCM	VC	JIANGSU
CHEN JIAZHONG	ALT					SCM		FUJIAN
CHEN JIEDI	NO				DEP CO		SCM	GUIZHOU
CHEN KAILU	NO				DEP CO	SCM	SCM	GUANGXI
CHEN KANG	FULL		DEP CO	KUNMING		SEC	VC	YUNNAN
CHEN MEIZAO	NO		PC	JINAN			SCM	SHANDONG
CHEN MINGYI	NO				CO	SEC	VC	XIZANG
CHEN SHUHUAI	NO					SCM	SCM	BEIJING
CHEN WEIDA	NO					DEP	VC	ZHEJIANG
CHEN XIANRUI	FULL		PC	BEIJING				
CHEN XILIAN	FULL	F	CO	BEIJING				
CHEN YI	NO					SCM	SCM	ANHUI
CHEN YONGGUI	FULL	F				SEC	VC	SHANXI
CHENG GUANGYUAN	NO					SCM	SCM	QINGHAI
CHENG YETANG	NO				DEP CO		VC	ANHUI
CHI MINGTANG	NO					SCM	VC	JIANGSU
CUI XIUFAN	ALT					SCM	VC	LIAONING
DA LUO	ALT					DS	VC	QINGHAI
DAI KELIN	NO				DEP CO	SCM	VC	ZHEJIANG
DAI SULI	NO					DS	VC	HENAN
DENG CUNLUN	NO					SEC	VC	NEI MONGGOL
DENG HUA	ALT						SCM	SICHUAN
DI ZICAI	NO					DS	RP	QINGHAI
DING FENGYING	NO					SCM	VC	HUBEI
DING GUOYU	FULL					SEC	VC	BEIJING
DING SHENG	FULL		CO	NANJING				
DONG CHUANJUN	NO				DEP CO	DS	VC	HENAN
DONG MINGHUI	FULL					MEM	SCM	HUBEI

NAME	CC	PB	MIL REG POS	MILITARY REGION	MIL DIS POS	PARTY POS	GOVT POS	PROVINCE
DU HEDI	NO				PC	SCM	SCM	HENAN
DU PING	FULL		PC	NANJING		SEC	SCM	JIANGSU
DUAN HUAIYU	NO				PC	SCM		QINGHAI
DUAN JUNYI	FULL					SEC	VC	SICHUAN
DUAN SIYING	NO		PC	KUNMING			SCM	YUNNAN
DUO JI	NO					MEM	MEM	XIZANG
FAN CHAOLI	NO		DEP CO	JINAN			SCM	SHANDONG
FAN PUQUAN	NO				PC		SCM	BEIJING
FAN XIAOJU	ALT						VC	JIANGSU
FANG MIN	NO					SCM	SCM	JIANGSU
FANG SHENGPU	NO					SCM	VC	SHAANXI
FENG GUOZHU	NO					SCM	VC	SHANGHAI
FENG KEDA	NO				DEP CO	SEC	VC	XIZANG
FU JIANWU	NO				DEP CO		SCM	SHANDONG
FU JIAXUAN	NO		DEP CO	JINAN			SCM	SHANDONG
FU KUIQING	NO					SEC	VC	HEILONGJIAN
GAO RUI	NO				CO	2S		NINGXIA
GAO SHUE	NO					SCM	SCM	JIANGXI
GAO ZHIRONG	NO				DEP CO	SCM	VC	SHANGHAI
GENG CHANGSUO	NO					SCM	VC	HEBEI
GENG QICHANG	FULL					SEC	VC	HENAN
GOU XIANXUE	NO				DEP CO		SCM	HUNAN
GU FENGMING	NO				PC		VC	SHAANXI
GU QIFENG	NO				PC	SCM	VC	HEBEI
GUAN ZHOU	NO					SCM	SCM	HEILONGJIAN
GUO FENGLIAN	NO					MEM	SCM	SHANXI
GUO GUANGZHOU	NO					SCM	VC	JIANGXI
GUO HONGJIE	FULL					SEC		ANHUI
GUO PENG	NO		DEP CO	LANZHOU			VC	GANSU
GUO QIANG	NO				PC		SCM	HEILONGJIAN
GUO XILAN	NO					SEC	VC	XIZANG
GUO YAOQING	ALT						SCM	GUANGXI
GUO YIQING	NO				PC		SCM	NEI MONGGOL
HAN DEFU	NO				PC		MEM	TIANJIN
HAN NINGFU	NO					SEC	VC	HUBEI
HAN SHIFU	NO				PC		SCM	GUANGXI
HAN XIANCHU	FULL		CO	LANZHOU				
HAN YING	FULL					SEC	VC	SHANXI
HAO JIANXIU	NO					MEM	MEM	SHANDONG
HE FENGSHAN	NO				DEP CO		SCM	NEI MONGGOL
HE GUANGYU	NO		DEP CO	KUNMING	CO	DS	VC	GUIZHOU
HE LINZHAO	NO		PC	URUMQI		SEC		XINJIANG
HE YOUFA	NO				CO	SEC	VC	JILIN
HE YUNFENG	NO					SEC	VC	SICHUAN
HE ZHIYUAN	NO				(1) PC	SCM	SCM	SHANDONG
HU DINGFA	NO				DEP CO		SCM	GANSU
HU JICHENG	NO		DEP CO	CHENGDU			SCM	SICHUAN
HU JIZONG	FULL					SEC	1VC	GANSU
HU LIANGCAI	ALT						VC	XINJIANG
HU WEI	ALT		DEP CO	LANZHOU		SEC	VC	SHAANXI
HU YONG	NO					MEM	VC	HUNAN
HUA GUOFENG	FULL	F PC		GUANGZHOU	1ST PC	1S	CH	HUNAN
HUA LINSEN	FULL					SCM	VC	JIANGSU
HUA YINFENG	NO					MEM	VC	ZHEJIANG
HUANG BINGXIU	ALT					SEC		HUNAN
HUANG CHUANLONG	NO					SCM	SCM	SHAANXI
HUANG JINGYAO	NO				CO	SEC	VC	SHAANXI
HUANG LIGONG	NO				DEP CO		SCM	HUNAN
HUANG MINGQING	NO				PC		SCM	HEILONGJIAN
HUANG RONGHAI	ALT		DEP CO	GUANGZHOU		SCM	VC	GUANGDONG
HUANG TAO	NO					SCM	SCM	SHANGHAI
HUANG XIAN	NO					SCM	VC	JIANGXI
HUANG YAGUANG	NO					SEC	VC	FUJIAN
HUANG ZHIZHEN	ALT					SEC		JIANGXI
HUANG ZUOZHEN	ALT				DEP PC	SEC	VC	BEIJING
HUO SHILIAN	NO					SEC	VC	SHAANXI
ISMAYIL AYMAT	FULL					SEC	SCM	XINJIANG
JI DENGKUI	FULL	F (1) PC		BEIJING		SEC	VC	HENAN
JIA TING	NO					SCM	VC	BEIJING
JIA TINGSAN	NO					DS	VC	GUIZHOU

NAME	CC	PB	MIL REG POS	MILITARY REGION	MIL DIS POS	PARTY POS	GOVT POS	PROVINCE
JIANG BAODI	ALT					SCM	SCM	ZHEJIANG
JIANG KE	NO					SCM	VC	JIANGSU
JIANG LIYIN	FULL					SCM	SCM	FUJIAN
JIANG WEIQING	ALT					1S		JIANGXI
JIANG XIEYUAN	FULL		DEP CO	GUANGZHOU				
JIANG YI	NO					SEC	SCM	HUBEI
JIANG YONGHUI	FULL		DEP CO	SHENYANG				
JIAO DEXIU	NO					SCM	VC	HUBEI
JIAO LINYI	FULL					SCM	VC	GUANGDONG
JIN ZUMIN	FULL					SCM	VC	SHANGHAI
JING LIN	NO				PC	MEM	SCM	HUNAN
KANG JIANMIN	ALT		PC	LANZHOU	1ST PC	1S	CH	NINGXIA
KANG LIN	ALT		DEP CO	BEIJING				
KANG YANZHONG	NO					SEC	VC	GUIZHOU
KONG QINGDE	NO		DEP CO	WUHAN		SEC		HUBEI
KONG SHIQUAN	FULL		PC	GUANGZHOU		SEC	1VC	GUANGDONG
LAI GUANGXUN	NO		DEP CO	URUMQI			SCM	XINJIANG
LAI KEKE	NO					DS	VC	ZHEJIANG
LAN GANTING	NO					SCM	VC	JILIN
LI BAOHUA	FULL					2S	VC	GUIZHOU
LI BINSHAN	NO				PC		SCM	SHANGHAI
LI BOQIU	NO					SEC	CH	LIAONING
LI CHANGMAO	NO					MEM	VC	TIANJIN
LI DAZHANG	FULL		PC	CHENGDU		SEC	VC	SICHUAN
LI DESHENG	FULL	F	CO	SHENYANG				
LI DINGSHAN	ALT					SCM	VC	ANHUI
LI FUQUAN	NO					SCM	VC	HUBEI
LI GUOLIANG	NO				DEP CO	SCM		JIANGXI
LI HUAMIN	ALT		DEP CO	WUHAN		SCM	SCM	HUBEI
LI JIANZHEN	NO					SCM	VC	GUANGDONG
LI KEZHONG	NO		PC	KUNMING		DS	VC	YUNNAN
LI LI	NO					DS	VC	GUIZHOU
LI RENZHI	FULL					SEC	VC	ANHUI
LI RUISHAN	FULL		PC	LANZHOU	1ST PC	1S	CH	SHAANXI
LI SHENGLI	NO					MEM	VC	ANHUI
LI SHUDE	NO					SCM	VC	NEI MONGGOL
LI SHUMAO	NO		DEP CO	LANZHOU			SCM	GANSU
LI SHUNDA	FULL					SCM	VC	SHANXI
LI SUWEN	FULL					SCM	VC	LIAONING
LI XIFU	NO				CO		SCM	YUNNAN
LI ZHENDONG	NO					MEM	SCM	ANHUI
LI ZHENJUN	NO				PC	SEC	VC	HUNAN
LI ZHIMIN	FULL		(1) PC	FUZHOU				
LI ZHONGQI	NO				DEP CO		SCM	BEIJING
LI ZHONGSHUN	NO				PC	SCM	SCM	HENAN
LIANG HUAXIN	NO					MEM	SCM	GUANGXI
LIANG JINTANG	FULL					SCM	VC	GUANGDONG
LIANG JIQING	NO				PC	SEC		ANHUI
LIANG RENJIE	NO				(1) PC		SCM	GANSU
LIANG RENKUI	NO				DEP CO		VC	HUBEI
LIANG XIUZHEN	NO					SCM	VC	GUANGDONG
LIANG ZHONGYU	NO		DEP CO	KUNMING		SCM	SCM	YUNNAN
LIAO BUYUN	NO				PC		VC	XIZANG
LIAO HAIGUANG	NO		PC	FUZHOU		SCM		FUJIAN
LIAO WEIXING	NO					SCM	VC	GUANGXI
LIAO ZHIGAO	ALT					1S	CH	FUJIAN
LIN LIMING	ALT					SEC	VC	GUANGDONG
LIN SHAN	NO				PC		SCM	QINGHAI
LIU ANG	NO				DEP CO	SCM		ZHEJIANG
LIU CHONGGUI	NO				PC	SEC	VC	GUANGXI
LIU CHUANXIN	NO					SCM	VC	BEIJING
LIU CHUNQIAO	ALT					SCM	SCM	HUNAN
LIU FAXIU	NO		DEP CO	URUMQI			SCM	XINJIANG
LIU GUANGTAO	ALT				1ST PC	2S	1VC	HEILONGJIANG
LIU HONGWEN	NO					SCM	VC	HENAN
LIU HUAXIANG	NO				DEP CO		SCM	NEI MONGGOL
LIU JIANXUN	FULL		PC	WUHAN	1ST PC	1S	CH	HENAN
LIU JUN	NO				DEP CO		SCM	NEI MONGGOL
LIU JUNXIU	NO					SCM	SCM	JIANGXI
LIU JUNYI	FULL					SCM		GUANGDONG

NAME	CC	PB	MIL REG POS	MILITARY REGION	MIL DIS POS	PARTY POS	GOVT POS	PROVINCE
LIU MINGHUI	NO					DS	VC	YUNNAN
LIU MINGQIAN	NO					SCM	VC	QINGHAI
LIU RUIFANG	NO		PC	LANZHOU			SCM	GANSU
LIU SHANFU	NO				DEP CO	SCM	VC	HUNAN
LIU SHAOWEN	NO					SEC	VC	BEIJING
LIU SHENGTIAN	FULL						VC	LIAONING
LIU SHIHONG	NO				PC	DS		SHANXI
LIU TIANCHEN	NO					SCM	VC	HEBEI
LIU TIANFU	NO					SCM	VC	GUANGDONG
LIU XICHANG	FULL					SCM	VC	BEIJING
LIU XING	NO					SEC	VC	XINJIANG
LIU XINGYUAN	FULL		1ST PC	CHENGDU		1S	CH	SICHUAN
LIU YAOZONG	NO				PC		VC	SHANGHAI
LIU YUN	NO					SCM	SCM	JIANGXI
LIU ZHENG	NO					SEC	VC	TIANJIN
LIU ZIHOU	FULL				1ST PC	1S	CH	HEBEI
LONG BINGCHU	NO					SCM	VC	GANSU
LONG GUANGQIAN	ALT					SCM	SCM	QINGHAI
LOU XUEZHENG	NO					SCM	VC	ANHUI
LU CUNJIE	ALT					SCM	VC	QINGHAI
LU DADONG	ALT						SCM	SICHUAN
LU HE	ALT						MEM	HEILONGJIANG
LU MEIYING	NO					MEM	SCM	SHANGHAI
LU MING	NO					SCM	VC	JIANGXI
LU RUILIN	FULL		DEP CO	KUNMING		1S	CH	GUIZHOU
LU SHENG	NO				PC	SCM	SCM	FUJIAN
LU YULAN	FULL					2S	VC	HEBEI
LU ZHIAN	NO				PC	DS		QINGHAI
LUO CHUNTI	ALT						VC	FUJIAN
LUO QIUYUE	NO					SCM	SCM	HUNAN
LUO YINGCHEN	NO				DEP CO		SCM	ANHUI
MA FU	NO					SCM	SCM	GUANGDONG
MA HUI	NO				CO	2S	VC	HEBEI
MA JIE	NO					2S	VC	HEBEI
MA LI	NO					DS	VC	HEBEI
MA QI	NO				PC	MEM	SCM	HUNAN
MA TIANSHUI	FULL					SEC	VC	SHANGHAI
MA XINGYUAN	NO					SCM	VC	FUJIAN
MA XISHENG	NO				DEP CO		VC	SHAANXI
MA XUELI	NO					SCM	VC	HUBEI
MAO YUANXIN	NO		DEP CO	SHENYANG		SEC	VC	LIAONING
MENG ZHAOYU	NO					SCM	SCM	ZHEJIANG
MO XIANYAO	FULL					MEM	SCM	ZHEJIANG
MU LIN	NO					SCM	VC	SHANDONG
NI NANSHAN	NO				1ST PC	SEC	SCM	FUJIAN
NI ZHIFU	FULL	A				SEC	VC	BEIJING
NI ZIWEN	NO				DEP CO	SCM	VC	NEI MONGGOL
NIAN JIRONG	FULL					SCM	VC	GANSU
PAN QIQI	NO				DEP CO	SCM	SCM	ANHUI
PAN SHIGAO	FULL					MEM	VC	JIANGXI
PAN ZHENWU	NO		PC	WUHAN		SEC	VC	HUBEI
PEI ZHOUYU	ALT		PC	URUMQI		SEC		XINJIANG
PENG CHONG	ALT					1S	CH	JIANGSU
PENG GUIHE	ALT					SCM	VC	YUNNAN
PENG SHENGBIAO	NO				PC		SCM	ANHUI
PI DINGJUN	FULL		CO	FUZHOU				
QIAO XIAOGUANG	NO					SEC	VC	GUANGXI
QILIN WANDAN	ALT					DEP	SCM	YUNNAN
QIN HEZHEN	NO					SCM	MEM	SHANDONG
QIN JIWEI	FULL		CO	CHENGDU				
QIU GUOGUANG	NO		DEP CO	GUANGZHOU		SCM	VC	GUANGDONG
RAO XINGLI	FULL					SCM	VC	HUBEI
REN RONG	ALT				1ST PC	1S	CH	XIZANG
REN SIZHONG	FULL		PC	GUANGZHOU			SCM	GUANGDONG
REN ZHIBIN	NO					SCM	SCM	ANHUI
REN ZHONGYI	NO					SEC	VC	HEILONGJIANG
RENZENG WANGJIE	NO					SCM	SCM	XIZANG
RUAN BOSHENG	ALT					SEC	VC	JILIN
SAIFUDING	FULL	A	1ST PC	URUMQI		1S	CH	XINJIANG
SHAN YINZHANG	NO					SCM	VC	GUANGDONG

NAME	CC	PB	MIL REG POS	MILITARY REGION	MIL DIS POS	PARTY POS	GOVT POS	PROVINCE
SHANG ZIJIN	NO					SCM	VC	HUNAN
SHE JIDE	ALT		PC	FUZHOU	1ST PC	SEC	CH	JIANGXI
SHEN CE	NO					SCM	VC	ZHEJIANG
SHEN MAOGONG	ALT					SCM	SCM	HENAN
SHEN XINFA	NO					SCM	VC	NEI MONGGOL
SHI LEI	NO				DEP CO	MEM	SCM	HUNAN
SHI XINAN	NO				(1) PC		VC	GUIZHOU
SONG CHANGGENG	NO				1ST PC	1S	CH	QINGHAI
SONG PEIZHANG	FULL				1ST PC	1S	CH	ANHUI
SONG PING	NO					SEC	VC	GANSU
SONG ZHIHE	NO					SEC	VC	XINJIANG
SU JUNLU	NO				PC		SCM	JILIN
SU MIN	NO				PC	SCM	VC	HEILONGJIANG
SU YIRAN	NO					SEC	VC	SHANDONG
SU YU	NO						VC	LIAONING
SUN BANGCHANG	NO					MEM	MEM	ANHUI
SUN BOWEI	NO				DEP CO	MEM	VC	GUANGXI
SUN GUOZHI	NO					SCM	VC	HUNAN
SUN HONGDAO	NO					SCM	SCM	SICHUAN
TAN KAIYUN	NO		PC	URUMQI			VC	XINJIANG
TAN QILONG	FULL				1ST PC	1S	CH	ZHEJIANG
TANG JINZHI	NO					MEM	VC	HEILONGJIANG
TANG KEBI	ALT						SCM	SICHUAN
TANG QISHAN	FULL					SCM	SCM	HENAN
TANG ZHONGFU	FULL					SCM	SCM	HUNAN
TIAN BAO	FULL				PC	SEC	VC	XIZANG
TIAN HUAGUI	FULL						VC	GUANGDONG
TIAN HUAYI	NO				PC		SCM	GUIZHOU
TIAN WEIYANG	NO		DEP CO	KUNMING			VC	YUNNAN
TIE YING	ALT				PC	SEC	VC	ZHEJIANG
TONG GUOGUI	NO				CO		SCM	SHANDONG
TU LIE	NO					SCM	VC	JIANGXI
WAN DA	NO					SEC	VC	HUNAN
WANG BICHEN	NO				PC	SCM	SCM	NEI MONGGOL
WANG BICHENG	FULL		CO	KUNMING		2S	1VC	YUNNAN
WANG BUQING	NO					SCM	VC	HUBEI
WANG CHENGJUN	NO					SCM	VC	SHANXI
WANG DAREN	NO					DS	RP	SHANXI
WANG GENYUAN	NO				DEP CO		SCM	HUBEI
WANG GUANGYU	NO					SEC	VC	ANHUI
WANG GUOFAN	FULL					SCM	SCM	HEBEI
WANG GUORUI	NO					SCM	VC	GANSU
WANG HONGWEN	FULL	F			PC	SEC	VC	SHANGHAI
WANG HUAIXIANG	FULL		PC	SHENYANG	1ST PC	1S	CH	JILIN
WANG HUI	NO				DEP CO	SCM	SCM	HENAN
WANG JIADAO	ALT		DEP CO	SHENYANG	CO	1S	CH	HEILONGJIANG
WANG JINGSHENG	ALT						VC	LIAONING
WANG JINSHAN	NO					SCM	VC	HEBEI
WANG LEI	NO					SCM	SCM	BEIJING
WANG LISHENG	NO				PC	SCM		HUNAN
WANG LIUSHENG	ALT		1ST PC	WUHAN		1S	CH	HUBEI
WANG LUMING	NO					SCM	VC	HEBEI
WANG MANTIAN	NO				PC	SEC	VC	TIANJIN
WANG QIAN	ALT					SEC		SHANXI
WANG SHAUYONG	NO					SCM	VC	SHANGHAI
WANG SHOUDAO	FULL					SEC	VC	GUANGDONG
WANG SHUZHEN	FULL					SCM	SCM	TIANJIN
WANG TI	ALT					SEC	VC	SHANXI
WANG TINGDONG	NO					DS	VC	SHANXI
WANG WANLIN	NO		PC	BEIJING			MEM	BEIJING
WANG WEIQUN	NO					DS	VC	HENAN
WANG XIANGQUN	ALT						SCM	SHANGHAI
WANG XIUZHEN	FULL					SEC	VC	SHANGHAI
WANG YI	NO				CO	SEC	VC	TIANJIN
WANG YILUN	NO					SEC	VC	HEILONGJIANG
WANG YINE	NO						SCM	SHANXI
WANG YINSHAN	NO				DEP CO		SCM	YUNNAN
WANG YOUHUA	NO				DEP CO	SCM	SCM	HUNAN
WANG YOUXIANG	NO					SCM	VC	ANHUI
WANG YUANHE	NO				PC	SCM	VC	TIANJIN

NAME	CC	PB	MIL REG POS	MILITARY REGION	MIL DIS POS	PARTY POS	GOVT POS	PROVINCE
WANG YUKUN	NO				DEP CO		MEM	HEBEI
WANG ZHIPING	NO					SCM	VC	SHANXI
WANG ZHIQIANG	ALT					DS	VC	NINGXIA
WANG ZHONG	NO					SCM	VC	ANHUI
WANG ZHONGJUN	NO				DEP CO		VC	HEILONGJIANG
WANG ZHUQUAN	NO					SCM	VC	SHANDONG
WANG ZIDA	NO					SCM	VC	ZHEJIANG
WEI BINGKUI	FULL						VC	LIAONING
WEI FENGYING	FULL						VC	LIAONING
WEI GUOQING	FULL	F	1ST PC	GUANGZHOU	1ST PC	1S	CH	GUANGXI
WEI JIANZHANG	NO					MEM	MEM	ANHUI
WEI KAIJIANG	NO				DEP CO	MEM		HUNAN
WEN DAOHONG	NO				PC	SEC	PC	JIANGXI
WEN XIANGLAN	ALT					SCM	SCM	HENAN
WU CONGSHU	ALT					SCM		ANHUI
WU DAI	NO		PC	BEIJING		2S	VC	TIANJIN
WU DASHENG	FULL		PC	NANJING	1ST PC	SEC	VC	JIANGSU
WU DE	FULL	F	PC	BEIJING	1ST PC	1S	CH	BEIJING
WU GUIXIAN	FULL	A					SCM	SHAANXI
WU HUA	NO				DEP CO		SCM	GUANGXI
WU TAO	FULL				1ST PC	SEC	VC	NEI MONGGOL
WU XIANGBI	ALT					SEC		GUIZHOU
WU ZHONG	ALT				CO	SEC	VC	BEIJING
XIA BANGYIN	FULL					MEM	SCM	HUBEI
XIA GUANGYA	NO					SCM	VC	HEILONGJIANG
XIA QI	NO				PC	SCM		ZHEJIANG
XIAN HENGHAN	FULL		1ST PC	LANZHOU		1S	CH	GANSU
XIAO CHUN	NO					SEC	VC	SHAANXI
XIAO DAOSHENG	NO					SEC	VC	JILIN
XIAO HAN	NO					SCM	SCM	GUANGXI
XIAO QIAN	NO		PC	WUHAN		SCM	SCM	HUBEI
XIAO YINGTANG	NO				DEP CO		SCM	NEI MONGGOL
XIAO YONGYIN	NO		DEP CO	NANJING		SCM		JIANGSU
XIE CHANGHUA	NO				DEP CO		VC	HEILONGJIANG
XIE JIATANG	ALT						SCM	SICHUAN
XIE JIAXIANG	FULL		PC	CHENGDU		SEC	VC	SICHUAN
XIE JINGYI	FULL					SEC	VC	BEIJING
XIE WANGCHUN	ALT					MEM	SCM	HUBEI
XIE XUEGONG	FULL				1ST PC	1S	CH	TIANJIN
XIE ZHENGHAU	NO					DEP	VC	ZHEJIANG
XIE ZHENHUA	ALT				CO	1S	CH	SHANXI
XIN JUNJIE	NO				CO	SCM	VC	HUBEI
XING YANZI	FULL					MEM	MEM	HEBEI
XIONG ZHENWU	NO				CO	SCM		JIANGXI
XU CHENG	NO					SEC	SCM	TIANJIN
XU CHI	ALT					SEC	VC	SICHUAN
XU GUOFU	NO		DEP CO	WUHAN			SCM	HUBEI
XU GUOZHEN	NO		DEP CO	LANZHOU		SCM	VC	GANSU
XU JIATUN	NO					SCM	VC	JIANGSU
XU JINGXIAN	FULL					SEC	VC	SHANGHAI
XU SHENGTING	NO				PC	SCM	SCM	GUANGXI
XU SHIYOU	FULL	F	CO	GUANGZHOU				
XU SHOUHENG	NO					SCM	VC	SHANXI
XU XIN	NO				PC		VC	TIANJIN
XU YAOZHOU	NO					MEM	SCM	SHANGHAI
XU YUQING	NO					SCM	SCM	FUJIAN
XUE HONGFU	NO					DS	VC	QINGHAI
YAN JINSHENG	NO				PC	SCM	RP	SHAANXI
YANG CHUNFU	FULL					SEC	VC	LIAONING
YANG DAYI	ALT				CO	SEC	VC	HUNAN
YANG DEZHI	FULL		CO	WUHAN				
YANG DI	NO		PC	SHENYANG			VC	LIAONING
YANG DONGSHENG	NO					SEC	VC	XIZANG
YANG FUZHEN	ALT					SCM	VC	SHANGHAI
YANG GUANGLI	NO					SEC	VC	JIANGSU
YANG GUI	ALT					SCM		HENAN
YANG GUOFU	NO		DEP CO	JINAN			SCM	SHANDONG
YANG HUANMIN	NO		DEP CO	LANZHOU			MEM	SHAANXI
YANG JIARUI	NO		DEP CO	LANZHOU			SCM	GANSU
YANG JUNSHENG	ALT				PC	SEC	VC	BEIJING

NAME	CC	PB	MIL REG POS	MILITARY REGION	MIL DIS POS	PARTY POS	GOVT POS	PROVINCE
YANG MEISHENG	NO		DEP CO	GUANGZHOU			SCM	GUANGDONG
YANG QI	NO				1ST PC		VC	LIAONING
YANG SHOUSHAN	NO					SCM	VC	BEIJING
YANG SILU	NO		DEP CO	FUZHOU		SCM	SCM	FUJIAN
YANG XIAOCHUN	NO					SCM	VC	ANHUI
YANG YONG	FULL		CO	URUMQI		2S	VC	XINJIANG
YANG ZONG	ALT						MEM	XIZANG
YAO SHUYIN	NO					SCM	SCM	GANSU
YAO TIANLU	NO				DEP CO	SCM	VC	JILIN
YAO WENYUAN	FULL	F				2S	VC	SHANGHAI
YE SONG	NO					SCM	VC	FUJIAN
YIN CHANZHEN	NO		PC	SHENYANG			VC	LIAONING
YONG WENTAO	NO					SCM	VC	GUANGDONG
YOU DEXING	NO					SCM	SCM	JIANGXI
YOU HAOYANG	NO		DEP CO	SHENYANG			SCM	HEILONGJIANG
YOU TAIZHONG	FULL		DEP CO	BEIJING	CO	1S	CH	NEI MONGGOL
YU HONGLIANG	FULL					SEC		HEILONGJIANG
YU MINGTAO	NO					SEC	VC	HUNAN
YUAN DELIANG	NO					SCM	VC	GUANGDONG
YUAN JIE	NO				DEP CO	SCM	SCM	HEBEI
YUAN KEFU	NO				PC	SCM	SCM	SHAANXI
ZENG MEI	NO				PC	SCM	VC	HEBEI
ZENG SHAOSHAN	FULL		(1) PC	SHENYANG		1S		LIAONING
ZENG SIYU	FULL		CO	JINAN				
ZENG ZHENG	NO				DEP CO	SCM	SCM	QINGHAI
ZHAN HUAYU	NO		PC	FUZHOU		SCM		FUJIAN
ZHANG CHUNQIAO	FULL	F	1ST PC	NANJING	1ST PC	1S	CH	SHANGHAI
ZHANG DUOSHU	NO				PC	SCM	SCM	HEILONGJIANG
ZHANG FUHENG	FULL					SCM	VC	TIANJIN
ZHANG GENSHENG	NO					SCM	VC	GUANGDONG
ZHANG GUIFU	NO					SCM	SCM	BEIJING
ZHANG GUIJIN	NO					SEC	VC	NINGXIA
ZHANG HAITANG	NO				CO		VC	LIAONING
ZHANG HENGYUN	FULL						SCM	GANSU
ZHANG HONG	NO				(1) PC	SCM		HUBEI
ZHANG HONGCHI	FULL					SEC		HEILONGJIANG
ZHANG HUAILI	NO				DEP CO	SCM	VC	NINGXIA
ZHANG JIANGLIN	ALT				CO	SCM	VC	QINGHAI
ZHANG JIECHENG	NO		DEP CO	URUMQI			SCM	XINJIANG
ZHANG JINGBIAO	NO					SCM	SCM	SHANGHAI
ZHANG LIANG	NO				DEP CO		VC	GUIZHOU
ZHANG LINCHI	ALT					SEC	VC	HEILONGJIANG
ZHANG LIXIAN	NO				PC	SEC	VC	HUNAN
ZHANG MING	NO					SCM	VC	GUIZHOU
ZHANG PEIRONG	NO				DEP CO		SCM	GUIZHOU
ZHANG PINGHUA	FULL				PC	2S	1VC	HUNAN
ZHANG RONGSEN	NO				DEP CO	SEC	VC	GUIZHOU
ZHANG RUSAN	NO		PC	JINAN			SCM	SHANDONG
ZHANG SHIZHONG	ALT					SCM		BEIJING
ZHANG SHUXIANG	NO				DEP CO	MEM		JIANGXI
ZHANG SHUZHI	FULL				CO	SEC	VC	HENAN
ZHANG SIZHOU	ALT						VC	SICHUAN
ZHANG WANCHUN	NO				DEP CO		SCM	HEILONGJIANG
ZHANG XIUZHI	NO					SCM	SCM	HEILONGJIANG
ZHANG YAODONG	NO					SCM	SCM	HENAN
ZHANG YIAI	NO				DEP CO		SCM	SHANGHAI
ZHANG YING	NO				PC	SCM	VC	JILIN
ZHANG YUANHE	NO				DEP CO		SCM	JIANGXI
ZHANG YUHUA	NO		PC	WUHAN		SEC		HUBEI
ZHANG ZE	NO					SCM	VC	SHAANXI
ZHANG ZHAOREN	NO				PC	SEC		JILIN
ZHANG ZHENDONG	NO					MEM	SCM	ANHUI
ZHANG ZHENGGUAN	NO		PC	BEIJING		MEM	MEM	BEIJING
ZHANG ZHIXIU	NO					SEC	VC	SHANDONG
ZHANG ZHIYONG	NO				PC	SCM		JIANGXI
ZHANG ZHONG	NO				CO	SEC	VC	GANSU
ZHAO CHUNZHENG	NO					SCM	VC	BEIJING
ZHAO GUANGEN	NO				PC	SCM	SCM	HUNAN
ZHAO MAOXUN	NO				DEP CO	SCM	SCM	GUANGXI
ZHAO XINCHU	ALT					SEC	VC	HUBEI

NAME	CC	PB	MIL REG POS	MILITARY REGION	MIL DIS POS	PARTY POS	GOVT POS	PROVINCE
ZHAO XINRAN	NO				DEP CO	SCM	VC	GUANGXI
ZHAO XIU	NO					SEC	VC	HUBEI
ZHAO ZHIXI	NO					SCM	MEM	BEIJING
ZHAO ZIYANG	FULL					1S	CH	GUANGDONG
ZHENG GUO	NO				PC	SCM	SCM	JIANGXI
ZHENG JIQIAO	NO					SEC	1VC	JILIN
ZHENG SANSHENG	ALT		DEP CO	BEIJING			VC	HEBEI
ZHENG ZHISHI	NO		DEP CO	CHENGDU			SCM	SICHUAN
ZHONG GUOCHU	NO				DEP CO		SCM	ANHUI
ZHOU CHUNLIN	FULL		DEP CO	NANJING	CO	SEC	VC	SHANGHAI
ZHOU GUANG	NO					SCM	VC	JILIN
ZHOU GUANWU	NO		PC	NANJING			SCM	JIANGSU
ZHOU JIANREN	FULL					SEC	VC	ZHEJIANG
ZHOU LIQIN	FULL					SCM	VC	SHANGHAI
ZHOU MANTIAN	NO					SCM	SCM	FUJIAN
ZHOU MAOQIN	NO					SCM	SCM	SHAANXI
ZHOU SHUIDUO	NO					SCM	SCM	SHANDONG
ZHOU XING	FULL		1ST PC	KUNMING		1S	CH	YUNNAN
ZHU CHUANLIN	NO					SCM	VC	ZHEJIANG
ZHU GANG	NO					SCM	SCM	YUNNAN
ZHU PEIPING	NO					SCM	VC	GANSU
ZHU SHAOQING	NO		DEP CO	FUZHOU		SEC	VC	FUJIAN
ZHU YAOHUA	NO		DEP CO	FUZHOU		SCM	VC	FUJIAN
ZHU YEKUI	NO				PC	MEM	VC	HUBEI
ZHUO XIONG	NO					SEC	VC	FUJIAN
ZONG XIYUN	FULL					SCM	VC	JILIN
ZOU YAN	NO		PC	SHENYANG			MEM	LIAONING

Appendix F: PRC Elites Holding Interlocking Positions (1982)

NAME	CC	PB	MIL REG POS	MILITARY REGION	MIL DIS POS	PARTY POS	GOVT POS	PROVINCE
AN PINGSHENG	FULL				1ST PC	1S		YUNNAN
BA SANG	FULL					SEC		XIZANG
BAI DONGCAI	FULL				1ST PC	1S		JIANGXI
BAI JIEFU	NO					SCM	VM	BEIJING
BAI JINIAN	NO					SCM	VG	SHAANXI
BATU BAGEN	ALT					SEC		NEI MONGGOL
BUHE	FULL					DS	GOV	NEI MONGGOL
CHEN GUANGYI	NO					DS	GOV	GANSU
CHEN GUODONG	FULL				1ST PC	1S		SHANGHAI
CHEN LEI	FULL					SEC	GOV	HEILONGJIANG
CHEN RENHONG	FULL		PC	JINAN				
CHEN SUZHI	ALT					SCM		LIAONING
CHEN WEIDA	FULL				1ST PC	1S		TIANJIN
CHEN XITONG	FULL					SEC	MAY	BEIJING
CHI BIQING	FULL				1ST PC	1S		GUIZHOU
DAI SULI	FULL					SEC		LIAONING
DONG JICHANG	ALT					SEC		SHAANXI
DUAN JUNYI	CAC				1ST PC	1S		BEIJING
DUOJI CAIRANG	NO					SCM	VG	XIZANG
DUOJIE CAIDAN	NO					SEC	GOV	XIZANG
FU KUIQING	FULL		PC	FUZHOU				
GAO DEZHAN	ALT						VG	JILIN
GAO YANG	CAC				1ST PC	1S		HEBEI
GAO ZHANXIANG	ALT					SEC		HEBEI
GE SHIYING	NO					SCM	VG	GANSU
GU XIULIAN	FULL					DS	GOV	JIANGSU
GUAN GUANFU	NO				1ST PC	1S		HUBEI
GUO FENG	CAC				1ST PC	1S		LIAONING
HAN PEIXIN	FULL				1ST PC	1S		JIANGSU
HE HAOJU	NO					SCM	VG	SICHUAN
HE ZHUKANG	ALT					DS	GOV	HENAN
HEI BOLI	ALT					SEC	GOV	NINGXIA
HU HONG	FULL					SEC		FUJIAN
HU LIJIAO	FULL					SEC		SHANGHAI
HU PING	ALT					SEC	GOV	FUJIAN
HUANG DEMAO	ALT		DEP CO	KUNMING				
HUANG HUANG	NO				1ST PC	1S		ANHUI
HUANG JINGBO	NO					SEC	GOV	QINGHAI
HUANG ZHIZHEN	FULL					SEC	GOV	HUBEI
ISMAIL AYMAT	FULL		PC	URUMQI		SEC	GOV	XINJIANG
JIANABUER	ALT					SEC		XINJIANG
JIANG MINKUAN	ALT					DS	VG	SICHUAN
JIANG YONGHUI	FULL		DEP CO	SHENYANG				
JIAO LINYI	FULL					SEC		HUNAN
JIN BAOSHENG	ALT					SEC		GUANGXI
JIN XUN	NO					SCM	VG	JIANGSU
LI BIN	NO				CO	SCM		GANSU

NAME	CC	PB	MIL REG POS	MILITARY REGION	MIL DIS POS	PARTY POS	GOVT POS	PROVINCE
LI CHANG'AN	ALT					SEC		SHANDONG
LI DESHENG	FULL	F CO		SHENYANG				
LI FENG	ALT					SCM	VG	HEBEI
LI GUIXIAN	NO					SCM	VG	LIAONING
LI HUAMIN	ALT		DEP CO	SHENYANG				
LI JIAN'AN	NO					SCM	VG	GUANGDONG
LI LI'AN	FULL				1ST PC	1S		HEILONGJIANG
LI LIGONG	FULL				1ST PC	1S		SHANXI
LI QINGWEI	NO					SEC	GOV	SHAANXI
LI RUIHAN	FULL					SEC	MAY	TIANJIN
LI SHOUSHAN	ALT					SCM		XINJIANG
LI TIEYING	ALT					SEC		LIAONING
LI XIPU	FULL					SEC		SHAANXI
LI XUEZHI	FULL				1ST PC	1S		NINGXIA
LI YUNHE	NO					DS	VG	NINGXIA
LI ZHEN	NO					DS	VG	SHANDONG
LI ZIQI	FULL				1ST PC	1S		GANSU
LIANG BUTING	FULL					SEC	GOV	SHANDONG
LIANG LINGGUANG	FULL					SEC	GOV	GUANGDONG
LIAO HANSHENG	FULL		1ST PC	SHENYANG				
LIN RUO	FULL					SEC		GUANGDONG
LIU GUIQIAN	ALT					SEC		NEI MONGGOL
LIU JIE	CAC				1ST PC	1S		HENAN
LIU SHUSHENG	ALT					SEC		YUNNAN
LIU YUNZHAO	NO					SCM	VG	JILIN
LIU ZENGKUN	NO					SCM	VM	TIANJIN
LIU ZHENG	NO					SEC	GOV	HUNAN
LIU ZHENGWEI	FULL					SEC		HENAN
LIU ZHENHUA	FULL		PC	SHENYANG				
LIU ZHIJIAN	FULL		1ST PC	KUNMING				
LU DADONG	FULL					SCM		SICHUAN
LU GONGXUN	ALT					SCM		SHANXI
LU MAOZENG	ALT					SEC		SHANDONG
LUO GAN	ALT					SEC		HENAN
LUO SHANGCAI	ALT						VG	GUIZHOU
MA SIZHONG	ALT					SCM	VG	NINGXIA
MA WEIHUA	ALT		DEP CO	BEIJING				
MA WENRUI	FULL				1ST PC	1S		SHAANXI
MA XINGYUAN	FULL					SEC		FUJIAN
MAO ZHIYONG	FULL				1ST PC	1S		HUNAN
NI XIANCE	NO					SCM	VG	JIANGXI
NIAN DEXIANG	ALT						VG	GANSU
PU CHAOZHU	NO					DS	GOV	YUNNAN
QIANG XIAOCHU	FULL				1ST PC	1S		JILIN
QIAO XIAOGUANG	FULL				1ST PC	1S		GUANGXI
QIAO XUETING	ALT		PC	CHENGDU				
QIN JIWEI	FULL	A CO		BEIJING				
QIN YINGJI	FULL					SEC		GUANGXI
QUAN SHUREN	NO					SEC	GOV	LIAONING
RE DI	FULL					SEC		XIZANG
REN RONG	ALT		PC	WUHAN				
REN ZHONGYI	FULL				1ST PC	1S		GUANGDONG
RUAN CHONGWU	NO					SEC	VM	SHANGHAI
SHEN YINLUO	FULL					SEC		HUBEI
SU GANG	FULL					SEC		GUIZHOU
SU HUA	NO					SCM	VG	ANHUI
SU YIRAN	FULL				1ST PC	1S		SHANDONG
SUN WEIBEN	ALT					SEC		LIAONING
TAN QILONG	FULL					SCM		SICHUAN
TIAN SHIXING	ALT		DEP CO	FUZHOU				
TIAN YING	NO					SCM	VG	HUBEI
TIEMUER DAWAMAI	FULL					SEC		XINJIANG
WAN HAIFENG	FULL		PC	CHENGDU				
WANG CHAOWEN	FULL					SEC	GOV	GUIZHOU
WANG CHENGHAN	FULL		CO	CHENGDU		SCM		SICHUAN
WANG DAOHAN	NO					SEC	MAY	SHANGHAI
WANG ENMAO	FULL		1ST PC	URUMQI		1S		XINJIANG
WANG FANG	FULL				1ST PC	1S		ZHEJIANG
WANG GUANGYU	FULL					SEC		ANHUI
WANG GUANGZHONG	FULL					SCM	VG	LIAONING

NAME	CC	PB	MIL REG POS	MILITARY REGION	MIL DIS POS	PARTY POS	GOVT POS	PROVINCE
WANG KEWEN	FULL					SEC		SHANXI
WANG MENG	FULL		PC	GUANGZHOU				HUBEI
WANG QUANGUO	FULL					SEC		HUBEI
WANG QUN	ALT				PC	SEC		HUBEI
WANG SENHAO	NO					DS	GOV	SHANXI
WANG YUZHAO	NO					SEC	GOV	ANHUI
WANG ZHUGUANG	NO					SCM	VG	GUANGXI
WEI CHUNSHU	NO					DS	GOV	GUANGXI
WEI JINSHAN	ALT		PC	NANJING				
WU LIE	NO		PC	BEIJING	PC	SCM		BEIJING
WU MINDA	NO					DS	VG	ZHEJIANG
WU SHENGRONG	NO		DEP CO	LANZHOU	CO	SCM		QINGHAI
WU ZHEN	NO					SEC	VM	TIANJIN
XIANG NAN	FULL				1ST PC	1S		FUJIAN
XIANG SHOUZHI	FULL		DEP CO	NANJING				
XIAO QUANFU	FULL		CO	URUMQI		SCM		XINJIANG
XIE FENG	FULL					SEC		HEBEI
XIE ZHENHUA	FULL		PC	KUNMING				
XIN JUNJIE	NO				CO	SCM		JIANGXI
XING CHONGZHI	ALT					SEC		HEBEI
XU QIN	ALT					SEC		JIANGXI
XU SHAOFU	FULL					SEC		LIAONING
XUE JU	FULL					DS	GOV	ZHEJIANG
YAN ZHENG	ALT		PC	WUHAN				
YANG CHENGWU	FULL		CO	FUZHOU				
YANG DI	FULL					SEC		SHANGHAI
YANG RUDAI	FULL				1ST PC	1S		SICHUAN
YANG XIZONG	ALT					DS	GOV	SICHUAN
YANGLING DUOJI	ALT					SEC		XIZANG
YIN FATANG	FULL		PC	CHENGDU	1ST PC	1S		XIZANG
YIN KESHENG	NO					SCM	VG	QINGHAI
YU MINGTAO	FULL					SEC		HENAN
YUAN FANGLIE	ALT					SCM		ZHEJIANG
YUAN JUN	ALT		DEP CO	SHENYANG				
ZHANG GENSHENG	ALT					SEC		JILIN
ZHANG JIANMIN	ALT					SCM		SHANXI
ZHANG SHENGZHEN	NO					SCM	VG	GUANGXI
ZHANG SHUGUANG	FULL					SEC	GOV	HEBEI
ZHANG XUDENG	ALT				CO			GUANGXI
ZHANG YUHUAN	NO					SCM	VG	GUIZHOU
ZHANG ZAIWANG	FULL					SEC		TIANJIN
ZHANG ZHAOWAN	NO					SCM	VG	ZHEJIANG
ZHANG ZHIXIU	FULL		CO	KUNMING				
ZHAO HAIFENG	FULL				1ST PC	1S		QINGHAI
ZHAO NANQI	FULL				PC	SEC		JILIN
ZHAO XINGYUAN	FULL		PC	SHENYANG	PC	SCM		HEILONGJIANG
ZHAO XIU	NO					SEC	GOV	JILIN
ZHAO ZENGYI	NO					SEC	GOV	JIANGXI
ZHAO ZHIJIAN	FULL					SCM		JIANGXI
ZHENG SANSHENG	FULL		DEP CO	JINAN				
ZHOU HUI	FULL				1ST PC	1S		NEI MONGGOL
ZHOU SHIZHONG	FULL		CO	WUHAN				
ZHU HOUZE	ALT					SEC		GUIZHOU

Bibliography

Books

Atkinson, Littleton B. Dual Command in the Red Army. Maxwell Air Force Base, Alabama: Air University Documentary Research Study, 1950.

Barnard, Chester I. The Functions of the Executive. Cambridge, Mass.: Harvard University Press, 1968.

Barnett, A. Doak. Cadres, Bureaucracy, and Political Power in Communist China. New York: Columbia University Press, 1967.

──────, ed. Chinese Communist Politics in Action. Seattle: University of Washington Press, 1969.

──────. Uncertain Passage--China's Transition to the Post-Mao Era. Washington, D.C.: The Brookings Institution, 1974.

Biographical Sketches of Chinese Communist Military Leaders, Taipei: Office of Military History, US Military Assistance Advisory Group, March 1971.

Brzezinski, Zbigniew, ed. Political Controls in the Soviet Army. New York: Research Program on the USSR, 1954.

Bureau of Intelligence, Ministry of National Defense, Republic of China, pamphlet, Fei Hsien Hsing Kuo Fang Tzu Chih Tse-Hsi (Current National Defense Organization System in Communist China), Taipei, Taiwan: 1976.

Carlson, Evans Fordyce. The Chinese Army: Its Organization and Military Efficiency. New York: Institute of Pacific Relations, 1940.

Central Intelligence Agency. Directory of Chinese Communist Officials: Provincial, Municipal and Military, A-69-5, April 1969.

──────. Directory of Chinese Communist Officials: Party, Provincial, Municipal and Military, A-70-13, May 1970.

──────. Directory of Chinese Communist Officials. A-71-14, May 1971.

_____. Communist China: Revolutionary Government in the Provinces. December 1968.
_____. Directory of the People's Republic of China, A-73-35, January 1974.
_____. Directory of Officials of the People's Republic of China, CR-78-16506, November 1978.
Chang, Parris. Power and Policy in China. University Park: Penn State University Press, 1975.
Chen, Jerome. Mao and the Chinese Revolution. London: Oxford University Press, 1965.
Ch'eng, J. Chester, ed. The Politics of the Chinese Red Army. Stanford, California: Stanford University Press, 1966.
Chi, Hsi-sheng. Warlord Politics in China, 1916-1928. Stanford, California: Stanford University Press, 1976.
Chiang, Kai-shek. Soviet Russia in China. New York: Ferrar, Straus, and Cudahy, 1958.
Chien, Yu-shen. China's Fading Revolution: Army Dissent Divisions, 1967-1968. Hong Kong: Centre of Contemporary Chinese Studies, 1969.
Chinese Military Leaders--1964. Taipei, Taiwan. MAAG Hqs, 1964.
Chiu, S.M. Chinese Communist Revolutionary Strategy, 1945-1949. Princeton, New Jersey: Princeton University Press, 15 December 1961.
Chung Kung Nien Pao (Yearbook on Chinese Communism). Taipei, Taiwan: Institute for the Study of Chinese Communist Problems, each year 1970-1982.
The Constitution of the People's Republic of China. Peking: Foreign Languages Press, 1975 and 1983.
Crozier, Michel. The Bureaucratic Phenomenon. Chicago: University of Chicago Press, 1963.
Defense Intelligence Agency, Handbook on the Chinese Armed Forces. DDI-2680-32-76, July 1976.
Deng, Xiaoping. Deng Xiaoping Wen Xuan (1975-1982) (Selected Works of Deng Xiaoping). Beijing: People's Press, 1983.
Dittmer, Lowell. Liu Shao-ch'i and the Chinese Cultural Revolution: The Politics of Mass Criticism. Berkeley: University of California Press, 1974.
Djilas, Milovan. The New Class. New York: Praeger, 1957.
Domes, Juergen. The Internal Politics of China, 1949-1972. New York: Praeger, 1973.
Ebon, Martin. Lin Piao: The Life and Writings of China's New Ruler. New York: Stein and Day, 1970.
Elegant, Robert S. China's Red Masters: Political Biographies of the Chinese Communist Leaders. New York: Twayne, 1951.
Fairbank, John K. The United States and China. Third Edition, Cambridge, Mass.: Harvard University Press, 1971.

Fedotoff-White, D. _The Growth of the Red Army_. Princeton, New Jersey: Princeton University Press, 1944.

Feng, Yu-lan. _A Short History of Chinese Philosophy_. ed. Derk Bodde, New York: MacMillan, 1948.

Finer, S.E. _The Man on Horseback_. New York: Praeger, 1962.

Fraser, Angus M. _The Changing Role of the PLA Under the Impact of the Cultural Revolution_. Research Paper P-524, Washington D.C.: Institute for Defense Analysis, July 1969.

Garvey, James E. _Marxist-Leninist China: Military and Social Doctrine_. New York: Exposition Press, 1960.

George, Alexander. _The Chinese Communist Army in Action: The Korean War and its Aftermath_. New York: Columbia University Press, 1967.

Gillin, Donald. _Warlord Yen Hsi-shan in Shansi Province, 1911-1949_. Princeton, New Jersey: Princeton University Press, 1967.

Gittings, John. _The Role of the Chinese Army_. London: Oxford University Press, 1967.

Godwin, Paul H. B. _The Chinese Defense Establishment: Continuity and Change in the 1980's_. Boulder, Colorado: Westview Press, 1983.

Goodman, David S.G., ed. _Groups and Politics in the People's Republic of China_. Armonk, New York: M. E. Sharpe Inc., 1984.

The Great Power Struggle in China. Hong Kong: Asia Research Centre, 1969.

Griffith, Samuel B. _The Chinese People's Liberation Army_. New York: McGraw-Hill Book Co., 1967.

_____. _Mao Tse-tung on Guerrilla Warfare_. New York: Praeger, 1962.

_____. _Peking and People's Wars_. London: Pall Mall Press, 1966.

Harrison, James P. _The Long March to Power--A History of the Chinese Communist Party, 1921-1972_. New York: Praeger, 1972.

Harding, Harry. _Organizing China: The Problem of Bureaucracy 1949-1976_. Stanford: Stanford University Press, 1981.

Hart, B. H. Liddel, ed. _The Red Army_. New York: Harcourt, Brace and Company, 1956.

Hinton, Harold C. _Leaders in Communist China_. Santa Monica: The Rand Corporation, 1956.

Hsieh, Alice L. _Communist China's Strategy in the Nuclear Era_. Englewood Cliffs, New Jersey: Prentice-Hall Inc., 1962.

Hsu, Francis L.K. _Americans and Chinese: Two Ways of Life_. New York: Henry Schuman, 1953.

Hsu, Kai-yu. _Chou En-lai: China's Gray Eminence_. Garden City, New York: Doubleday and Co., 1968.

Hsiung, S. I. _The Life of Chiang Kai-shek_. Shanghai: China Publishing Co., 1937.

Huang, Chen-hsia. *Mao's Generals*. Hong Kong: Research Institute of Contemporary History, 1968.
Institute for the Study of Chinese Communist Problems, *1981 Yearbook on Chinese Communism*, (Taipei: 1981). Also from other years from 1976-1983.
Jencks, Harlan W. *From Muskets to Missiles: Politics and Professionalism in the Chinese Army, 1945-1981*. Boulder, Colorado: Westview Press, 1982.
Joffe, Ellis. *The Chinese Red Army: Growth and Professionalism and Party-Army Relations, 1949-1963*. Cambridge, Massachusetts: East Asian Research Center, Harvard University, 1963.
_____. *Party and Army, Professionalism and Political Control in the Chinese Officer Corps, 1949-1964*. Cambridge, Massachusetts: Harvard University Press, 1965.
Johnson, Chalmers A. *Peasant Nationalism and Communist Power*. Stanford, California: Stanford University Press, 1962.
Kao, Michael Ying-mao, ed. *The Lin Piao Affair: Power Politics and the Military Coup*. White Plains, New York: International Arts and Sciences Press, 1975.
_____. *The People's Liberation Army and China's Nation-Building*. White Plains, New York: International Arts and Sciences Press, 1973.
_____, et al. *The Political Work System of the Chinese Communist Military*. Providence: East Asia Language and Area Center, Brown University 1971.
Klein, Donald W. and Anne B. Clark. *Biographic Dictionary of Chinese Communism, 1921-1965*. 2 Volumes. Cambridge, Massachusetts: Harvard University Press, 1971.
Kolkowicz, Roman. *The Soviet Military and the Communist Party*. Princeton, New Jersey: Princeton University Press, 1967.
Lewis, John W. *Leadership in Communist China*. Ithaca, New York: Cornell University Press, 1963.
Lifton, Robert J., *Revolutionary Immortality: Mao Tsetung and the Chinese Cultural Revolution*. New York: Random House Vintage Books, 1968.
Lindbeck, John M. H., ed. *China: Management of a Revolutionary Society*. Seattle: University of Washington Press, 1971.
Linebarger, Paul M. A. *The Political Doctrines of Sun Yat Sen*. Taipei: China Publishing Company, 1957.
Liu, F. F. *A Military History of Modern China, 1924-1949*. Princeton, New Jersey: Princeton University Press, 1956.
Liu, Shaoqi. *Liu Shaoqi Ji Xuan Ji* (Selected Works). 2 Volumes. Beijing: People's Press, 1981.
Maitan, Livio. *Party, Army and Masses in China--A Marxist Interpretation of the Cultural Revolution and its Aftermath*. London: Humanities Press, 1976.

Mao, Tse-tung. *Selected Military Writings*. Peking: Foreign Languages Press, 1963.

_____. *Selected Works*. 5 Volumes. New York: International Publishers, 1954.

Ministry of National Defense. *Cheng Chih Tso Chan Shih Lieh* (Historical Examples of Political Warfare), 4 Volumes. Taipei: Ministry of National Defense, History Bureau, 1964.

Moody, Peter R. Jr. *Chinese Politics After Mao*. New York: Praeger, 1983.

Mouzellis, Nicos P. *Organization and Bureaucracy: An Analysis of Modern Theories*. Chicago: Aldine Publishing Co., 1967.

Muller, David G. Jr. *China as a Maritime Power*. Boulder, Colorado: Westview Press, 1983.

National Foreign Assessment Center, *Directory of Officials of the People's Republic of China* (Washington D.C.: US Government Printing Office, October 1977).

Nelsen, Harvey W. *The Chinese Military System: An Organizational Study of the Chinese People's Liberation Army*. Boulder, Colorado: Westview Press, 1977.

Payne, Robert. *Portrait of a Revolutionary: Mao Tse-tung*. New York: Abelard-Schuman, 1961.

Peters, Thomas J. and Robert H. Waterman, Jr., *In Search of Excellence: Lessons from America's Best-Run Companies*. New York: Warner Books, 1984

Phipps, Ramsay Weston. *The Armies of the First French Republic*. 5 Volumes. London: Oxford University Press, 1926.

Political Warfare Historical Editing Committee, *KuoChun Cheng-gung Shihkao* (History of Political Work in the National Army). 3 Volumes. Taipei: Ministry of National Defense, 1960.

Political Warfare Staff College. *Cheng Chih Tso Chan Kai Lun* (General Discussion of Political Warfare). Fuhsingkang, Taiwan: Political Warfare Staff College, May 1960.

Pool, Ithiel de Sola. *Satellite Generals: A Study of Military Elites in the Soviet Sphere*. Stanford, California: Stanford University Press, 1955.

Powell, Ralph L. *Politico-Military Relationships in Communist China*. Washington D.C.: External Research Staff, Bureau of Intelligence and Research, United States Department of State, 1963.

Price, Jane L. *Cadres, Commanders, and Commissars--The Training of the Chinese Communist Leadership, 1920-1945*. Boulder, Colorado: Westview Press, 1976.

Pye, Lucian. *The Dynamics of Factions and Consensus in Chinese Politics: A Model and Some Propositions*. Santa Monica, California: Rand Corporation, 1980.

_____. *The Dynamics of Chinese Politics*. Cambridge, Massachusetts: Oelgeschlager, Gunn and Hain Publishers, 1981.

Reischauer, Edwin O., and John K. Fairbank. *East Asia, The Great Tradition*. Boston: Houghton Mifflin Company, 1958.

Rice, Edward E. *Mao's Way*. Berkeley: University of California Press, 1972.

Rigg, Robert B. *Red China's Fighting Hordes*. Harrisburg, Pennsylvania: Military Service Publishing Co., 1951.

Rhoads, Edward J. M. *The Chinese Red Army, 1927-1963: An Annotated Bibliography*. Cambridge, Massachusetts: Harvard University Press, 1964.

Roberts, Thomas C. *The Chinese People's Militia and the Doctrine of People's War*. Washington D.C.: National Defense University Press, 1983.

Robinson, Thomas. *A Politico-Military Biography of Lin Piao, Part I, 1907-1949*. Santa Monica, California: Rand Corporation, 1971.

Scalapino, Robert A., ed. *Elites in the People's Republic of China*. Seattle: University of Washington Press, 1972

Schram, Stuart R. *Mao Tse-tung*. New York: Simon and Schuster, 1967.

Schurmann, Franz. *Ideology and Organization in Communist China*. 2nd Edition. Berkeley: University of California Press, 1968.

Segal, Gerald and William T. Tow. *Chinese Defense Policy*. London and Basingstroke: The MacMillan Press, 1984.

Selznick, Philip. *Leadership in Administration*. Evanston, Illinois: Row and Peterson, 1957.

Sheridan, James E. *Chinese Warlord: The Career of Feng Yu-hsiang*. Stanford, California: Stanford University Press, 1966.

Simon, Herbert A. *Administrative Behavior--A Study of Decision-Making Processes in Administrative Organization*. 2nd Edition. New York: Free Press, 1956.

Smedley, Agnes. *The Great Road: The Life and Times of Chu Teh*. New York: Monthly Review Press, 1956.

Snow, Edgar. *The Other Side of the River: Red China Today*. New York: Random House, 1962.

Snow, Helen Foster. *The Chinese Communists: Sketches and Autobiographies of the Old Guard*. Westport, Connecticut: Greenwood Publishing, 1972.

Solomon, Richard. *Mao's Revolution and the Chinese Political Culture*. Berkeley: University of California Press, 1971.

Starr, John B. *Ideology and Culture*. New York: Harper and Row, 1973.

Starr, John B. and Nancy Dyer. *Post-Liberation Works of Mao Zedong: A Bibliography and Index*. Berkeley: Center for Chinese Studies, 1976.

Sun, Chin-ming. *Chungguo Pingchihshih* (A History of Chinese Military Systems). Taipei: United Publishers Center, 1960.

Sun, Yat Sen. *San Min Chu I*. Taipei: China Publishing Co., n.d.

Swanson, Bruce. *Eighth Voyage of the Dragon: A History of China's Quest for Seapower*. Annapolis, Maryland: Naval Institute Press, 1982.

Tanham, George K. *Communist Revolutionary Warfare--From the Vietminh to the Vietcong*. New York: Praeger, 1961.

Taylor, Frederick W. *Scientific Management*. New York: Harper and Row, 1911.

Teiwes, Frederick. *Provincial Party Personnel in Mainland China, 1956-1966*. New York: Occasional Papers of the East Asian Institute, Columbia University, 1967.

_____. *Leadership, Legitimacy and Conflict in China*. Armonk, New York: M. E. Sharpe Inc., 1984.

Thompson, James D. *Organizations in Action*. New York: McGraw-Hill, 1967.

Townsend, James R. *Political Participation in Communist China*. Berkeley: University of California Press, 1969.

The Twelfth National Congress of the CPC (September 1982). Beijing: Foreign Languages Press, 1982.

Union Research Institute. *Hierarchies in the People's Republic of China, March 1975*. Hong Kong: Union Research Institute, 1975.

_____. *Source Book on Military Affairs in the People's Republic of China*. Hong Kong: Union Press Ltd., 1965.

_____. *Who's Who in Communist China*. Hong Kong: Union Research Institute, 1965.

United States Department of State, Bureau of Intelligence and Research. *Directory of Party and Government Officials of Communist China*. 2 Volumes. BD. 271, July 20, 1960.

United States Senate, Committee on Government Operations, Subcommittee on National Policy Machinery. *National Policy Machinery in Communist China*. Washington D.C.: Government Printing Office, 1960.

Vogel, Ezra F. *Canton Under Communism: Programs and Politics in a Provincial Capital, 1949-1968*. Cambridge, Massachusetts: Harvard University Press, 1969.

Wallon, Henri. *Les Representants du Peuple en Mission et la Justice Revolutionnaire dans les Departments en l'an II (1793-1794)*. 5 Volumes. Paris: Hachette, 1889-1890.

Wang Sheng. *Political Warfare*. Taipei: Ministry of National Defense, 1963.

Weber, Max. *The Theory of Social and Economic Organization*. Trans. A. Henderson and T. Parsons. London: William Hodge, 1947.

Whiting, Kenneth. *The Chinese Communist Armed Forces*. Maxwell Air Force Base, Alabama: Air University, 1967.

Whitson, William W. *Chinese Military and Political Leaders and the Distribution of Power in China, 1956-1971.* Santa Monica, California: The Rand Corporation, R-1091-DOS/ARPA, May 1973.

_____, ed. *The Military and Political Power in China in the 1970's.* New York: Praeger, 1972.

Whitson, William W., and Chen-Hsia Huang. *The Chinese High Command--A History of Chinese Military Politics, 1927-1971.* New York: Praeger, 1973.

Wilson, Amy Auerbacher; Greenblatt, Sidney Leonard; Wilson, Richard W. (Eds).*Methodological Issues in Chinese Studies.* New York: Praeger, 1983.

Zhongguo Gongchandang Di Shierce Quanguo Daibiao Dahui Wenjian, (Documents of the 12th Party Congress of the Chinese Communist Party), Hong Kong: Joint Publishing Co., September 1982).

Articles

"Against One-Sided Emphasis on Modernization." *Liberation Army News* in *Joint Publications Research Service.* 1357 N (March 16, 1959): 1-4.

"Actively Launch Criticism and Self-Criticism." *Red Flag* 16 (16 April 1981): 2-4,22.

Almond, Gabriel A. "Interest Groups and the Political Process" in Roy C. Macridis and Bernard Brown, eds. *Comparative Politics: Notes and Readings.* Homewood, Illinois: The Dorsey Press, 1968: 181-197.

An, Thomas S. "Mao Tse-tung Purges Military Professionalism." *Military Review,* 48 (August 1968): 88-98.

Barber, Charles H. "China's Political Officer System." *Military Review,* 33 (July 1953): 11-21.

Barnett, A. Doak. "Social Stratification and Aspects of Personnel Management in the Chinese Communist Bureaucracy." *China Quarterly,* 28 (Oct.-Dec. 1966): 8-39.

Baum, Richard D. "'Red and Expert': The Politico-Ideological Foundations of China's Great Leap Forward." *Asian Survey,* 4 (September 1964): 1048-1057).

Bennett, Gordon A. "Elites and Society in China: A Summary of Research and Interpretation," in Robert A. Scalapino, ed. *Elites in the People's Republic of China.* Seattle: University of Washington Press, 1972: 3-37.

_____. "Military Regions and Provincial Party Secretaries: One Outcome of China's Cultural Revolution." *China Quarterly,* 54 (April/June 1973): 294-307.

Bullard, Monte R. "Political Warfare in Vietnam." *Military Review*, 49 (October 1969): 48-59.
_____. "The US-China Defense Relationship." *Parameters*, Vol. XIII, No. 1 (March 1983): 43-50.
Candlin, A. H. S. "China: The Army, the Party, and the People." *Military Review*, 51 (February 1971): 24-32. Longer version in the *Journal of the Royal United Service Institution* (Great Britain)(September 1970): 1-11.
Chamberlain, Heath B. "Transition and Consolidation in Urban China: A Study of Leaders and Organizations in Three Cities, 1949-1953," in Robert A. Scalapino, *Elites in the People's Republic of China*. Seattle: University of Washington Press, 1972: 245-301.
Chang, Parris. "Mao's Last Stand." *Problems of Communism*, 4 (July-August 1976): 1-17.
_____. "Changing Patterns of Military Roles in Chinese Politics," in William W. Whitson, ed. *The Military and Political Power in China in the 1970's.* New York: Praeger, 1972: 47-72.
_____. "Decentralization of Power." *Problems of Communism*, 21 (July/August 1972): 67-74.
_____. "Mao Tse-tung and His Generals: Some Observations on Military Intervention in Chinese Politics," in Frank B. Horton, et al., eds., *Comparative Defense Policy*. Baltimore: Johns Hopkins University Press, 1974: 121-128.
_____. "Political Profiles: Wang Hung-wen and Li Teh-sheng." *China Quarterly*, 57 (January-March 1974): 124-131.
_____. "Provincial Party Leaders' Strategies for Survival During the GPCR," in Robert A. Scalapino, ed., *Elites in the People's Republic of China*. Seattle: University of Washington Press, 1972: 501-539.
_____. "Regional Military Power: The Aftermath of the Cultural Revolution." *Military Review*, 53 (May 1973): 80-94. Reprinted from *Asian Survey*, (December 1972): 999-1013.
Cheng, Chester J. "The Dynamics of the Chinese PLA: Regularization and Revolutionization 1949-1959." *Military Review*, 54 (May 1974): 79-89.
_____. "Problems of Chinese Communist Leadership as seen in the Secret Papers." *Asian Survey*, 4 (June 1964): 861-872.
Chien, S. M. "The Chiang Ch'ing Faction and Peping's Military Forces." *Issues and Studies*, 12 (January 1976): 12-30.
Chiu, S. M. "The Chinese Communist Army in Transition." *Far Eastern Survey*, 21 (November 1958): 168-175.
_____. "Chinese Communist Military Leadership." *Military Review*, 39 (March 1960): 59-66.

_____. "The PLA and the Party: Recent Developments." *Military Review*, 43 (June 1963): 58-66.

_____. "Political Control in the Chinese Communist Army." *Military Review*, 41 (August 1961): 25-35.

Chu Teh. "People's Army, People's War." *Jen Min Jih Pao* (Peking), 31 July 1958.

Cole, D. M. "Political Commissars--Past and Future." *Army Quarterly*, 40 (February 1943): 202-204.

"Communique: Of the Third Plenary Session of the 11th Central Committee of the Communist Party of China," *Beijing Review* 52 (29 December 1978).

Deane, Michael J. "The Main Political Administration as a Factor in Communist Party Control over the Military in the Soviet Union." *Armed Forces and Society*, 3 (Winter 1977): 295-324.

deB. Mills, William. "Generational Change in China." *Problems of Communism* Vol XXXII (Nov-Dec 1983): 16-35.

Dick, Glen G. "The General Political Department" in William W. Whitson, ed., *The Military and Political Power in China in the 1970's*. New York: Praeger, 1972: 171-184.

Domes, Juergen. "The Cultural Revolution and the Army." *Asian Survey*, 8 (May 1968): 349-363.

_____. "Generals and Red Guards." *Asia Quarterly*, (January 1971): 3-32 and (February 1971): 123-160.

_____. "Problems of the Chinese Communist Armed Forces," in Richard F. Staar, ed., *Aspects of Modern Communism*. Columbia, South Carolina: University of South Carolina Press, 1968: 259-285.

_____. "The Role of the Military in the Formation of Revolutionary Committees, 1967-1968." *China Quarterly*, 44 (Oct-Dec 1970): 112-145.

_____. "Some Results of the Cultural Revolution in China." *Asian Survey*, (September 1971): 932-940.

Doolin, Dennis J. "'Both Red and Expert': The Dilemma of the Chinese Intellectual." *Current Scene*, 2 (1 September 1963): 1-9.

Dreyer, June Teufel. "China's Military in the 1980's." *Current History*, 83-294 (September 1984): 276-278.

Elegant, Robert S., and Sidney C. Liu. "Red China's Divided Army." *Military Review*, 47 (November 1967): 31-38.

Elmquist, Paul. "The Internal Role of the Military," in William W. Whitson, ed. *The Military and Political Power in China in the 1970's*. New York: Praeger, 1972: 269-290.

Ermarth, Fritz. "Soviet Military Politics." *Military Review*, 48 (January 1968): 32-36.

Falkenheim, Victor C. "Continuing Central Predominance." *Problems of Communism*, 21 (July-August 1972): 75-83.

_____. "Provincial Leadership in Fukien: 1949-1966," in Robert A. Scalapino, ed. *Elites in the*

People's Republic of China. Seattle: University of Washington Press, 1972: 199-244.

_____. "Bureaucracy, Factions and Political Change in China," Pacific Affairs, 57-3 (Fall 1984): 471-480.

Fan Ke. "The Orientation of Political Work for the Army." Jen Min Jih Pao (Peking)(28 July 1961): trans. in Survey of the China Mainland Press, 2556, (11 August 1961): 1-12.

Fang, Chun-kuei. "Military Dictatorship Under Mao's Regime." Issues and Studies, 8 (October 1971): 23-37.

"Four Sets of Regulations on Political Work in Company-Level Units of PLA Promulgated for Enforcement." Survey of the China Mainland Press, 2630 (December 1, 1961): 1-3.

Galay, Nicolai. "The Relationship between the Structure of Society and the Armed Forces as Illustrated by the USSR." Bulletin, 13 (November 1966): 3-20 and 13 (December 1966): 3-16.

Gittings, John. "Army-Party Relations in the Light of the Cultural Revolution," in John W. Lewis, ed. Party Leadership and Revolutionary Power in China. Cambridge: Cambridge University Press, 1970: 373-403.

_____. "The Chinese Army," in Jack Gray, ed. Modern China's Search for a Political Form. London: Oxford University Press, 1969: 187-224.

_____. "China's Militia." China Quarterly, 18 (April-June 1964): 100-117.

_____. "The 'Learn from the Army' Campaign." China Quarterly, 18 (April-June 1964): 153-159.

_____. "Military Control and Leadership, 1954-1964." China Quarterly, 26 (April-June 1966): 82-101.

_____. "Political Control of the Chinese Army." World Today, 19 (August 1963): 327-336.

Godwin, Paul H. B. "The PLA and Political Control in China's Provinces." Comparative Politics, 9 (October 1976): 1-20.

Gregor, William J. "The Political Problem of the People's Army." Military Review, 55 (April 1975): 3-14.

Halperin, Morton H., and John Wilson Lewis. "Communist China Army-Party Relations." Military Review, 47 (February 1967): 71-78.

_____. "New Tensions in Army-Party Relations in China, 1965-1966." China Quarterly, 26 (April-June 1966): 58-67.

Harding, Harry. "China After Mao." Problems of Communism, 26 (March-April 1977): 1-18.

_____. "China: The Fragmentation of Power." Asian Survey, 12 (January 1972): 1-15.

_____. "Competing Models of the Chinese Communist Policy Process: Toward a Sorting and Evaluation," in *Issues and Studies*, XX (February 1984): 13-36.

_____. "The Evolution of Chinese Military Policy," in Frank B. Horton et al., eds., *Comparative Defense Policy*, Baltimore: Johns Hopkins University Press, 1974: 216-232.

_____. "Leadership Succession in the People's Republic of China." *Symposium Proceedings: Perspectives on National Leadership Succession*. Washington D.C.: Mathematica Inc., June 1975: 82-86.

Harrigan, Anthony. "Men Over Weapons." *Military Review*, 45 (January 1965): 12-16.

Hinton, Harold C. "Political Aspects of Military Power and Policy in Communist China," in Harry L. Coles, ed., *Total War and Cold War: Problems in Civilian Control of the Military*. Columbus, Ohio: Ohio State University Press, 1962: 266-292.

Hsiao Hua. "Participation in National Construction is a Glorious Task of the PLA." *Hung Ch'i* (August 1, 1959). *Survey of China Mainland Magazines*, 182 (September 1, 1959): 1-8.

Hsieh, Alice L. "China's Nuclear Missile Programme: Regional or Intercontinental?" *China Quarterly*, 45 (January-March 1971): 85-89.

_____. "China's Secret Military Papers: Military Doctrine and Strategy." *China Quarterly*, 18 (April-June 1964): 79-99.

Hua Kuo-feng. "Speech at the Second National Conference on Learning from Tachai in Agriculture," trans. in *Peking Review*, 1 (January 1977): 43-44.

Jencks, Harlan W. "People's War Under Modern Conditions: Wishful Thinking, National Suicide or Effective Deterrent?" *China Quarterly*, 98 (June 1984): 305-320.

Joffe, Ellis. "The Army After Mao, " *International Journal*, 34 Autumn 1979)| 568-584.

_____. "The Chinese Army After the Cultural Revolution: The Effects of Intervention." *China Quarterly*, 55 (July-September 1973): 450-477.

_____. "The Chinese Army in the Cultural Revolution: The Politics of Intervention." *Current Scene* (7 December 1970): 1-7.

_____. "The Chinese Army under Lin Piao: Prelude to Political Intervention," in J. M. H. Lindbeck, ed., *China, Management of a Revolutionary Society*. Seattle: University of Washington Press, 1971: 343-374.

_____. "The Communist Party and the Army." E. Stuart Kirby, ed. *Contemporary China*, Volume 4. Hong Kong: Hong Kong University Press, 1961: 55-69.

_____. "The Conflict Between Old and New in the Chinese Army." *China Quarterly*, 18 (April-June 1964): 118-140.

_____. "Conflict in Red China's Army." *Military Review*, 44 (December 1964): 70-82.

_____. "Contradictions in the Chinese Army." *Far Eastern Economic Review*, 41(July 11, 1963):123-126.

_____. "The PLA in Internal Politics." *Problems of Communism*, 24 (November-December 1975): 1-12.

_____. "The Soldier's Role." *Far Eastern Economic Review*, 29 (September 1, 1960): 477-479.

Joffe, Ellis and Gerald Segal, "The Chinese Army and Professionalism." *Problems of Communism*, 27 (Nov-Dec 1978): 1-19.

Johnson, Chalmers. "Caesarism in China." *Encounter* (December 1976): 76-83.

_____. "Lin Piao's Army and Its Role in Chinese Society." *Current Scene*, (1 July 1966): 1-10 and (15 July 1966): 1-11.

Johnston, Alastair I. "Changing Party-Army Relations in China 1979-1984", *Asian Survey* 10 (October 1984): 1012-1040.

Jordan, James D. "The Maoist vs the Professional Vision of a People's Army," in William W. Whitson, ed., *The Military and Political Power in China in the 1970's*. New York: Praeger, 1972: 25-45.

_____. "Political Orientation of the PLA." *Current Scene*, 9 (November 1973): 1-15.

Jowitt, Ken. "An Organizational Approach to the Study of Political Culture in Marxist-Leninist Systems." *The American Political Science Review*, 68 (September 1974): 1171-1191.

Kashin, A. "The Ideology of Military Control," in William Liu, *Chinese Society Under Communism*. New York: Wiley, 1967: 141-150.

Kao, Michael Ying-mao and P. M. Perrolle. "Politics of Lin Piao's Military Coup." *Asian Survey*, 14 (June 1974): 558-577.

Kong, Allen S. H. "Comradeship in Arms: An Analysis of Power through Associations in the CPLA--February 1970 to February 1974." *Asian Survey*, 14 (July 1974): 663-677.

Lewis, John W. "China's Secret Military Papers: 'Continuities' and 'Revelations'." *China Quarterly*, 18 (April-June 1964): 68-78.

Li, Ming-hua. "The CCP Leadership and Party Works in 1975." *Issues and Studies*, 12(February 1976):53-79.

_____. "The Chinese Communist Leadership Reorganization." *Issues and Studies*, 12(March 1976): 61-83.

Lieberthal, Kenneth. "China in 1975: The Internal Political Scene." *Problems of Communism*, 24 (May-June 1975): 1-11.

Ling, William P. Y. "A Longitudinal Study of Chinese Military Factionalism, 1949-1973." *Asian Survey*, 15 (October 1975): 896-910.

Lin Piao. "March Ahead Under the Red Flag of the General Line and Mao Tse-tung's Military Thinking." Peking Review (October 6, 1959): 13-20, and in Ten Glorious Years, Peking: Foreign Languages Press, 1960: 67-89.

MacFarquhar, Roderick. "Communist China's Intra-Party Dispute." Pacific Affairs, 31 (December 1958): 603-618.

Mao, Tse-tung. "On Ten Major Relationships." Survey of the China Mainland Press, 4000 (14 August 1967): 16.

_____. "On the Correct Handling of Contradictions Among the People," People's Daily, 19 June 1957.

"Members of the Hunan Military District Leading Body," Radio Changsha, FBIS HK 060404, 1 June 1983.

"Moves to Curb the PLA and Provincial Groups." Current Scene (10 March 1973): 17-18.

Mozingo, David. "The Chinese Army and the Communist State" in Nee, Victor and David Mozingo (Eds). State and Society in Contemporary China. Ithaca and London: Cornell University Press, 1983.

Nathan, Andrew. "A Factionalism Model for CCP Politics." China Quarterly, 53 (January-March 1973): 34-66.

Nelsen, Harvey W. "Military Bureaucracy in the Cultural Revolution." Asian Survey, 14 (April 1974): 372-395.

_____. "Military Forces in the Cultural Revolution." China Quarterly, 51 (July-September 1972): 444-474.

_____. "Regional and Paramilitary Ground Forces," in William W. Whitson, ed., The Military and Political Power in China in the 1970's, New York: Praeger, 1972: 135-152.

Nethercut, Richard D. "Deng and the Gun: Party-Military Relations in the People's Republic of China," Asian Survey", 8 (August 1982): 691-705.

_____. "Leadership in China: Rivalry, Reform and Renewal," Problems of Communism, 32 (March-April 1983): 30-47.

"New Appointees in Government and Military Posts." Current Scene (August 1972): 23-26.

Ng-Quinn, Michael. "Deng Xiaoping's Political Reform and Political Order", Asian Survey, 12 (December 1982): 1187-1205.

Oksenberg, Michel. "Local Leaders in Rural China, 1962-1965: Individual Bureaucratic Positions and Political Recruitment," in A. Doak Barnett, ed., Chinese Communist Politics in Action. Seattle: University of Washington Press, 1969: 155-215.

Oksenberg, Michel and Richard Bush. "China's Political Evolution: 1972-1982", Problems of Communism, 31 (Sept-Oct 1982): 1-19.

Oksenberg, Michel and Steven Goldstein. "The Chinese Political Spectrum." Problems of Communism, 23 (March-April 1974): 1-13.
Parrish, William. "Factions in Chinese Military Politics." China Quarterly, 56 (October-December 1973): 667-699.
Pavlov, K. "The Political Morale of Mao's Army." Bulletin (Institute for the Study of the USSR), 11 (March 1964): 5-16.
"Peking Reshuffles Top Regional Commanders." Current Scene (February 1974): 19-23.
Powell, Ralph L. "Commissars in the Economy: 'Learn from the PLA' Movement in China." Asian Survey, 5 (March 1965): 140-151.
_____. "Continuity and Purge in the PLA." Marine Corps Gazette (February 1968): 20-30.
_____. "The Increasing Power of Lin Piao and the Party-Soldiers, 1959-1966." China Quarterly, 34 (April-June 1968): 38-65.
_____. "The Military Affairs Committee and Party Control of the Military in China." Asian Survey, 3 (July 1963): 347-356. Also in William Liu, Chinese Society Under Communism, New York: Wiley, 1967: 154-163.
_____. "The Military and the Struggle for Power in China." Current History, 63 (September 1972): 97-102.
_____. "The Party, the Government and the Gun." Asian Survey, 10 (June 1970): 441-471.
_____. "The Power of the Chinese Military." Current History, 59 (September 1970): 129-133.
_____. "Soldiers in the Chinese Economy." Asian Survey, 11 (August 1971): 742-760.
"PRC Military Service Law." People's Daily, 5 June 1984.
"PRC Provincial Military Districts." Current Scene (March 1974): 16-21.
"Raise Aloft the Great Red Banner of the Thought of Mao Tse-tung, Resolutely Implement Regulations Governing PLA Political Work," editorial in Liberation Army News (May 8, 1963). In Survey of the China Mainland Press, 2632 (December 5, 1961): 1-8.
"Raise Our Army's Education and Training to a Higher Level." Liberation Army News (4 December 1980): 1.
"Regulations Governing Work of YCL Branch in Company-Level Units of the PLA." China's Youth (November 24, 1961). In Survey of the China Mainland Press, 2632 (December 5, 1961): 1-3.
Reid, George H. "The Political Commissar in the Red Army." Military Review, 28 (April 1948): 14-20.
Robinson, Thomas W. "Lin Piao: A Chinese Military Politician," in William W. Whitson, ed., The Military and Political Power in the 1970's. New York: Praeger, 1972: 73-92.

_____. "Lin Piao as an Elite Type," in Robert A. Scalapino, ed., *Elites in the People's Republic of China*. Seattle: University of Washington Press, 1972: 149-195.

_____. "Chinese Military Modernization in the 1980's," *China Quarterly*, 90 (June 1982): 231-253.

Scalapino, Robert A. "The CCP's Provincial Secretaries." *Problems of Communism*, 24 (July-August 1976): 18-35.

_____. "The Transition in Chinese Party Leadership: A Comparison of the Eighth and Ninth Central Committees," in Robert A. Scalapino, ed., *Elites in the People's Republic of China*. Seattle: University of Washington Press, 1972: 67-148.

Shambaugh, David L. "China's Defense Industries: Indigenous and Foreign Procurement," in Paul H. B. Godwin, *The Chinese Defense Establishment: Continuity and Change in the 1980's*. Boulder, Colorado: Westview Press, 1983: 43-89.

Simmonds, John D. "The New Gun-Barrel Elite," in William W. Whitson, ed., *The Military and Political Power in China in the 1970's*. New York: Praeger, 1972: 93-114.

_____. "P'eng Teh-huai: A Chronological Re-examination." *China Quarterly*, 37 (January-March 1969): 120-138.

Skilling, H. Gordon. "Interest Groups and Communist Politics." *World Politics*, 18 (April 1966): 435-451.

"The Spirit of the Army." *China News Analysis*, 436 (September 7, 1962): 1.

Starr, John B. "From the Tenth Party Congress to the Premiership of Hua Kuo-feng--The Significance of the Colour of the Cat." *China Quarterly*, 67 (September 1976): 480-484.

Stowe, Leland. "The Evolution of the Red Army." *Foreign Affairs*, 22 (October 1943): 94-105.

Strong, Anna Louise. "Political Work of the Chinese Army." *Amerasia*, 2 (August 1938): 304-308.

"Study Documents Well and Grasp Key Links," joint editorial in *Peoples Daily*, *Red Flag*, and *Liberation Army News*: (7 February 1977): 1.

Su Yu, "Great Victory for Chairman Mao's Guideline on War," *Peking Review*, 34 (19 August 1977): 6-15.

Sung, George C. S. "China's Regional Politics: A Biographical Approach." *Asian Survey*, 15 (April 1975): 346-365.

T'an, Cheng. "Questions of Political Work at the New Stage of Army-Building." *Eighth National Congress of the Communist Party of China*. Peking: Foreign Languages Press, 1956: 259-78.

Teiwes, Frederick C. "Provincial Politics in China: Themes and Variations," in John M. Lindbeck, ed.,

China: *Management of a Revolutionary Society*. Seattle: University of Washington Press, 1971: 116-192.

Trotsky, Leon. "Creating the Russian Communist Army." *New York Times Current History Magazine*, 11 (November 1919): 309-312.

Van Fleet, James A. "The Truth About Korea: From a Man Now Free to Speak." Part I, *Life* (11 May 1953): 132-135.

Vogel, Ezra. "From Revolutionary to Semi-Bureaucrats: The 'Regularization' of Cadres." *China Quarterly*, 29 (January-March 1967): 36-60.

Walker, Richard L. "The Chinese Red Army." *New Republic*, 136 (May 13, 1957): 39-42.

Wang Ting. "The Succession Problem." *Problems of Communism*, 22 (May-June 1973): 13-24.

Weggel, Oskar. "The PLA in the Cultural Revolution: Grassroots Level Organization and Mass Work." *Revue de Sudest Asiatique et de l'Extreme Orient*, 2 (1969): 243-254.

White, Lynn. "Leadership in Shanghai, 1955-1969," in Robert A. Scalapino, ed., *Elites in the People's Republic of China*. Seattle: University of Washington Press, 1972: 302-377.

_____. "The Liberation Army and the Chinese People." *Armed Forces and Society*, 1 (Spring 1975): 364-384.

Whitson, William W. "The Concept of Military Generation: The Chinese Communist Case." *Asian Survey*, 8 (November 1968): 921-947. Reprinted as "Chinese Military Generations." *Military Review*, 49 (April 1969): 39-55.

_____. "Domestic Constraints on Alternative Chinese Military Policies and Strategies in the 1970's." *Annals* (July 1972): 40-54.

_____. "The Field Army in Chinese Communist Military Politics." *China Quarterly*, 37 (January-March 1969): 1-30.

_____. "Organizational Perspectives and Decision-making in the Chinese High Command," in Robert A. Scalapino, ed., *Elites in the People's Republic of China*. Seattle: University of Washington Press, 1972: 381-415.

"Who's Who in Peking? Leadership and Organization in the Chinese Party, Government and Army." *Current Scene* (8 August 1966): 1-17.

Yelenin, I. and A. Pamor. "The Militarization of Social Life in China." *Current Digest of the Soviet Press*. (29 March 1972).

Yung Wei. "Elite Conflict in Chinese Politics: A Comparative Note." *Studies in Comparative Communism*, (Spring-Summer 1974): 64-73.

Yu Yang. "Mao Kung Tui Chun Fang Chung Yao Jen Shih Te Tiao Cheng" ("Shift of Military Leaders"), *Chung*

Kung Yen Chiu (Studies in Chinese Communism), 10 (May 1976): 50-57.

"Zhou Enlai's Report on the Work of the Government," 13 January 1975 at the 1st Session of the 4th National People's Congress. People's Daily (21 January 1974): 1.

Unpublished Works

Bobrow, Davis B. "The Political and Economic Role of the Military in the Chinese Communist Movement, 1927-1959." Ph.D. dissertation, Massachusetts Institute of Technology, Cambridge, Massachusetts, 1962.

Bullard, Monte R. "Political Cadre Systems in the Military". Thesis, Command and General Staff College, Ft. Leavenworth, Kansas, June 1970.

Chang, Chen-pang. "Why Hua Kuo-feng?" Paper presented to the Fifth Sino-American Conference on Mainland China, Taipei, Taiwan, June 1976.

Ch'in, Yung-fa. "The Impact of the Lin Piao Affair on the People's Liberation Army." Paper presented to the Third Sino-American Conference on Mainland China, Taipei, Taiwan, December 1974.

Chiu, S. M. "A History of the Chinese Communist Army." Ph.D. Dissertation, University of Southern California, 1958.

DeLuca, A. P. "Leadership in the Chinese Communist Army". Thesis, Command and General Staff College, Fort Leavenworth, Kansas, June 1964.

Domes, Juergen. "The Relationship Between Party, Army, and Government in Communist China." Paper presented to the Fifth Sino-American Conference on Mainland China, Taipei, Taiwan, June 1976.

Heinlein, Joseph J. Jr. "The Political Establishment in the Army of the Republic of China." Thesis, Command and General Staff College, Fort Leavenworth, Kansas, June 1967.

Kau, Michael Y. M. "The Role of the Military in Transition: The Politics of Mao's Army Building." Paper presented to the Fifth Sino-American Conference on Mainland China, Taipei, June 1976.

MacFarquhar, Roderick. "The Whampoa Military Academy." Harvard Papers on China, Cambridge, Massachusetts, August 1955.

Oksenberg, Michel. "Occupational Groups in Chinese Society and the Cultural Revolution." Paper prepared for the Year-in-Review Conference, University of Michigan, Center for Chinese Studies, Ann Arbor, Michigan, 1968.

Thornton, Richard. "Teng Hsiao-p'ing and Peking's Current Crisis: A Structural Interpretation." Paper presented to the Fifth Sino-American Conference on Mainland China, Taipei, Taiwan, June 1976.

Ts'ao, Ch'ih-ching. "Structural and Personnel Changes in Military Regions and Factions in CHICOM Military Politics." Paper presented to the Fifth Sino-American Conference on Mainland China, Taipei, Taiwan, June 1976.

Tseng, Yung-hsien. "The Party Military Relationship and the Centralized Leadership on the Mainland." Paper presented to the hsien. "The Party Military Relationship and the Centralized Leadership on the Mainland." Paper presented to the hsien. "The Party Military Relationship and the Centralized Leadership on the Mainland." Paper presented to the Third Sino-American Conference on Mainland China, Taipei, Taiwan, December 1974.

Yao, Meng-hsuan. "The Chinese Communist Internal Struggle During the Power Transition." Paper presented to the Fifth Sino-American Conference on Mainland China, Taipei, Taiwan, June 1976.

Periodicals

Hong Kong

Current Background
Survey of China Mainland Magazines
Survey of China Mainland Press

People's Republic of China

Beijing Review (Formerly Peking Review)
China Daily
Hong Qi (Red Flag)
Jie Fan Jun Bao (Liberation Army News)
Liaowang (A Chinese Communist Party Monthly)
Nan Fang Shi Bao (Southern Times)
Ren Min Ri Bao (People's Daily)

Taiwan

Chung Kung Yen Chiu (Studies in Chinese Communism)
Issues and Studies

Index

Accountant (in PLA), 77
Advisor (to PLA), 32-34, 72
Afghanistan, 21
Age limits (in PLA), 23, 30
Agriculture (in Four Modernizations), 20
Air Force, 21, 38
American Military Assistance Advisory Group, 73
Anhui, 61, 64, 93, 98, 105-109, 111-113, 115-116, 119-121, 123-125, 128-129, 131-135, 137-139, 146
Anti-Dengists, 4, 11
Anti-individualism, 76
Antiaircraft (PLA unit), 27
Antichemical (PLA unit), 35
Antitank, 26, 27
Army groups, 7, 76
Army-government, 29, 57, 90, 96, 100-103, 114, 118, 127, 130, 136
Artillery, 27, 35
Authoritarian tradition, 69
Baowei,
  see security section
Battalion political officers, 81
Beijing Military Region, 12, 95, 99, 128-129, 131-135, 137-139, 146
Beijing, 12, 61, 92-94, 96-97, 99, 101, 104-105, 107-109, 111-113, 115-116, 119-121, 123-125, 128-129, 131-135, 137-139, 146
Bolshevik Military Revolutionary Committee, 67
Bolsheviks, 67
Bourgeois conservatism, 9
Bourgeois liberalism, 9
Bureaucratic model, 1-5, 16
Bureaucratic roles, 46
Cadre
  administrative, 38
  air force, 38
  army, 38
  commanding, 38
  medical, 38
  military law-enforcement, 38
  militia and people's armed force, 38
  navy, 38
  political, 38
  staff, 38
  supply, 38
  technical, 38
  veterinary, 38
  central, 28-29, 140, 152-153
  government, 28-29, 38, 140
  grassroots, 28-29, 140
  local, 28-29, 140
  military, 10, 19, 27-29, 32, 65, 140
  nonparty-member, 28-29,

65, 140
Cadre
  party-member, 28-29, 48, 57-58, 65, 65, 152-153
  state/collective enterprise, 28-29
Canmou ganbu,
  see cadre (staff)
Center, 5, 10, 13-15, 42, 47, 56, 90, 150-152, 154
Center-region relationship, 43-44, 47, 51-57, 91-93, 96, 150
Central Advisory Commission (CAC), 106, 109-111, 136-137, 141
Central Committee of CCP, 5, 15, 41, 42, 45-48, 81, 92, 99-111, 114, 131-136, 140-145
Central Directive-18, 21
Central Military Council (CMC), 41-45, 47
Centralization, 7, 52
Centralization-decentralization, 52, 62
Chairman of the Chinese Communist Party, 4
Charismatic-type revolutionaries, 19
Checks and balances
  in PRC political system, 13, 35
Chen Yun, 52
Chengdu MR, 39, 94-95, 99, 101, 128-129, 131-135, 137-139, 146
Chiang Kai-shek, 69, 73, 86
Chiefs-of-staff, 47, 99, 132-134
China Youth League, 77
Chinese Communist Party (CCP), 5, 7, 29, 37, 58 72-73, 76
Chuishiban,
  see mess squad
Class struggle, 20
Clerk (in PLA), 77
Cliques, 3, 6, 10-11, 13, 16
Collective leadership, 12
College entrance exam, 26, 31

"Command by consensus", 79
Command system, 49, 90, 94, 96-104, 106-110, 112, 132-133, 152
Commandism, 49, 83, 154
Commerce (in PRC), 53, 56
Communications clerk (in PLA), 77
Company level political officer, 78
Company political branch 78
Compartmentation (as a PLA problem), 36
Confucius, 69, 71
Consensus decisionmaking, 7, 11-12, 17
Conservatives, 11
Constitution (state),
  Article-4, 12
  Article-86, 12, 18
Constitution (party), 29, 38
Corps, 30, 35, 45, 73, 76-77
Cultural affairs instructor, 77
Cultural affairs unit, 77
Cultural section, 77
Dangweihui, see division and corps party committee
Decentralization, 13, 45, 52-56, 61, 91
Defense industries, 20, 37
Demobilization, 32-34, 45
Democratic centralism, 13, 57, 78
Deng Xiaoping, 3, 6-8, 11-12, 17, 44, 149, 152, 155
Dengists, 4, 6, 12-14, 16-17
Deterrent (Chinese capability), 21
Dichotomies (as an analytical method), 3-4, 11
Difang ganbu,
  see cadre (local)
Director (in PLA political department), 25, 30-31, 47, 76, 99

Divisions and corps party committees, 45, 80-81
Divisions, 21, 33, 36, 45, 54, 76, 81
Djilas, 57, 63
Doctrine (PLA) 52, 58-59, 68, 72-75, 155
Dual positions
  party-army, 20, 56-57, 90, 102-103, 106, 112-119, 122, 130, 136, 143
  party-government, 56-57, 90, 94, 97, 106, 112-118, 122, 126, 130, 143
  army-gvovernment, 90, 96, 101-104, 114, 117-118, 122, 126, 130, 136, 142-143
Dual rule, 52-54, 140
Dual/triple positions, 11, 93-98, 100, 107, 122, 136, 140, 143
Dynastic cycle, 98
Economic transformation, 20
Egalitarianism, 21
"Eight-legged essay", 9
Eighth Central Committee, 42-43, 53, 91-94, 101, 110, 117, 122, 146, 150
Eighth Party Congress, 42, 53, 58
Eleventh Central Committee, 45
Eleventh Party Congress, 42
Elite analysis, 1-2, 6, 15, 51
Elite conflict, 1-7
Elite roles (general use in analysis), 31, 46-47, 50, 90
Elite roles (military)
  commander, 5, 12, 30, 39, 45, 47, 49-50, 55, 58, 66-67, 69-73, 75-82, 99-100, 102, 114-133, 142-143, 147, 153
  deputy commander, 31, 39, 47, 49, 91, 100, 132-133
  deputy political commissars, 30, 91, 103, 134, 138-139
  first political commissar 6, 39, 47, 80, 90, 99-100, 102-103, 117-144, 152
  political assistant, 77
  political commissars, 6, 15, 39, 47, 49-50, 58-59, 67-87, 91, 97, 101-111, 131-144, 150-154
  second political commissar, 47, 102, 134-137
Elite roles (party or state)
  standing committee member 49-50, 69, 111-117, 122-124, 126-127, 130, 136
Elite roles (party)
  deputy secretaries, 47-49
  first secretaries, 6, 44-48, 53-61, 90, 96-119, 126-130, 134-144, 153
  general secretary, 43, 47, 123
  second secretaries, 47, 48, 61, 96-98, 100-104
  secretaries, 43, 55, 47, 78, 81, 114, 126-127, 151-154
  senior secretary, 47-48, 100, 104, 110
  third secretaries, 47-48, 101
Elite roles (state)
  chairman, 100-103, 108, 113-121, 130, 135, 151
  first vice-chairman, 100-103, 119-121, 127, 129-131
  first vice-governor/first vice-mayor, 50, 119-121
  governor/mayor, 47-50, 98, 104-110, 114-125, 130-134, 151
  vice-governors/vice-mayors, 47, 50, 80, 114, 117, 119-125, 130
Engineers (in PLA), 17, 27
"Experts", 3, 12, 89
"Extreme leftism", 9
Factional politics model 2-3
Factions, 4, 10-12, 14, 16, 154
Feedback mechanism, 79

Field sanitation personnel, 77
Fifth Plenum of the Fifth NPC, 12
Finance (PRC regulations on), 54
First Plenum of the Eleventh Party Congress, 42
First Republic (France), 66
Forward defense (as a military strategy), 24
"Four basic principles" (of Communist Party), 13, 24
"Four cadre transformations", 28
"Four modernizations", 20-22
France, 67-68, 74
French Revolution (as a source of the political commissar system), 67
Fujian, 93-94, 105, 107-109, 111-113, 115-116, 119-121, 123-125, 128-129, 131-135, 137-139, 146
Fuzhou MR, 95, 99, 101, 128-129, 131-135, 137-139, 146
Gang-of-Four, 4, 11, 42, 55
Gansu, 61, 93, 105, 107-109, 111-113, 115-116, 119-121, 123-125, 128-129, 131-135, 137-139
Gao Gang, 56
Geminghua see revolutionization
General Logistics Department (GLD), 30
General Political Department (GPD), 25, 30-33, 39
General Staff Department (GSD), 30-33, 35, 39
General branch (battalion party organization), 80
George, Alexander, 76, 87
Germans, 72-73
Great Leap Forward, 9, 98
Great Proletarian Cultural Revolution, 7, 10-13, 29, 42-44, 55, 57, 89-90, 96-97, 100, 151, 155
Guangdong, 93, 103, 105, 107-109, 111-113, 115-116, 119-121, 123-125, 128-129, 131-135, 137-139, 146
Guangxi, 93-94, 103, 105, 107-109, 111-113, 115-116, 119-121, 123-125, 128-129, 131-135, 137-139
Guangzhou MR, 39, 94, 95, 99, 128-129, 131-135, 137-139, 146
Guerrilla warfare, 23-27
Guizhou, 61, 93, 105, 107-109, 111-113, 115-116, 119-121, 123-125, 128-129, 131-135, 137-139, 146
Haijun ganbu, see cadre (navy)
Hebei, 61, 93, 105, 107-109, 111-113, 115-116, 119-121, 123-125, 128-129, 131-135, 137-139
Hegel, 9
Heilongjiang, 61, 93-94, 101, 105-109, 111-113, 115-116, 119-121, 123-125, 128-129, 131-135, 137-139, 146-147
Henan, 61, 62, 93-94, 105, 107-109, 111-113, 115-116, 119-121, 123-125, 128-129, 131-135, 137-139
High command (PLA), 4, 16, 34-35, 44, 61, 63, 84
Horizontal linkages, 117
Hua Guofeng, 3, 16
Hubei, 61, 93-94, 105-109, 111-113, 115-116, 119-121, 123-125, 128-129, 131-135, 137-139, 146-147
Hunan, 32, 38, 61, 93, 105, 107-109, 111-113, 115-116, 119-121, 123-125, 128-129, 131-135, 137-139, 146
Identity-forming experience, 2, 4, 46, 65, 90
Independent kingdoms, 51,

56
India, 21
Indochina, 21
Industry (PRC), 20
Intellectualization, 31-32, 38
Intellectuals, 20
Interest group, 3, 6, 11-13, 16, 141
Interlocking directorate, 5-7, 10-11, 15, 20, 36, 41-45, 51, 90-91, 104, 114, 143, 149, 154-155
Interlocking roles, (evolution of), 35
Interlocking roles, 5-6, 15, 51, 104, 117-118, 123 126-127, 131, 136, 143, 151-154
Ismail Aymat, 151
Jiangsu, 61, 93-94, 105-109, 111-113, 115-116, 119-121, 123-125, 128-129, 131-135, 137-139, 146
Jiangxi, 93, 105, 107-109, 111-113, 115-116, 119-121, 123-125, 128-129, 131-135, 137-139
Jiceng ganbu,
  see cadre (grassroots)
Jilin, 93, 105, 107-109, 111-113, 115-116, 119-121, 123-125, 128-129, 131-135, 137-139, 146
Jinan MR, 94-95, 99, 128-129, 131-135, 137-139, 146
Jishu ganbu,
  see cadre (technical)
Junfa ganbu, see cadre (military law-enforement)
Junxu ganbu,
  see cadre (supply)
Junyi ganbu,
  see cadre (medical)
Kongjun ganbu,
  see cadre (air force)
Korean War, 19, 58
Kuaiji,
  see accountant
Kunming MR, 94-95, 99, 128-129, 131-135, 137-139, 146

Kuomintang (KMT), 72
Lanzhou MR, 39, 64, 94-95, 99, 128-129, 131-135, 137-139, 146
Lardy, Nicholas, 54
Lateral transfer (from PLA), 26, 32-34
"Leadership responsiblity system", 12, 49
Leadership, 5, 8, 13, 17, 20, 24, 28, 32, 43, 48, 51-52, 55, 57, 59, 63, 141-144, 153
Leftism, 9, 25
Li Desheng, 12, 30
Liaoning, 61, 92-93, 105-109, 111-113, 115-116, 119-121, 123-125, 128-129, 131-135., 137-139, 146-147
Liberals, 11
Lin Biao Incident, 151
Lin Biao's Fourth Field Army Group, 7
Lin Biao, 7
"Line, principles and doctrine", 24
Liu Shaoqi, 9, 17
Lixiu,
  see retirement
Local force units, 31, 35, 38-39, 96
Logistics (in PLA), 23
Louis Napoleon, 67
Louis Philippe, 67
Lujun ganbu,
  see cadre (army)
Lure deep (military strategy), 21-24
Main force units, 24, 30, 35, 38, 45, 81, 96, 151
Managers, 53, 55, 58
Mao Zedong, 8, 11, 11-19, 25, 29, 37, 52, 56-57, 61-62, 86, 155
Marxist-Leninist/Maoist, 14, 29, 47
Mass organizations, 28, 48
Mensheviks, 67
Mess squad (in PLA), 66
Micro-political analysis, 2, 5
Middle-range theory, 3

Military Affairs Commission of the CCP (MAC), 35, 43, 45, 47, 76-77, 97
Military academies
  Academy of Military Sciences, 27
  Logistics Academy, 27
  Military Academy, 27
  Political Academy, 27
Military district elites, 49-50, 96, 98, 140-141
Military district, 5, 29, 31, 34, 36, 44-45, 47, 49, 65, 76-77, 90-95, 97-99, 104-110, 118-120, 126-135, 137-147, 150-153
Military modernization, 20
Military region elites, 49, 50, 90, 98, 104, 141
Military region representation (at the Center), 90, 94-97, 110
Military region, 5, 15, 27-29, 34-36, 44-47, 49, 60, 76-77, 95, 99, 118-120, 126, 128-129, 131-135, 137-145, 147
Military sub-district, 35, 76, 127, 152
Militia, 20, 31, 35, 38-39, 45, 65, 96, 152-153
Minbing
  see militia
Ministry of Defense, 33-34, 83
"Moderates", 89-90
Modernization process, 19-20, 22, 149, 153
Modernization, 19-20, 23-24, 34-37, 44, 59
"Modernizers", 19
Monarchy (French), 66
"Mountaintopism", 153
Nanjing MR, 39, 94-95, 99, 128-129, 131-135, 137-139, 146
National Defense Science, Technology and Industry Commission, 35, 39, 44
National Party Congress, 38
National People's Congress (NPC), 12, 18, 39, 41, 44, 60
National reconstruction, 20
Navy, 30, 39
Nei Monggol, 50, 93, 95-96, 99, 101, 105, 107-109, 111-113, 115-116, 119-121, 123-125, 128-129, 131-135, 137-139, 146
"New Communist Man", 75-76, 82-83
"New socialist man", 89
Nicholas I, 67
Nicholas II, 67
Ningxia, 61, 93, 105, 107-109, 111-113, 115-116, 119-121, 123-125, 128-129, 131-135, 137-139, 146
Ninth Party Congress, 42
North Vietnamese, 72
Nuclear, 21, 27, 63
"On Contradiction", 16-17
Opportunists, 11, 25, 70, 78
Organization section (of PLA staff), 66-68
Organization sub-committee (of PLA unit), 78-80
Organizational change, 4, 22, 34-36, 54
Organizational structures 8, 26, 44, 72, 76, 82, 149
Overaged (Cadre), 30-34
PLA Cadre Service Regulaions, 30, 32
Party branch (of PLA unit), 77, 79-80
"Party commands the gun", 20, 57, 73, 152
"Party conservatives", 89
Party rectification movement, 25, 54
Party representative, 50, 74, 94, 97
Party-army relations, 20, 56-59, 81-82, 90, 112-119, 136
"People's War", 19, 21-24

"People's war under modern conditions", 20
Politburo, 10, 44-48, 91, 96-97
Political Commissar System, 15, 19, 25, 47-49 65-76, 80-82, 85, 103-104 142-144, 152-154
Political culture, 17, 46, 85
Political indoctrination, 27, 78
Political warfare, 73, 83, 85
"Political work", 10, 13, 78-80
Political-military, 1, 5, 14-15, 20, 41, 65, 68, 150-153
"Positive appeal", 68, 83, 153-154
Pragmatic attitudes, 51
"Pragmatists", 89
Premier, 3-4, 12, 39
Production unit, 52, 55
Professionalization (PLA) 25-26, 32, 38, 44, 149
Promotion criteria, 28
Propaganda section (of PLA unit), 77
Province government, 5, 34, 50, 63, 145
Province party, 5-6, 45, 47, 90-91, 94, 106, 116, 130, 144
Province repesentation (at Center), 90, 92, 94-97, 150-153
Qinghai, 61, 93, 105-109, 111-113, 115-116, 119-121, 123-125, 128-129, 131-135, 137-139, 146
Qingniantuan, see youth league
Quartermaster, 77
ROC Army, 69, 72-73, 86
"Radicals", 3, 7, 90
Rank system, 34
Rao Shushi, 56, 86
Recentralization, 55, 97
Recruitment (into PLA), 4, 20, 26-27, 79
Rectification campaign, 8, 10, 25, 54
Rectification, 2, 7
Red Army, 21, 67, 72, 84
Red guards, 16, 55
Red-expert, 3, 57
Regimental Youth League, 77
Regimental party committee, 77, 81
Regional force, 152
Regionalism, 51, 56, 60
Regularization, 22, 25, 26, 37
Rejuvenation, 28, 30-31, 38
"Representents en Mission", 33-67
Republic of China (ROC), 69
Retirement (from PLA), 26, 32-33, 93, 150
"Return to barracks" (PLA), 96-97, 149, 152
Revolutionization, 38
Role linkages, 41, 90, 150
"Rose like helicopters", 25
Rural youths, 26-27
Russian Commissars, 67
SS-20 missiles, 21
Scalapino, Robert, 1, 3, 16
School of citizenship (PLA as), 77
"Second United Front", 73
Security section (of PLA unit), 77
Self-reliance (PLA principle), 20, 22
Sense of urgency (PLA lack of), 21
Shaanxi, 93, 98, 105, 107-109, 111-113, 115-116, 119-121, 123-125, 128-129, 131-135, 137-139
Shandong, 61, 93-94, 105-109, 111-113, 115-116, 119-121, 123-125, 128-129, 131-135, 137-139, 146-147
Shanghai, 48, 61, 92-94,

96-97, 105, 107-109, 111-113, 115-116, 119-121, 123-125, 128-129, 131-135, 137-139
Shanxi, 61, 93, 98, 105, 107-109, 111-113, 115-116, 119-121, 123-125, 128-129, 131-135, 137-139, 146
Shenyang MR, 12, 30, 92, 94-97, 99, 101, 128-129, 131-135, 137-139, 146
"Shifting coalitions", 6, 11
Shouyi ganbu,
see cadre (veterinary)
Sichuan, 61, 92, 93, 105, 107-109, 111-113, 115-116, 119-121, 123-125, 128-129, 131-135, 137-139, 146-147
Signal Corps, 35
Sino-Japanese War, 19, 52
Sino-Vietnam "lesson", 58
Siwuzhang,
see quartermaster
Social control, 153
Social transformation, 20
"Socialist spiritual civilization", 77
Soviet Communist Party (CPSU), 72
Soviet Far East, 21
Soviet Union, 75, 77, 80, 152
Soviet political commissar, 67
Soviet, 21-22, 26, 72-73, 84-86
Spectrum of acceptable conflict (PLA perspective), 8
Standing Committee of the Politburo, 43
State Central Military Council (CMC), 35, 43-45
State Council, 12, 44-45, 53
Strategy (PLA), 21, 23, 26, 63
Subjectivism, 9
Sun Yat-sen, 65
Tactics, 8, 23
Ten Great Relationships, 56
Tenth Central Committee, 10, 45, 50, 91-92, 94, 100, 110, 150
Tenth Party Congress, 42, 114
The Three Transformations 22-34
Third Plenum of the Tenth Party Congress, 55
Threat perception (PRC), 20-21
Three People's Principles 69
Three-in-one committees, 55
Tianjin, 61, 93, 105, 107-109, 111-113, 115-116, 119-121, 123-125, 128-129, 131-135, 137-139, 146
Tongxinyuan,
see communication clerk
Training/schooling, 26-29
Triple position government-party-army, 28, 143, 152
Tuiwu,
see demobilization
Tuixiu,
see retirement
Twelfth Central Committee 45, 48, 60-61, 92, 115, 146
"Two whateverists", 21
USSR,
see Soviet Union
Ulanfu, 99
United States, 31, 39, 69
"Unity of command", 73
Urban youths, 26-27
Urumqi MR, 94-95, 99, 128-129, 131-135, 137-139, 146
Vertical linkages, 117 122, 140
Vertical rule, 52
Vietnam, 21, 31, 36
Voluntaristic motives, 72
Wang Sheng, 66, 83, 85-86
War of Liberation, 19, 33
Warlord Period, 68, 84
Wei Guoqing, 25
Weishengyuan, see field

sanitation personnel
Welfare subcommittee
    (of PLA unit), 79
Wengongdui,
    see cultural affairs unit
Wenhua jiaoyuan,
    see cultural affairs
    instructor
Wenhua,
    see cultural section
Wenshu,
    see clerk
Whampoa Military Academy,
    72, 86
Wuhan MR, 39, 93-94, 99,
    128-129, 131-135, 137-
    139, 146
Wuzhuang ganbu,
    see cadre (militia and
    people's armed police)
Xielijun,
    see political assistant
Xingzheng ganbu,
    see cadre (administrative)
Xinjiang, 61, 92-95, 98-
    100, 104-105, 107-109,
    111-113, 115-116, 119-
    121, 123-125, 128-129,
    131-135, 137-139, 146
Xiuzheng,
    see streamlining
Xizang, 93, 95, 98-101,
    103-105, 107-109, 111-
    113, 115-116, 119-121,
    123-125, 128-129, 131-
    135, 137-139, 146
Xuanchuan,
    see propaganda section
Youth activities, 48
Yu Qiuli, 25, 39
Yunnan, 61, 93, 105, 107-
    109, 111-113, 115-116,
    119-121, 123-125, 128-
    129, 131-135, 137-139,
    146
Zhejiang, 61, 93-94, 98,
    105, 107-109, 111-113,
    115-116, 119-121, 123-
    125, 128-129, 131-135,
    137-139, 146
Zhengguihua,
    see regularization
Zhengwei,
    see political commissar
Zhengzhi ganbu,
    see cadre (political)
Zhihui ganbu,
    see cadre (commanding)
Zhongyang ganbu,
    see cadre (central)
Zhou Enlai, 3, 37
Zhuanye,
    see lateral transfer
Zhuanyehua,
    see professionalization
Zong zhibu,
    see general branch
Zuzhi,
    see organization section